The Guitar

The Guitar

A Guide for Students and Teachers

Compiled and Edited by

Michael Stimpson

Oxford New York

OXFORD UNIVERSITY PRESS

1988

Oxford University Press, Walton Street, Oxford OX2 6DP

Oxford New York Toronto
Delhi Bombay Calcutta Madras Karachi
Petaling Jaya Singapore Hong Kong Tokyo
Nairobi Dar es Salaam Cape Town
Melbourne Auckland
and associated companies in
Beirut Berlin Ibadan Nicosia

Oxford is a trade mark of Oxford University Press

Published in the United States
by Oxford University Press, New York

British Library Cataloguing in Publication Data

The Guitar: a guide for students and teachers.
1. Guitar—Methods
I. Stimpson, Michael, 1948–
787.6'1'0714 MT582
ISBN 0–19–317419–7
ISBN 0–19–317419–9 Pbk

Library of Congress Cataloging-in-Publication Data

The Guitar: a guide for students and teachers.
Bibliography: p. 271
Includes index.
1. Guitar. I. Stimpson, Michael.
ML1015.G9G825 1988 787.6'1 87–5622
ISBN 0–19–317419–7
ISBN 0–19–317421–9 (pbk.)

Phototypeset by Latimer Trend & Company Ltd, Plymouth
Printed in Great Britain
at the University Printing House, Oxford
by David Stanford
Printer to the University

Foreword

YEARS ago an esteemed and reliably traditional English composer remarked to me how magical was the sound of just the open strings of a guitar when he heard a young person strumming on a railway platform. How right he was and how ironic it is that this very observation should highlight the guitar's problem as a musical instrument; the sound has an extra-musical and captivating charm which can so easily camouflage poor music-making!

In the 'old' days, from the sixteenth to the early eighteenth century, the vihuela and the baroque guitar had musical and technical styles more akin to the lute, but the six-string guitar of the early 1800s was really a different instrument. It developed in the age of Boccherini and Paganini and in the same way that these composers exploited the technique of the cello and violin, so did Fernando Sor, Mauro Giuliani, and many others on the guitar. Their music was nearly all solo, both because of the guitar's small sound and because these performer/composers mostly did not know how to write for other instruments (certainly not with the skill of the great composers). Even Giuliani had to enlist Diabelli and Moscheles for his string and piano writing. The guitar was to contribute little to the development of nineteenth-century music, both for these reasons and because its tuning and eccentrically difficult technique was not understood by composers who did not play it. They would have also found its small and distinctive sound unsuitable for the flowering of romantic, nationalist, and impressionist expression.

This has been the pattern until well into this century when some leading composers have written important works (perhaps owing to the freedoms of a more eclectic age) under the inspiration and persuasion of well-known performers. Nevertheless, the guitar has been on the sidelines in the development of European 'art' music or 'classical' music of the last five hundred years and the resulting lack of experience is the reason that guitarists, performers, teachers, and students alike, are inferior to most other instrumentalists at sight-reading, listening, phrasing, and playing together. This isolation in turn has encouraged even more concentration on difficult solo music to the point where the classical guitar seems to have its own rules on rhythm and phrasing. The instrument's acceptance by the main music colleges has made these problems yet more obvious to those involved.

But this is the good news! We have become aware of the situation not only at a time when we are equipped to do something about it but at a time when the guitar itself can help and even give a lead in a radical re-assessment of European classical music in relation to other musical cultures and the popular traditions they have maintained: jazz is often considered as the most obvious and important example but the same values apply to many others. The guitar has always been a popular instrument and this is its ultimate strength. It can be the bridge from the popular to the classical traditions and vice versa, but it must learn from both to do it well.

That is why whether student or teacher, beginner or advanced, amateur or professional, this book is a must for anyone who is involved and interested in the future of the guitar. When giving specific guidance and viewpoints many of the chapters are necessarily more subjective than others. However, I particularly enjoyed the chapters which deal with classroom teaching, arranging, elementary repertoire, and classical guitar technique and consider that they give invaluable advice which I believe is unequalled elsewhere. The conjunction and interdependence of all these factors in the one book make it unique.

John Williams

Editor's Preface

As the twentieth century approaches its final decade, it becomes increasingly clear that the guitar has enjoyed its most successful period ever. The classical instrument has, by now, attracted some significant compositions. This, together with an increasing awareness of the music of other continents and a broadening of the transcribed material, has enabled the classical guitar to become almost universally established in the concert hall. As a non-classical instrument the guitar has played such a fundamental role in the development of other styles of music, that at times it is difficult to imagine the style existing without the guitar. The thought of rock music without a lead and bass guitar, or the blues singer or modern-day folk singer without the steel-string guitar is almost inconceivable. The characteristic sound of the guitar has so often added a different dimension to the jazz ensemble. Meanwhile, although the flamenco guitarist has never lost sight of his or her role in the whole flamenco ensemble, flamenco guitar has become so established in its own right that solo performers are now accepted world-wide.

It is not surprising, therefore, that with such development and diversity, the guitar gradually became incorporated into the educational system. The groundwork for the entry of the guitar into education was carried out in the 1950s when the classical guitar was first taught in music college. By the end of the 1960s, the guitar was more widely recognized by the music colleges, diplomas had been set up for the performer and the teacher, and the guitar had begun to be examined by bodies such as the Associated Board of the Royal Schools of Music (in 1967). The result is, that by the mid-1980s, all the music colleges have departments that accept about four students each year, and that the number of candidates who take classical guitar examinations (with the Associated Board) matches the numbers of some important representatives of other instrumental groups—oboe, viola, horn, and singing.

Clearly, there would be a 'knock-on' effect into other areas of education as well as further independent development. Guitarists, on occasion, are accepted in the music departments of universities and colleges of higher education, although, given the number of candidates referred to above, it is uncertain why in some departments this appearance is such a rarity. Some local education authorities are open to the same question. By 1980–1 (the information updated in 1984), a considerable number of authorities had failed to introduce the guitar either at all, or in any significant amount. 'Thirty of the local authorities that provided the relevant information (that is, 50%) offered less than 3% of their instrumental provision to the guitar, and of these local authorities, twenty (that is one-third of the total that replied) offered no guitar teaching at all. Yet a number of authorities have well over one thousand hours of instrumental teaching per week.'[1] When questioned on which instruments were taught, it emerged that the full range of orchestral instruments was offered; whenever children were questioned on which instrument they wished to try or learn, the guitar invariably rated amongst the highest.

One important contributory factor to this is the influence of the electric guitar. It will not have escaped attention that all the above information refers to the classical guitar—other styles receive virtually no recognition at all. The electric guitar, for example, is an infrequent visitor to school, college of higher education, university, or music college, the last three being predominantly responsible for the training or 'production' of guitar teachers. Equally, at the time of writing, Holland is the only country in Europe to create a comprehensive course on flamenco guitar at music college level. This limiting of the instrument—'we are trying to eradicate folk guitar', as one music adviser said in an attempt to give the guitar a classical respectability—is a fundamental error for education to make because it is the very diversity of the guitar that is among its greatest strengths.

The subject of the training of guitar teachers is one which warrants some mention because, as with other musical instruments, the qualification for teaching is almost solely based on a proven ability to play, not to teach. The amount of 'teacher training' on some courses is often negligible, the Post Graduate Certificate in Education being one of the few courses to make a substantial attempt to relate a student's playing skill to the profession of teaching. Many courses that are responsible for the training of guitarists do not have the necessary graduate status for students to go on to a course such as the PGCE. Meanwhile, the

1. Stimpson, M. (March 1985). 'The Guitar in English Music Education', *British Journal of Music Education*, Vol. 2, No. 1, Cambridge.

obtaining of a Teachers' Diploma is not a satisfactory training for anyone who may teach in school. Until some radical restructuring can reflect the art of instrumental teaching there should, at the very least, be a move in some courses towards establishing a supervised teaching practice, a recognition of the various musical styles with which the guitar is associated, and some acceptance of the educational areas which are essential for any prospective teacher.

This then provides the background for this book, which, while in part a recognition of the progress that the guitar has made, is also a call for a broader approach to the training of guitar teachers in order to meet the varying needs of today's children. However, it is equally intended for the new guitar teacher who may need to prepare for school work or the teaching of beginners; the guitarist who has been trained in one style of music and needs to diversify; the class music teacher who wishes to bring the guitar into the classroom; and, of course, 'the student'.

Some comment may be helpful concerning the direction of the individual chapters. 'The Peripatetic Teacher' and 'The Private Teacher' are predominantly intended for the new guitar teacher, establishing some of the issues involved and some pointers toward counteracting the somewhat haphazard approach that can easily be taken. 'The Guitar as a Classroom Instrument', primarily for the class music teacher, explores ways in which the guitar can be used with schoolchildren who may not have a high degree of facility on the instrument. An argument is made for a closer co-operation between the class teacher and the visiting guitar teacher. If this takes place, the latter may be called upon to work with instruments other than the guitar. In addition, the class teacher might decide to involve guitars without the help of a visiting specialist—'Arranging for the Guitar and Other Instruments' (and Appendices I, II, and III) offers the essential information. 'Examinations' is a chapter for both students and teachers, providing a most detailed survey of examinations for all levels of classical guitar. The following three chapters, 'Classical Repertoire' ('Elementary', 'Intermediate', and 'Advanced'), reflect the problems of teaching and playing at their respective levels, as well as discussing the repertoire. Two immediate questions arise concerning what to include and at which level a piece is graded. The former has been directed by the various examination syllabuses, the latter generally by the level of difficulty in the majority of the pieces or movements. It does not take long for anyone writing about technique to come up against the problem of a technique being, to some extent, highly individual. Nevertheless, 'Classical Technique' follows closely the fundamental principals of guitar-playing. The chapters on Rock, Bass, Folk, Flamenco, and Jazz Guitar, have been structured to include a brief history, notes on the instrument itself, techniques individual to that style, and repertoire. Each author has, of course, applied a personal emphasis within these subject areas, and these chapters are essential reading if an individual's reservation, or at worst, prejudice, is to be dissipated. A collection of Appendices has been added to provide the most relevant information for the less experienced guitarist.

I began work on this project in 1984 and have been fortunate indeed that such specialists have become involved. I would, therefore, like to extend my sincere thanks to the contributors (who, by the way, may not necessarily adhere to the sentiments of this preface or chapters other than their own) who have given me considerable amounts of their time. Furthermore, my thanks to Oxford University Press, Tom Dupré and my other friends, and particularly to my wife Frances for their support and assistance.

MICHAEL STIMPSON

Acknowledgements

Acknowledgement is made to the following for permission to reproduce copyright material: Boosey and Hawkes, for an extract from Sonata opus 47 by Alberto Ginastera; Chappell, for a chord sequence of *All the Things You Are* by Jerome Kern and Oscar Hammerstein; Chester Music, for an extract from *Homenaje* by Manuel de Falla; J. D'Addario & Company, Inc. for their drawing of guitar strings; EMI Music, for the melody *In the Caribbean* from *Reggae Schooldays* by Pearle Christian and Michael Burnett; Kahler, for their drawing of a bridge-unit and tremolo arm; OUP, for an extract from *Introduction to the Guitar* by Hector Quine; Pan Music, for an extract from *Freight Train* by Elizabeth Cotton; G. Ricordi & Co. (London) Ltd., for extracts from *Ten Short Chorales* by Erik Satie (arr. Michael Stimpson) and *Play Purcell* (arr. Gerald Tolan); Schott and Co., for extracts from *Nocturno* by Federico Moreno Torroba (ed. Andrés Segovia), *Tres Piezas Españolas* by Joaquín Rodrigo, *Fandanguillo* by Joaquín Turina; Thames, for an extract from *Playground* by Michael Stimpson; Éditions Musicales Transatlantiques/UMP, for an extract from *Tellur* by Tristan Murail; and Sean Milner and Micky Moody for information used in Chapter 12.

Contents

Notes on Contributors

MARJORIE GLYNNE-JONES is Inspector for Music with the Inner London Education Authority and was formerly Principal Lecturer and Music Chairperson at Middlesex Polytechnic. She is a member of the Executive of the UK Council for Music Education and Training and a former Chair of the Association for the Advancement of Teacher Education in Music. She is on the editorial board of the British Journal of Music Education and has served on the Music in School and Teacher Training Commission of the International Society for Music Education. She is a regular contributor to national and international conferences; publications include *Music* (Macmillan, Basic Books in Education), and contributions to *Music Education Review II* (Chappell/NFER), *Fundamentals in the First School* (Blackwell), and the *International Journal of Music Education.*

JOHN GAVALL studied violin, guitar, and singing. Between 1951 and 1954 he made many radio and television broadcasts. In 1955 he became a Music Adviser in the West Riding of Yorkshire, and in 1961 he appointed and trained the first peripatetic school guitar teachers in the UK. In 1962 he became the county's Senior Music Adviser. In 1972 he became a Lecturer in Music at Moray House, Edinburgh. Since 1979 he has concentrated on his private teaching. He has approximately fifty guitar publications to his name, including *Learning Music Through Guitar*, Vols. 1–5 (Belwin Mills), *First and Second Book of Solos* (OUP), and *Great Baroque Arias* (Ricordi).

MICHAEL BURNETT is Principal Lecturer in Music at Roehampton Institute of Higher Education. Previous posts have included secondment to the Jamaica School of Music as Senior Tutor, and Assistant Organist at Coventry Cathedral. He has written and presented *Music Box* for BBC Schools Radio, and other programmes on pop and Jamaican music. Publications include reviews and contributions to the *New Oxford Companion to Music, Music Teacher, The Times Educational Supplement, Music Education Review* (ed.) (Chappell/NFER), and the *Oxford Topics in Music* series. Compositions include *Suite Blaen Myherin* for brass quartet (Ricordi) and *Five Pieces for Two Guitars* (Boosey and Hawkes).

MARTIN TEALE has held the post of Syllabus Secretary to the Associated Board of the Royal Schools of Music since 1969. He has previously studied violin and classical guitar, and has taught the latter. Amongst his somewhat diverse interests, studies, and appointments, he has carried out the research for two volumes of early Italian songs and arias which are published by the Associated Board. He is, at present, actively involved as a partner in the publisher, European Music Archive, which specializes in early instrumental music.

MICHAEL STIMPSON originally trained as a scientist, then studied guitar with Hector Quine at the Royal Academy of Music and later became an Associate of the Institute of Education, University of London. Publications include contributions to *Music Education Review* (Chappell), the *British Journal of Music Education, The Times Educational Supplement, Guitar International, Music Teacher,* and *Classical Music.* His music, *Café Music, Suite for Solo Guitar* (Ricordi) and *Playground* (Thames) is currently included in the syllabuses of the Associated Board of the Royal Schools of Music and the Guildhall School of Music and Drama respectively. Other music includes *Studies at Dusk* for two guitars (Ricordi) and arrangements for guitar ensemble. At present, he teaches guitar at the Roehampton and West London Institutes of Higher Education.

CHARLES RAMIREZ was first taught guitar by William Gomez. He continued his studies at the Royal College of Music, winning the guitar prize there. Since making his professional debut in 1974, he has been a contributor to BBC Radio 3, has played regularly on London's South Bank, and given master classes both in Britain and abroad. He has also given many duo recitals in partnership with Helen Kalamuniak, arranging many substantial works for the medium. He was appointed, in 1979, Professor of Guitar at the Royal College of Music, and also teaches at the college's junior department.

CARLOS BONELL studied guitar at the Royal College of Music where he was appointed the youngest ever Professor of Guitar immediately upon completing his studies. He has given concerts in all of the world's major musical centres and has recorded with ASV, CBS, Decca, EMI, and Fonit Cetra, receiving some of the highest instrumental awards from the recording industry. Publications include editions of the standard repertoire, arrangements, and original compositions—*The Romantic Guitar, The Classical Guitar* (ed.) (International Music

Publications), *First Pieces* (Ricordi), *Three Spanish Folk Songs for Three Guitars* (arr.) (Schott), and *Spanish Folk Songs and Dances* (Music Sales).

DAVID RUSSELL was first taught guitar by his father, then studied with Hector Quine at the Royal Academy of Music, and latterly with José Tomás in Spain. He has won first prize in many competitions, most notably, the Julian Bream prize in 1971 and 1972, the Concurso Andrés Segovia in 1977, and the Certamen Francisco Tárrega, also in 1977. Each year since 1976 he has toured the USA and has performed in most of the countries in Western Europe. He has recorded both solo and guitar duets on a number of occasions in the United Kingdom and Canada.

BRIAN MAY trained as a physicist, taking four years of post-graduate study in astronomy. Since college, he has been lead guitarist with the band Queen, recording fifteen albums to date; the many hit singles include *Bohemian Rhapsody* and *We are the Champions*. He has played throughout the world, notably, Sao Paulo, Brazil, in 1981, and Live Aid, in 1985. With Queen, he wrote the music for the film, *Flash Gordon* (nominated for the BAFTA award 'Best Film Title Track') and *Highlander*. His solos have been published under the *Star Licks* series.

ALPHONSO JOHNSON, born in Philadelphia, USA, began studying the bass viol at the age of nine, and at the age of eighteen took up the electric bass guitar. After moving to Los Angeles in 1976 he joined the group Weather Report. Since then he has toured and recorded with a number of artists including Phil Collins, Carlos Santana, The Crusaders, John McLaughlin, Didiel Lockwood, and Pino Daniele. In 1983 he composed the soundtrack for a children's animated film, *Sound of Sunshine . . . Sounds of Rain*, which was nominated for an Academy Award in the category of Best Animated Film.

BERT JANSCH has performed both as a solo artist and with the groups Pentangle and Conundrum. He has recorded with the labels Making Waves, Transatlantic, Warner Brothers, and Charisma. He has played throughout the world, and his concerts include the Carnegie Hall and the Royal Albert Hall with Pentangle, and the Queen Elizabeth Hall as a solo performer. He has written the music for the television series, *You Can't See the Wood* (David Bellamy), and with Pentangle, for *Take Three Girls*. *The Songs and Guitar Solos of Bert Jansch* is published by New Punchbowl Music.

PACO PEÑA, born in Córdoba, Spain, made his London debut in 1967. In 1970 he founded a company of dancers, guitarists, and singers, and since then his world-wide tours, both as a soloist and with his company, have included performances at the major music festivals from Edinburgh to Hong Kong, and London Seasons at the Royal Festival Hall, Barbican Centre, and Sadler's Wells Theatre. In 1981 he founded the Centro Flamenco Paco Peña in Córdoba. The centre offers the opportunity to experience the art of flamenco and organizes an annual guitar festival at which the most renowned artists have appeared. He is Professor of Flamenco at the Rotterdam Conservatory.

JOHN ETHERIDGE became a professional guitarist in 1971. He joined the band Soft Machine in 1975, recording three albums. In 1977 he began working with Stephane Grappelli, with whom he toured all over the world. He has recorded with EMI/Harvest, Concorde Jazz, and Doctor Jazz, and concerts have included the Carnegie Hall, the Royal Albert Hall, and the Royal Festival Hall. Since 1981 he has worked in a variety of contexts, touring as leader of his own group, and playing alongside leading English jazz musicians. He has published with *Guitar International* and his teaching appointments include the Wavendon All Music Plan, Barry Summer School, and Dartington College.

1 The Peripatetic Teacher

Marjorie Glynne-Jones

PERHAPS the most helpful way to begin will be to outline present educational provision in England and Wales and the ways in which music's contribution is organized. The diagram (Fig. 1) shows the provision made by Local Education Authorities—LEAs—for children, young people, and adults.

Music provision in schools

Class work

Most secondary schools have music departments which provide a music curriculum for all pupils in the first two or three years, and, from the third or fourth year upwards, for those who choose to do music. Minimum group sizes for option groups are being stipulated by LEAs. Heads of department, sometimes called directors of music, may have one, or perhaps two, assistant teachers. The departments may be administered quite separately from other arts departments in the school, or they may form part of a creative or performing arts faculty. In both forms of organization, collaborative and integrative work in the arts is being developed.

Provision in primary schools is by contrast more varied and much less satisfactory. If there is a teacher with responsibility for music, or for the arts (creative arts), he or she:

(*a*) may or may not be a postholder (i.e. have an incremental allowance);
(*b*) may or may not be a music specialist;
(*c*) may teach only music, or may teach music only to her/his own class;
(*d*) may or may not act in an advisory capacity for other teachers in the school;
(*e*) may or may not be a full-time teacher in the school.

Where there is no postholder or other person responsible for music, headteachers take responsibility for this aspect of the primary curricu-

Fig. 1.1

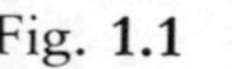

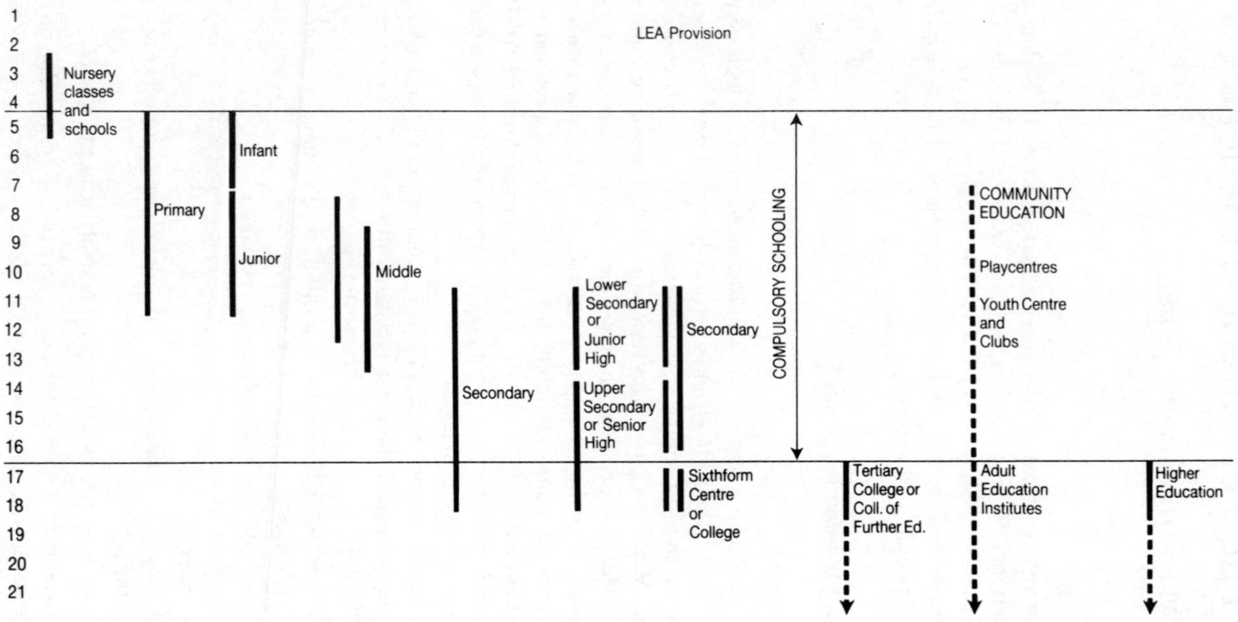

Note. Pattern varies between LEAs. Separate 16–19 provision being developed.

lum. It is generally recognized that music should be an integral part of children's curriculum experience in primary school.

In middle schools, provision may be made either on the primary or on the secondary pattern.

Instrumental tuition

Most LEAs provide an instrumental teaching service for pupils of school age, which, in establishment and mode of operation, varies from authority to authority. Teachers are recruited either to a team led by the LEA adviser or inspector, or to panels of approved teachers who may then be appointed to schools. It is normally expected that instrumental teachers will hold qualified teacher status (QTS). Scale one appointments are made on a full-time or part-time basis, while appointments at scale two or above usually involve some additional responsibility. Instrumental 'heads' may be appointed to posts at scale three or four. Instrumentalists who are not qualified teachers are normally appointed as instructors, usually on an hourly or sessional basis. Maximum permitted hours may be stipulated.

Instrumental teaching takes place in schools during lesson time; in breaks and before or after school; and/or in LEA music centres which operate after school or on Saturdays. In secondary schools, and some middle schools, instrumental lessons are usually scheduled on a weekly basis, either at a fixed time each week or on a rota system. Where lessons coincide with other subject periods, pupils are often withdrawn for music. Such arrangements can only be made with the support of the headteacher and after consultation by the head of music with other members of staff. Though more complicated to administer and remember, the rota system causes less interruption to pupils' other studies than fixed time systems. Similar arrangements are made in primary schools and other middle schools, though the greater flexibility of school organization makes timetabling an easier task, given that space is no problem. Instrumental teachers are expected to keep attendance and lateness records using the system in operation by the school or the particular department. They should also contribute to the school's procedure for profiling pupils' progress through writing regular reports on individual pupils two or three times a year.

Music provision in the youth service and adult education

In youth centres and adult education institutes, instrumental classes may operate during the day or in the evening. Tutors may be recruited to panels of approved teachers, or by the centres and institutes themselves, in response to identified local need. Minimum class sizes are being stipulated.

Initial contacts

Instrumental teachers first come into contact with schools either through LEA team arrangements or through making preliminary visits to schools with teaching vacancies. In either circumstance a first visit should involve, if possible, a meeting with the headteacher and some identifying of the ethos and policies of the school. Sufficient time should be allowed for discussion with the head of department, or with the liaison person in a primary school, about the music policy in the school; the systems for administering the instrumental teaching programme, for selecting pupils, and for recording pupils' achievements; and the arrangements for preparing rooms for teaching—particularly important where there is shared usage. The calendar for performance events and for meetings which involve instrumental teachers should be available. It would be reasonable to expect these to be scheduled on a termly basis.

Similarly, visits to youth centres and adult institutes should involve discussion with the head of centre or the head of department about policy, resources, accommodation, and administrative procedures.

Accommodation

It is appropriate to expect that music-teaching spaces are carpeted in order that sound levels are reduced, and the ambient noise levels created by bodies, bags, and chairs are minimized; that they are not over-reverberant and are relatively free from sound disturbance from outside; that south-facing rooms are fitted with sun blinds; and that lighting levels are adequate for reading notation. As far as resources are concerned, it is reasonable to expect that chairs and stools are of an appropriate height; that footstools, music stands, a keyboard, amplification and isolating equipment, and an adequate number of socket outlets are provided; and that recording equipment can be made available.

Instrumental teachers and the music curriculum

There is a notion, which dies hard, that because a person can play an instrument, he or she is automatically well qualified to become a teacher of that instrument. Indeed, the labels we use to identify people who do this job—instrumental teachers, peripatetic teachers, visiting teachers, instrumental specialists—reflect the specialist nature of the skill involved as well as the fact that the work usually necessitates travelling to different institutions and centres. The commonly held view of what pupils receive from instrumental tuition tends to focus on the level of technical skill achieved, the underlying assumption being of an enterprise predominantly concerned with a technical specialism for which tuition on an individual basis is essential. However, it is increasingly recognized that such a view is limited and inadequate since it fails to take account of those aspects of music education with which present developments in the field are concerned. So, what should replace it?

The first point to make is that educators are very aware of the need to look at the whole educational and social context in which children, young people, and adults learn and develop. In schools, there is a major concern for the coherence of pupils' learning experiences, or to put it another way, a concern to minimize the discontinuities which have existed for pupils between their experiences in primary and secondary schools; between their experiences of different subject areas in the curriculum; and between what happens in school and what happens outside or post school. (I am sure that readers will have experienced some, if not all of these discontinuities when they were pupils themselves, and may be experiencing them now as parents, or indeed as teachers.) The implications of this concern for all areas in the school curriculum are that liaison between primary and secondary schools, and between schools and community education, needs to be developed; that teachers will need to contribute to the development and implementation of whole-school policies, for example, about the approaches to teaching which should take place in all subject areas; and that schools need to create closer contacts with parents and with groups in the local community. There are similar implications for the youth service and adult education. As far as the music curriculum is concerned, this means minimizing the discontinuities which often exist between different aspects of music activity in schools, particularly between class work and instrumental tuition. I remember having this brought forcibly to my attention some years ago by a 13-year-old, who, in response to my question 'Do you use your clarinet in music (class) lessons?' replied, 'Oh, we don't use our instruments in music lessons'!

Things have certainly been changing since then. It is now generally accepted that a fundamental aim of music education in schools is the creation of opportunities for the musical experience and development of all pupils. Work in class is therefore considered to be of central significance. As a consequence, instrumental teachers need to see their work as contributing to the learning experiences of pupils through extending what might be called the core curriculum of class music activities. To put it another way, they will be contributing to the musical experiences of pupils, and to their person-to-person experiences, in a very particular way—through musicianship activities with the focus of one particular instrument.

Secondly, the relevance of what pupils learn is seen as a critical aspect of this coherence. In music, this means that what is done in school should be relevant to the ways people do music outside school—making music, making up music, and developing and following up individual preferences as listeners. The music experienced in school should be relevant to the musical interests of children and young people, and should take account of Afro-American styles as well as those in the Western European tradition, and of the variety of cultural traditions in world music. The resources available in schools and centres for making and recording music should reflect technological developments in the field.

It immediately becomes clear that 'passing through and doing your own thing', as one instrumental teacher put it, is likely to contribute precious little to the coherence being considered here. Quite the contrary, there will be a continuing need for discussion, for exchange of information, and for collaboration between all those who have responsibility for music activities with pupils and students.

Organization of instrumental lessons

One of the issues receiving much present attention is the question of group teaching, and, as tends to happen when different ways of doing things are being developed, the arguments have become polarized—almost on a for or against basis. Since group teaching for the guitar is fairly well established, or at least for pupils in the early stages of playing the instrument, we might look to guitar teachers to develop strategies for handling group teaching situations. However, that would presuppose that genuine group learning experiences were taking place and not the sort of situations in which three or four players are grouped together for a thirty- or forty-minute session, receive individual tuition for ten minutes or so, and wait, doing nothing, for the rest of the time.

A pattern of lesson or session organization is needed which takes account of the learning situations which best support the learner. Of course, at all stages of learning, pupils (young people and adults) will need individual tuition/coaching, and of course, the length and frequency of coaching sessions will vary according to the experience of the player and the tasks being undertaken. At all stages in their development players will also need ensemble opportunities, not merely in a clutch of their own instrument, but in mixed ensembles as well—no less if they are guitar or keyboard players than if they play single-line instruments. However, if instrumental tuition is organized only on the basis of these two situations (individual tuition and ensemble work), learning will be impoverished, for we know that there is considerable benefit for pupils/students in working and discussing with their peers. Where this is encouraged, learning is usually more successful than it is in exclusively teacher/tutor-directed activities.

Pupils and students in groups learn more readily to be both critics and players since there are opportunities both for the separation and for the combination of these roles. As they play and listen to each other, pupils should be involved in analysing aurally, in discussing and appraising what other players, or they themselves, have done; in offering alternative solutions to technical and interpretative problems and demonstrating them; in comparing the relative merits of suggested solutions; in developing coaching techniques and deciding on practice strategies; in taking part in group improvisations and in contributing to group compositions; and in exploring the musical ideas in pieces they meet. These experiences cannot be matched in a one-to-one situation. What is problematic is that such collaborative teaching/learning requires additional strategies on the part of the teacher to those used in what might be called the 'telling mode'. For rather than always telling pupils/students what to do, it requires that teachers help them to learn to find solutions themselves, and encourage them to make musical decisions and take musical initiatives: in other words, to be independent learners. It therefore requires strategies for questioning and for promoting discussion. This is an approach which has long been established in all areas of primary education, and is receiving considerable attention at secondary level and in community education. It was reflected in a comment made by an instrumental teacher at the end of a group session: 'Have we done enough (explored/played/talked) for you to figure it (a piece) out for yourselves?'

The place of imitation

Encouraging pupils to be independent learners in this way means that it is not acceptable in teaching to use, either solely or predominantly, the strategy of 'do it like this', that is, of presenting models to be imitated. Of course, there are situations for which it is a necessary strategy. For example, teachers need constantly to present models of tone in order that pupils can develop their own image of a desired sound—their own internal standard, if you like. Also, teachers need to play during lessons, not only performing music being learned and sharing in improvisations, but also contributing to the exploration of ways of playing certain parts or phrases. And clearly, the acquisition of technique on an instrument involves precise coaching of physical skills within stylistic conventions. In games and exercises too, aimed towards the development of aural analysis and memory, short rhythmic, melodic, or harmonic patterns need to be presented for imitation through echo-playing, clapping, or singing.

However, there is another aspect of music teaching which involves imitation, though it is not often thought of in this way. It is that the music studied is usually, perhaps exclusively, by other people—published music, or music arranged or composed by the teacher. In considering this aspect we need to refer again to 'the musician's fundamental activities of performing, composing and listening',[1] and their place at the heart of curriculum experience in music, whatever the educational setting. Their centrality is acknowledged in the music criteria for the single examination at 16-plus, the General Certificate of Secondary Education (GCSE), which has one 'paper' for each of these activities.[2] Composing, improvising, and arranging have been accorded equal importance to performing in the GCSE for a number of reasons. First, taking up an earlier point, if school music activity and the assessment of it is to be relevant to music activity 'in the world', it has to involve those behaviours which go with being involved with music. Second, pupils' understanding of music is enhanced by direct experience of having and handling musical ideas themselves. Third, the genuine conferral of responsibility on pupils and students for their own actions requires that they have opportunities to initiate musical ideas as well as to imitate the ideas of others. Activities can range from question-and-answer improvisations framed by the teacher, to compositions for which pupils are entirely responsible themselves from start to finish, working in duos, trios, or quartets, for example, or by themselves. Instrumental sessions which do not include opportunities for pupil/student-initiated activities, interpreting as well as improvising and composing, will be very undernourishing affairs. Looking at musical experience in the context of human experience in the arts should serve to remind us that the arts 'are not only for communicating ideas, they are ways of having ideas, of creating ideas, of exploring experience in particular ways and fashioning our understanding of it into new forms'.[3]

There is a further point to make which concerns another of those notions which die hard: that is, that creating (making up) music is only possible when a basic technique and some basic theory are properly established. This is something akin to the idea of learning the notes and then putting the expression in! Approaches based on this view result in very lopsided experiences for learner-musicians because, through failing to recognize that 'techniques and creative purposes grow together by mutual stimulation',[4] they ignore both the nature of musical activity and the nature of learning and development in music. Let us make no mistake: making a piece is possible as soon as a beginner can sound one note. Individuals' one-notes, or the collection of one-notes in a group, can be shaped into pieces, without additions; with an accompaniment or counterpart added by the teacher; with an accompaniment by other members of the group using tuned and untuned percussion, or voices; or by members of another instrumental group.

Voices have an important contribution to make to instrumental sessions. Here I am not only talking about singing, though obviously songs will often play an important part in guitar tuition, but about the vocalizing of phrases, intervals, and melodies—top lines and bass lines. For the learner, such vocalizing provides a means of coming to feel and to understand melodic shape, and of exploring how melodic lines may be expressed. Vocalizing, muttering even, is a way of getting to know a piece from the inside: it is part of the music-learning process.

The place of notation, tutors, and syllabuses

This is another much-debated issue. Present attitudes are reflected in the ritual that must be replicated thousands of times each year when beginners take up the recorder or guitar. A visit is made to the local music shop to buy the necessary equipment: instrument, case, and book. The book is usually recommended by the teacher and can play a powerful role in pupils' learning experience as it is often treated as a syllabus and its contents worked through from lesson to lesson. In a similar way, examination pieces are often treated as a complete syllabus in themselves, to the exclusion of other pieces of music and other musical activities. It does not take much imagination to see how inappropriate both these situations are.

If we take notation first. Music educators are continually reminding themselves of the primacy of aural perception in musical behaviour, and of the fundamental significance of the 'inner ear', that is, of musical imaging and memory. Yet, with notable exceptions, a model of teaching orchestral instruments has become established which often relegates this essential musical behaviour to a place of lesser importance than is accorded to music-reading. The practice has extended to recorder and guitar-teaching, and even to teaching in musical styles where the tradition is aural! I think it should be stated unequivocally that in the early stages of acquiring a particular instrumental skill, that is in the early stages of making a relationship with a particular instrumental sound, the essential experiences should be physical and aural, whatever the style involved. The focus should be on acquiring, in music-making situations, the necessary physical control to produce a desired sound, the qualities of which will be progressively internalized from models presented by the teacher and from performances heard. As has been suggested earlier, it is very soon possible to plan initiating, as well as imitating activities. In discussion, pupils and students will gradually pick up appropriate verbal labels as they talk about what has been done and what needs to be practised—given the relevant introduction of labels, everyday words, and technical terms, by teachers. It is only when these are being handled confidently and purposefully that it is appropriate to introduce, where relevant, the additional aspect of notations. Given the criterion of relevance, a balance should then be achieved between aurally-based work and notationally-based work—reading (on-the-spot, or studying) published or arranged music and writing compositions and arrangements. It is helpful, therefore, to plan in the first instance for a minimum of one term's work for beginners on an exclusively aural basis, whether or not pupils have handled notations in other musical spheres. At the end of this time there should be a review of progress with all interested parties.

The argument now needs to progress to the idea of syllabuses. It has been noted that published instrumental tutors and examination syllabuses are often treated as complete teaching schemes—we would probably all recognize the practice of ticking and initialling pieces (or pages) in the book as they are 'done'. Where this happens the diet is meagre indeed. One resultant phenomenon might be described as the 'etiolated Grade 8s', young players who, in studying music in the Western European tradition, have been sold short by their teachers through having their musical energies channelled into learning a linear progression of pieces, with no possibility of branching out to explore the riches on the way. If this is combined with imitation-based teaching, pupils' musical personalities, and the initiative, curiosity, and critical thinking characteristic of music activity, have little opportunity to develop. Auditions for courses of higher education in music bear sad witness to this phenomenon.

The problem with instrumental tutors (the printed variety) and similar syllabuses is that they assume that everyone's growth and development will, and should, follow the same pattern. In some ways, of course, this is true. There are some necessary sequences of events in the acquisition of technical skills, particularly in the early stages. Similarly, in the development of musical concepts, a stable sense of pulse is, for example, a prerequisite for getting the feel of, and making sense of, rhythmic patterning. But, at the same time, what catches the attention and interest of individuals, and what comes to have meaning for them, is particular and distinctive. Teachers need to recognize the quality and the powerful motivation of this response. If they are to key into it, no method, no tutor, and no examination syllabus will do on its own as a basis for planning. On the contrary, a scheme of work, while incorporating material from such sources as and when appropriate, needs to be based on teachers' knowledge of pupils' developing interests and abilities. It requires that teachers listen to what pupils do and say, and, as it were, learn to listen to music with their ears.

It is interesting that this individuality of response and development is one of the reasons put forward for the necessity of individual tuition. Where group teaching is thought to consist of a number of pupils all learning the same piece, mixed ability, mixed technical ability in particular, is seen as an insuperable difficulty. Yet, I think this can only be so where the outworn teaching strategies to which earlier reference has been made are still being employed. Given the collaborative practice of teaching and learning being urged in their place, the mixed ability/mixed experience/mixed response teaching characteristic of group situations opens up possibilities for challenging players to achieve their best.

Profiling progress

If teachers work in the ways being suggested here, they are able to build up a detailed picture of pupils' interests, abilities, and activities. This will be particularly helpful when it comes to the recording and reporting on pupils' progress which schools are being asked to undertake. Systems are being developed for doing this throughout the period of schooling so that at points of transfer, for example, from primary to secondary school, or when young people leave school, there will be enough information available for the task to be done satisfactorily. The Government has set the policy objective of 'establishing by the end of the decade arrangements under which all pupils leaving school will be provided with a record of achievement'.[5] As far as instrumental teaching is concerned, a move away from reports which focus only on technical achievements—or technical problems—is clearly needed. It is helpful to think of a profile as a cumulative record of pupils' engagement with music through composing, performing, and listening experiences in class work, in instrumental sessions, in performance groups, and through outside-school activities. The drawing up of an individual's music profile should be discussed by all the teachers or tutors who work with that individual. Comments need to be expressed in a way that is readily understandable, and appropriately informative, for pupils, parents, headteachers, form teachers, and governors. And in line with the emphasis being given to pupils taking responsibility for their own learning, they should contribute to the drawing up of their own profile.

In order to ensure that what is said genuinely gives information about individual interests, abilities, and activities, an approach similar to that used in drawing up a curriculum vitae is helpful. Comments might be made about the following.

PERFORMING

recent experience	instrument(s)
	occasion(s) (could be in a lesson)
	location(s)
	audience(s)
	role(s)
	piece(s)
	style(s)
	recordings
range of experiences	pupil/student-organized groups
	teacher/tutor-organized groups
	solo playing/singing
	leading, coaching, conducting
	arts projects
	community activities
	cultural traditions

particular interests and preferences—established/recent

COMPOSING, IMPROVISING, ARRANGING

recent work, recent performances, recent recordings

CONCERTS/SHOWS ATTENDED

ASSESSMENTS UNDERTAKEN

DEVELOPING SKILLS

established, emergent, will be tackled next

Broadening perspectives

Some of the headings suggested for inclusion in a profile need some amplification. First, whatever instrument/voice is taken up in schools and music centres, whatever the expectations and preferences of the learner, and whether or not an advanced study or performing outcome is the aim, no instrumental music programme should operate on a monocultural basis, though, of course, it may well have a particular emphasis. While that emphasis may quite properly increase as players identify their particular sphere of interest and as their skills become more advanced, experience of musics should be integral in the early stages of learning. By this I mean that music-making activities should include music, or involve musical ideas, from a variety of styles. Only through such direct experience can an informed understanding of different music languages begin to develop, and only if this is so can young people begin to develop a respect for cultural values and traditions other than their own.

Second, particular attention should be given to ensuring that leadership roles are taken by both girls and boys, both in discussion and group work in lessons, and in rehearsals and performances. Being concerned that girls should have equal opportunities requires that we should not only seek to eliminate gender bias in the take-up of instruments, rock guitar, for example, but also that we should look carefully at the role played by girls in lessons. Perhaps more difficult is the task facing all teachers of making certain that their language and tone of voice, and their expectations of pupils, are free of gender bias and discrimination; that a similar balance of challenge and encouragement is being offered to girls and boys; and that both are contributing to the collaboration considered in this chapter.

Aims and outcomes

A fairly common reaction to the ideas being put forward here goes something like this: 'That's fine, all those extra things, but standards have got to be kept up, and there's not time for it all.' Here is the very nub of the argument. If our aim is to promote the development of 'musicianliness' rather than mere technical, dot-following competence—and surely it is; if we seek to promote the independence of the learner, and if we value his or her individuality—and surely we must; if there is a wish to encourage and challenge pupils and students to achieve their best—and surely there is; and if we have a concern for the wholeness and quality of persons' experiences—and surely we do; then, far from being 'extra things', the processes and activities suggested in the preceding pages are essential to any programme of instrumental learning and teaching. Their inclusion might bring about more of a match between musical aims and musical outcomes!

Author's note

Since this chapter was written, GCSE courses have begun in schools. There has been a growing awareness on the part of teachers, class and instrumental, that common approaches to instrumental work need to be developed across the music curriculum.

New conditions of service for teachers will come into effect in the Autumn 1987.

Notes

1. DES (1985). *Music from 5 to 16*, HMSO.
2. DES/Welsh Office (1985). *GCSE The National Criteria Music*, HMSO.
3. Robinson, K. (ed.) (1982). *The Arts in Schools; principles, practice and provision*, Caloustie Gulbenkian Foundation.
4. Small, C. (1977). *Music. Society. Education.*, John Calder.
5. (1985). *Better Schools*, HMSO.

Further reading

Evans, C. (May, June, July, 1985). 'Attitudes and Change in Instrumental Teaching', *Music Teacher*.

Paynter, J. (1982). *Music in the Secondary School Curriculum*, Cambridge.

Reimer, B. (1970). *A Philosophy of Music Education*, Prentice-Hall.

Stimpson, M. (Mar. 1985). 'The Guitar in English Music Education', *British Journal of Music Education*, Vol. 2, No. 1.

Swanwick, K. (1979). *A Basis for Music Education*, NFER.

Thompson, K. (July, 1984). 'An Analysis of Group Teaching', *British Journal of Music Education*, Vol. 1, No. 2.

2 The Private Teacher

John Gavall

THE comments on private teaching which follow are intended for guitarists who see this aspect of their work as now becoming one of the recognized music professions. They are for those who plan to take such work seriously and who intend to develop their teaching skills, studio equipment, and rules of professional behaviour.

To some extent, as a result of the belated and relatively recent introduction of classical guitar teaching in our main schools and colleges, the skilled and qualified private guitar teacher is still something of a rarity. Any guitarist who undertakes private teaching is not joining an established profession, but is embarking on the work of creating a new one, the national image of which is forged by the quality of musicianship and artistic responsibility brought to it. It should be clear, therefore, that this necessarily involves a good deal more than just being a competent guitar player who is prepared to teach some scales and solos to any pupils who may chance to apply for lessons (which are to be fitted in at such times as the guitarist is resting from the priority of performance work). Private guitar tuition is a profession which needs the most careful fostering.

The market: children and adults

Today, although the guitar is in a much more respected artistic position than it was twenty years ago, it is still not seen by the general public, and therefore by parents, as an obvious choice of instrument on which to arrange for a child to take the first steps in studying music. The piano retains its age-long place as the most comprehensive practical entry to the musical arts. The next most probable parental choice will still normally fall on one of the standard orchestral instruments, the study of which not only provides the social opportunities of playing in an orchestra or band, but also offers experience of a wide range of musical repertoire of high calibre. Hence, the private teacher of guitar tends to encounter much less of an automatic and favourably predisposed market, and therefore receives a far smaller flow of requests for lessons. One consequence of this is that the private guitar teacher may encounter a smaller percentage of young children than is the case of a neighbouring private piano teacher. The obvious disadvantage is that some musical training calls for a start to be made in childhood, usually around the age of eight, if not earlier. The later after that age that a start is made, the less easy it is to achieve the highest levels of musical performance.

With the adult pupil, the motivation often tends to be quite powerful. Many an adult has felt attracted towards doing something active in music, but was not given any opportunity in school life to do anything positive about it. It is a fact that many a child has been permanently put off music by some thoughtless and insensitive remark by someone in authority. The adult, who in later life decides nevertheless to take up a musical instrument, is making a very special personal effort to seek a form of self-realization. The teacher needs to see the task as one of helping a person to develop, not merely as transmitting a few musical skills in return for a fee. Indeed, the private teacher should try to acquire some knowledge of the adult pupil's general way of life, enthusiasms, and problems, as part of finding the means to help along this effort. Clearly, there must not be the tiniest hint of the teacher prying into a pupil's personal activities, but many a pupil will quite spontaneously comment on some current personal activity, project, or problem. The alert teacher will take note of this as an integral part of the lesson.

Private teaching is not merely a matter of selecting only the very obviously talented pupils. The essential criterion for the teacher to apply is whether there is progress, however small, in musical understanding, interest, and skill. There are many gradations of musical abilities, all of which are well worth cultivating. A dedicated guitar teacher will normally teach this wide range of abilities, all hopefully growing steadily, even if some may be moving slowly.

It is not always fully realized by a teacher new to the profession, that an adult pupil who is making tentative steps in learning a musical instrument tends to be extremely nervous at the start of a lesson. This generally differs from the child pupil who is more accustomed to being told that he or she has made a mistake. The adult has grown to expect to make a reasonable success of a task and has lost much resilience in the face of direct correction and criticism. Any such setback makes the adult feel disproportionately more bothered than a child would tend to be in similar circumstances. It can be quite surprising to the inexperienced teacher to find just how much an adult can be inhibited, and even partly go to pieces, out of fear of looking foolish. One of the essential tasks of the teacher is therefore to spot this when it arises, and to take specific steps to deal with it.

A truly vital concern of the teacher should be to ensure that the music for a pupil is chosen in careful relation to an assessment of the pupil's current abilities and musical likings, so as to make the next step forward interesting, easy, and comfortable. At all costs the teacher must avoid leading a pupil into an attempt at a given musical task which results in a feeling of utter defeat. This obviously does not mean that the teacher has to avoid every step forward which involves a pupil in making special effort, but at such points the pupil's progress needs to be monitored very carefully. If even an incipient defeat shows signs of developing, the teacher should unobtrusively find some means of exit from the task and move smoothly on to something where the pupil's self-confidence will be fully re-established. This policy can only be carried out successfully if the teacher has a wide range of carefully graded musical items and tasks.

Studio equipment and routine

For each pupil the teacher will need to open a pupil's work diary sheet, with room at the top for the pupil's name, telephone number, and address. There should be some half-dozen lines drawn vertically in order to create a series of boxes, about two inches square. In the left margin of each box the teacher may log the date of the lesson and perhaps the fee paid or the number of the lesson in a contract of ten. The main area of the box can be used for the teacher's notes on the work done in the lesson, with comments on progress and future work to be tackled. The right margin can be reserved for any special remarks. From time to time the teacher will wish to look back in the work diary files in order to check the general trend of the pupil's progress, and this provides an invaluable guide. It is best to keep all of the work diaries in a filing cabinet, with an initial cap for each file. This will carry a large number of files, alphabetically indexed, plus a good deal of music that is likely to be needed. Obviously, the teacher needs a calendar diary in which to record all engagements. At the end of a lesson the teacher should be careful to fill in both the calendar diary and the pupil's work diary sheet. This important task is easy to forget, especially if one lesson follows immediately on from another.

The teacher will often need to break off from music-making to explain some point of notation, time-keeping, musical terminology, or to write out a musical exercise. The teacher should therefore keep near at hand, a notepad, manuscript paper, pen, pencil, and eraser. Sometimes, the teacher may decide to edit out one or more notes from a piece of music or amend the fingering. For this, it is useful to have a bottle of correction fluid. The teacher may at times wish to emphasize certain parts of a musical texture, to bring out the melody, or clarify the movement of an inner voice. This can be done effectively by using a fluorescent yellow crayon or textliner.

The studio must obviously contain a chair, without arms and of the correct height, and footstools for both the teacher and the pupil. The parent of a younger child may sometimes like to sit in on one or more of the lessons, and it is therefore useful to have an easy chair available. At least one, and preferably two, good music stands are absolutely essential, as are a tuning-fork and metronome. Many teachers also like to have an electronic guitar tuning device, and the well-prepared teacher should keep some spare sets of strings in case of breakage or for the occasion when a string is so dead that it warrants changing. To deal with this, a geared machine-head winder is invaluable. Further equipment should include a nail-cutter, nail-scissors, emery boards, and polishing devices for the nails.

A pupil who goes for a piano lesson naturally expects to play on one of the teacher's instruments. Although a guitar pupil can easily carry the instrument to a lesson, and many pupils prefer to use their own guitar, it is found to be inconvenient by some to have to bring the instrument to every lesson (possibly from the office, by public transport, or for a long distance). Hence, the teacher should have a spare instrument to allow for use by pupils who prefer to avoid bringing a guitar to every lesson. The loan of a guitar can also help a pupil to realize what it is like to play a guitar of some quality, and this may be just the stimulus that the pupil needs to consider purchasing a new instrument.

A cassette recorder, microphone, and a separate loudspeaker(s), are essential items of equipment. They allow the teacher to make recordings of difficult passages for a pupil to take home as an aid to practice. This also allows for the introduction of commercial recordings which relate to the piece of music being tackled. This should not be restricted to recordings of guitar-playing, but embrace as wide a musical field as the teacher can devise. Every opportunity should be taken in a guitar lesson to lead a pupil towards a wider appreciation of music, and indeed, the teacher may sometimes plan the next piece for a pupil with just this in mind. Finally, it will help to have a small collection of photographs of well-known guitarists, sitting in good playing positions. This will assist the teacher in emphasizing to new pupils the importance of the correct playing positions of the arms, hands, and trunk, etc.

Advertising

It is obviously sensible to ensure that the teacher's name, address, telephone number, and qualifications are printed in the main monthly magazines that are concerned with the guitar. These do, however, tend to be read by people who already play the guitar, and the teacher should not expect to tap the local market for beginners. For this, it will be necessary to advertise in non-specialist ways. The most straightforward method is to have printed the very best-looking professional card that spares nothing in good layout and quality of print and paper. If it is about the size of a postcard, it will then be suitable for window display in local newsagents, post offices, and other businesses. This is usually the cheapest form of advertising, although the local parish magazine can be both useful and relatively inexpensive. A wider circulation is covered by the local press, and here an advertisement is likely to cost about £3.00 or £4.00 per week for the minimum detail. It will be necessary to run the advertisement for more than one week to measure the response truly, but a ten-week series, for example, that costs in the order of £35.00, may be considered as a worthwhile and not too expensive experiment. A larger panel in the local press is, of course, more expensive and the soundness of this should be measured carefully. The same applies to the general music magazines in which an advertisement costs approximately £5.00 per publication. A longer-term method of advertising that requires a greater investment is the music teacher's section of the British Telecom Yellow Pages. Lineage can be purchased, but it is more effective to use a small panel because this allows the same amount of information as on the professional card that was referred to above. A name under the heading Musicians, with no indication of instrument or qualifications, is of little use. Advertising in Yellow Pages is not cheap and costs between £200 and £400 per year according to the area to be circulated. However, such figures should be compared with the fees that can be earned from giving forty lessons in one year to one pupil. Experience has shown that it is an excellent advertising medium, and if it provides the teacher with a well-supplied practice, it will have been an invaluable investment.

The management of lessons

When a pupil buys a lesson, he or she is in fact buying a certain amount of the teacher's professional time. It is important that the pupil understands from the outset that the teacher expects pupils to arrive on time and be ready to leave promptly at the end of the lesson. Any questions should be raised during, and not at the end of the lesson. It is, of course, helpful to have some place where a pupil who arrives early for a lesson may wait, but real punctuality should be striven for and the teacher must see his or her own reliability of attendance and punctuality as a matter of basic professional self-respect. Hence, it is desirable for a clock to be visible to the pupil and teacher. It can, however, subtly dilute the favourable atmosphere of a good lesson if either the pupil or teacher is consciously seen to be glancing at the clock. The implication is that one of them wishes the lesson were over.

It can occur that a pupil simply forgets a lesson. This is most likely to happen with children in holiday periods, when their weekly school-based routine has been dropped and a lesson has lost its connection with a given day of the week. Some teachers prefer to stop lessons during school holidays for this and other reasons. Moreover, if a lesson is forgotten, provided that it has been paid for in advance as part of some package, it is a simple matter to debit the parents for the lesson as if it had been given. After all, the teacher will have reserved the lesson time, possibly refused to allocate it to another pupil, and probably done some preparatory work in expectation of the lesson. The teacher is, therefore, fully entitled to be paid for the time that has in effect been lost. It is essential, however, that this arrangement should be made quite clear at the start of any dealings concerning lessons. It is useful to have this stated in writing so that there can be no argument over the arrangement. Some degree of flexibility can, of course, be exercised. An adult is less likely to forget a lesson but may be more likely to request cancellation at the last minute. It is, therefore, essential that the point be made (in writing) that any cancellation of less than a week's notice seriously disrupts the teacher's professional work, and if a cancellation is made as late as twenty-four hours before the lesson then it will be charged for in full. With some people it can be necessary to state quite forcefully that cancellation means a loss of money to the teacher, quite apart from the inconvenience caused. The teacher can occasionally find that the nicest person is incapable of behaving responsibly in this matter, and in such cases it may be best to terminate the lessons.

The actual length of a lesson traditionally tends to be thirty minutes. I prefer forty minutes, although the choice ultimately must be decided by the teacher's own style of work. The frequency of lessons is normally one a week. These are not, however, successful if the pupil does not do the necessary practice between them and some pupils really cannot manage the work inside a week. These may do better with a fortnightly arrangement.

The teacher should keep a simple and accurate record (ledger diary) of every single professional incoming and outgoing, updated regularly so that it can be referred to when preparing accounts for the Inland Revenue. The teacher should also set aside every piece of paper which will substantiate the entries made in the ledger diary because a self-employed teacher is expected by the tax inspector to claim for professional expenses each year. These would include such items as stationery, strings, advertising, travel, subscriptions, sheet music, music books, scores, cassettes, and LP records used in work. The teacher's annual accounts must show exactly what has been earned and exactly what has been spent in the process. It is on the difference between these two sets of figures that the teacher will eventually pay tax. In addition to outlays such as those mentioned above, the teacher is entitled to claim a reasonable proportion of basic living costs (rates, gas, electricity, telephone, etc.) as being an essential part of expenditure in carrying out professional work. The paying of quite costly fees to a professional accountant may only be justified if the teacher has a very complex set of accounts to keep. Few private teachers have such a problem. The first step for a new teacher to take is to call at the local tax office and seek detailed advice from the inspector.

The single most useful thing that a new private guitar teacher can do is to join the Private Teachers' Section (PTS) of the Incorporated Society of Musicians: ISM, 10 Stratford Place, London W1N 9AE; telephone: 01-629-4413. This professional organization has collected the combined wisdom and experience of generations of private teachers and it can assist the new teacher in many ways. A teacher new to the field can find it extremely helpful to have concrete advice on the scale of fees for private music lessons. So long as we have inflation with us, fees will need to be raised periodically, and the ISM publishes what might be called a rising norm, to which the teacher can refer pupils or parents, should the need arise. It is advisable to give adequate warning of a future rise in costs well in advance of the actual date of implementation. The new private teacher can feel rather isolated unless linked with other teachers, and membership of the ISM can give much support.

The ISM tends to advocate giving lessons lasting thirty minutes, grouped in contracts of ten lessons and payable in advance. The teacher who wishes to maximize the number of pupils must take note of the fact that many people today are in occupations which do not permit them to attend with absolute regularity. To meet this, it is a simple matter for the teacher to offer such people the opportunity to telephone to see if the teacher happens to have a period free. Similarly, some people who cannot easily manage to find the whole cost of ten lessons can nevertheless have no difficulty in managing the price of one lesson at a time. A teacher should try to offer lessons in a manner which can meet the needs of as many as possible of the people who live locally.

The lesson

Before the lesson begins, the teacher should study the pupil's work diary to see which music will be needed, and to note any matters discussed in the last lesson. The pupil, on arrival, should feel that he or she is meeting a helpful friend. Someone who regards the pupil coolly, as a passing customer who will pay a fee, will not put the pupil at ease.

Many pupils need to warm up before tackling the main piece of music that they have been practising. The teacher is advised to teach by rote, quite early in a course of lessons, a one octave scale pattern (for example C major in fifth position). This can then be used to cultivate the pupil's closest possible attention to the various aspects of left- and right-hand technique. The purpose of teaching this item is twofold: not only to focus the pupil's attention on left- and right-hand action, but also to provide the pupil with a totally absorbing warm-up exercise on which to get busy on arrival. Once so absorbed, the pupil has no time to think about nerves and can therefore move on more efficiently to the main music-making part of the lesson.

Every pupil will make mistakes. It is essential, therefore, that the teacher should analyse and describe the causes of any mistakes as clearly as possible. One standard cause of mistakes is the tendency of every beginner to try to do everything faster than the level of skill will permit. The teacher will need to keep slowing the pupil down until the speed is reached at which the music can be played accurately. Mistakes occur a great deal in the reading of time-values. The teacher should therefore realize that if trouble is taken in the early stages to instil a solid sense of time-keeping, an important sense of security and skill will be established.

The teacher will need to have a planned set of carefully-graded repertoire files that include: introductory reading exercises; first, second, and third-level solos; hispanic solos; solos from the sixteenth and seventeenth centuries; baroque solos; nineteenth-century solos; twentieth-century solos; and those of other musical styles. Further files are required on scales, studies, and solos grouped to deal with mastering the use of certain positions on the finger-board.

However wide the repertoire the teacher may have gathered, he or she will receive occasional requests for solos which are not known to exist in published form. These requests may often only be met by the teacher's own arrangement(s) of the music concerned. Hence, the teacher should take pains to develop skills in arranging and composition, as a positive contribution to building up a stock of music to meet the varied needs of all pupils.

The teacher needs to make the most of the fact that the guitar is especially suitable for illustrating all kinds of harmonic structure, and should be alert to exploit opportunities for the analysis of progressions encountered in the repertoire studies.

It is desirable that a pupil be led towards frequent playing in ensemble. Initially, this will be practical only in the playing of duos with the teacher, but later this should evolve into work with fellow pupils. Few things develop musicianship so powerfully as regular ensemble playing.

At the end of a lesson the teacher will need to wind up the work tidily and on time. The pupil should be set clear targets for practising and the lesson concluded with a few particular aims to strive for, and some words of encouragement. Poor lessons will undoubtedly take place and in certain circumstances the teacher will feel that a series of lessons should be discontinued. This decision is difficult because rates of progress vary, as does the degree of fulfilment and enjoyment that each individual gains from studying the guitar. Nevertheless, one major factor that contributes to making a good teacher is the capacity to analyse the lesson, both during and after. It may, however, be some time before a new teacher has the confidence to recognize that a teaching arrangement has run its productive course.

The teacher should not only try to develop good performances of pieces but also a general growth of musical understanding. Furthermore, the teacher should seek to lead the pupil to an interest in the whole field of music and not merely confine it within the realms of guitar literature. The guitar should be seen as a gateway to music interest generally, not just as an end in itself.

3 The Guitar as a Classroom Instrument

Michael Stimpson and Michael Burnett

THE relative importance of music within the school curriculum is a question which has at times come under intense discussion. Too often, music has been relegated to the depths of a league table of priorities, and it has rarely become fashionable to recognize that music has a unique contribution to make to the curriculum and that it should therefore be given equal status to other subjects in school. The reasons for music's poor standing are complex and varied, but there can be no doubt that in a climate of economic cut-backs it has become all the more important to question the relevance of the music curriculum to today's children. Time and again it becomes apparent that some music educators have made so little effort to avoid stagnation that it is a wonder that the subject has maintained even its present position—and this in a century when music, like society itself, has undergone almost unbelievable change. With the advent of mass world travel, complex technological progress, and, indeed, of significant new developments within the subject itself, music has flowered into a truly multifaceted twentieth-century discipline, capable of catering in different ways for the needs of each member of society. Yet, in addition to showing little propensity for development, music education has exhibited a divisiveness of approach which has alienated a substantial proportion of its recipients, often ensuring in the process that any benefits which these children may gain are accidental rather than intended. And of all musical instruments it is perhaps the guitar which has suffered most as a result of the confines of twentieth-century music education.

Throughout the century the guitar has been at the forefront of the development of a number of contrasting musical styles. There are many reasons for this: the instrument's portability, its suitability for accompaniment, and its role in the music of certain groups within society, all have played a part. Many guitarists would argue, however, that the most fundamental reason is the instrument's extraordinary range of sound capabilities, both acoustic and amplified; indeed, it is difficult to think of any other instrument which can match the ability of the guitar to vary its tone quality from, on the one hand, the delicacy of timbre of a passage of harmonics in a classical piece, to, on the other, the expressive use of feedback in rock.

Certainly, the suitability of the Spanish guitar for the performance of twentieth-century music has made a substantial contribution to its acceptance by classical musicians. Outside classical music, of course, the guitar has been accepted more readily, although the popular image of the instrument has often merely served to arouse reservations about it on the part of the classical music establishment. The fact that the guitar, in all its forms, has such power in the hands of non-classical musicians militates against its acceptance as an instrument worthy of a place alongside instruments that are associated more obviously with the great composers of the past. The danger here is that tacit assumptions concerning the guitar's inferiority can result in a failure to recognize the true capabilities and integrity of the instrument and, indeed, the very force that lies behind the development of the modern guitar and its music.

For example, the use of the guitar as an instrument for accompaniment by the class music teacher has been a dominant one for many years now and is based on assumptions concerning the instrument's ease of playing, portability, and relatively low cost—factors which are only a part of the true picture. Here, the guitar is seen merely as an adjunct to the main activity, that of class singing, which of course has a high priority in many schools. Indeed, the use of the guitar primarily for its ability to support another, more important, musical activity has been strongly advocated by music educators for decades and it is still the case that most teacher-training courses (including in-service) endorse the self-same view. Many examples of this sort of approach could be quoted; suffice it to say that the true capabilities of the guitar are considerably greater than such limited use implies. It is the purpose of this chapter to suggest a number of more varied classroom activities involving the instrument.

Before considering project work for the classroom, brief reference should be made to the role of the visiting teacher. It is common for the work of the visiting teacher to be seen as entirely separate from that of the class teacher and, although this is a topic more fully dealt with in Chapter 1, the relationship between the two forms of teaching deserves further emphasis here. Many of the problems that face the visiting teacher derive from a lack of involvement in the working of the school and its curriculum. The class teacher, although unlikely to be a specialist in the guitar, will almost certainly have a broader perspective of each child and an awareness of what will work in the classroom. The issue in this chapter is the use of the guitar in non-specific areas of the curriculum, not the production of players, and although the visiting teacher will be tempted to shy away from involvement in the classroom, the class teacher should make every effort to use the specialist knowledge of the instrumental teacher. The potential contribution of a visiting teacher to work in the classroom can be most valuable and should not be viewed merely as a loss of lesson time for the small number of individual pupils that would normally be taught. A classroom lesson that makes use of the skills of these particular children will serve the dual purpose of exhibiting those skills and also of demonstrating the instrument's capabilities to those who are not studying it.

Project 1: Sound and the construction of the guitar

From an early age a child learns to distinguish and select specific sounds, and a project for younger children which helps demonstrate the sound capabilities allied to the structure of the guitar can be both stimulating and illuminative. The aim is for the children themselves to discover as many different sounds as they can, and for these discoveries to be listed by the teacher as they emerge. In the classroom the children should be divided into as many groups as there are guitars. If the school owns only one instrument it will be necessary for the children to pass this round and for each member of the class to attempt to produce a different sound from those made previously. It is important that the children are as quiet as possible during this activity as sounds can easily be made accidentally by, for example, merely handling the instrument. Some characteristic guitar sounds are listed below, although it should be emphasized that there are far more to be discovered than are mentioned here.

Common musical sounds

Single note, normal tone, played over the sound-hole.
Single note, ponticello tone, played near the bridge.
Single note, flautando tone, played where the neck of the guitar meets the body of the instrument.

Two, three, or four strings played simultaneously with varying tone qualities.

Strum—note that the speed of the strum can be varied, that a crescendo or diminuendo may be added, and that individual notes may be highlighted. The tone may be varied by using the thumb nail or tip (flesh), or the finger-nails as in flamenco style (*rasgueado*).

Less common musical sounds

(For technical explanation see Chapter Nine.)

Glissando.

Harmonics—these may be played in single note and chord form.

Pizzicato.

Portamento.

Tambour—note that the balance between the sound of the wood and the strings can be varied depending on where the guitar is struck.

Vibrato—note that the speed and pitch of the vibrato can be varied considerably.

Unusual sounds

A high-pitched sound can be created by sounding the strings between the nut and the rollers.

A sound reminiscent of a creaking door being opened can be produced by running a finger-nail along a metal-wound string.

A lighter version of this sound, familiar to all guitarists, is that produced by running the fleshy fingertip along the string.

A considerable range of percussive sounds can be made by striking the guitar (gently!).

Talking, whistling, or blowing into the guitar.

Rubbing the body of the guitar with a wet finger gives a high pitched squeak.

External material may be used to make a variety of sounds which can be useful in relation to creative music making in the classroom. In the writers' experience children prove to be highly imaginative in this respect; for example, paper may be threaded between the strings or a bottle slid along them. Particular care must, of course, be taken of the instrument(s) during experiments such as these.

Project 2: Musical games

The exploration of the various sounds of which the guitar is capable is just one of many musical games that are possible with the instrument. Before referring to some of these, it is important to stress that musical games should not be seen as a substitute for more formal work, but as a potential method of producing musical awareness by the stimulus of less usual means. In addition, musical games help foster children's social skills and interaction, and provide some experience of an instrument that may otherwise be denied. Games cover a variety of topics and may be used to facilitate the development of concentration, pitch recognition, awareness of rhythm, imagination, self-expression, and improvisation.

(i) Higher or lower?

For this game one guitar only is required and the children may work in teams or as individuals. The teacher, or a child, should play first one, then a second, different, note on the guitar. Participants must then decide whether the second note is higher or lower.

(ii) Alternative uses for the guitar

The purpose of this game is for the children to suggest alternative uses for the various parts of the guitar. The game is intended for very young children who, in the process of playing it, will discover much about the construction and working of the instrument, including the names of its components. Such children have, in the writers' experience, proved to be highly imaginative in thinking up unusual uses for these. One five-year-old felt that sawing off the neck of a guitar and removing its strings would leave an ideal boat for her pet rabbit. Another child suggested that the strings, tied together, would make a useful washing line. Other children thought of many and varied uses for the strings, pegs, rollers, etc.

(iii) Memory game

A short game for two, three, or four children, each with a guitar. In its simplest form this game is intended to help reinforce the natural notes found in one position. The teacher should initially show and name the notes to be used as the basis of the game (for example, open string E, F, and G on the first string). The first child should play and name one of these notes (for example E). This note should then be played by the second child, who names and plays another one of the set (for example G). One of the notes from the set is then added by each child in turn, a child dropping out of the game when he or she fails to remember the sequence of notes played by the preceding participant. The winner is the last child remaining. The game can be adapted to meet the needs of more advanced groups by introducing sharps, flats, and more extended sets of notes.

(iv) Melodic patterning

This game emphasizes the melodic capabilities of the guitar and will assist in developing some basic scale technique. It will thus prove suitable for older children and will also serve as a useful preliminary to the extemporized melodies suggested later. First, the teacher should specify and demonstrate a one, or two, octave scale (not necessarily diatonic) which will constitute the nucleus of melodic material. (For example, a one octave C major scale starting in fifth position.) The teacher should then ask the children each to practise the scale and to construct a variety of short melodic fragments from it, using conjunct as well as stepwise movement. A time-signature (for example 4/4) and speed (moderato) should subsequently be indicated and the teacher should then play an opening phrase of a simple melody. A child should then be asked to respond to the teacher's opening phrase by adding a second, using notes selected from the nucleus and rhythms similar to those used by the teacher. (This phrase may draw upon the melodic shapes already constructed, but not necessarily.) For example, a potential opening phrase (Ex. 3.1), might be followed by (Ex. 3.2). The teacher should then continue the melody by repeating the first phrase and asking another child to invent a fourth and final phrase (such as Ex. 3.3). (A tape-recorder will prove a useful aid to

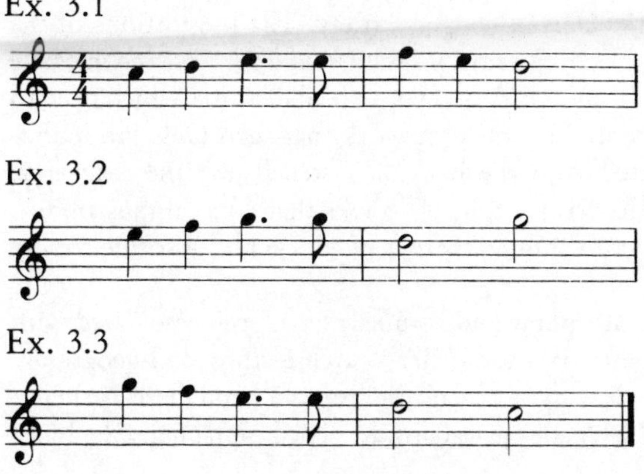

analysis and discussion of the complete melody.) The melody game should be repeated using the same opening phrase until all the children have had an opportunity to join in. Then other scales and opening phrases should be tried out (such as Ex. 3.4).

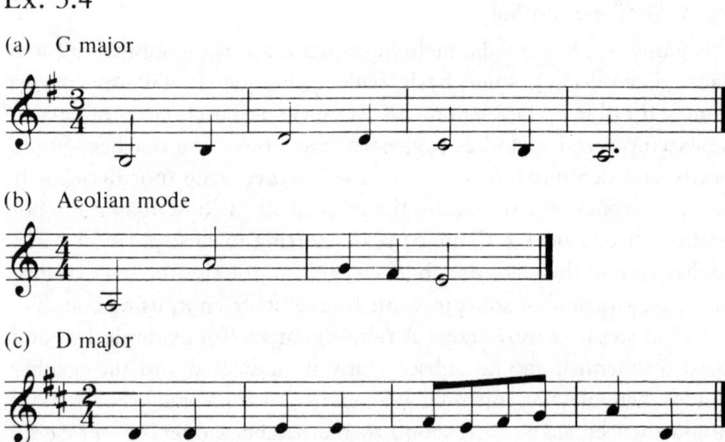

Project 3: Art work and other subjects

For the junior classroom, the guitar provides an ideal theme for general work such as painting and drawing. In relation to the latter, the shapes and dimensions of guitars have, over the years, changed considerably and many children will now be used to seeing, on television, solid-bodied electric guitars that are oblong or triangular in shape, as well as the classic, winged variety. The proportions of the body shapes and necks of the various guitars, and the drawing in of the frets, strings, bridge, nut, head, and pegs are all features which need to be taken into account. The intricate work that surrounds the sound-hole can be imitated with the help of a stencil and the teacher is referred to Appendix VII for a list of books that contain illustrations of all kinds of guitars, although there is of course no substitute for the real thing.

More generally, the guitar and its music have been associated with many different aspects of history, dress, architecture, and geography etc. (the latter is dealt with more fully in Project 5), and there are many connections that the teacher may consider worth pursuing. The blues guitar and its links with slavery, the electric guitar and the 1960s, the importance of the guitar in the music of the South American countries, the life and music of Andrés Segovia, and the planning of a rock concert or tour—these are just a few ideas for differing age-ranges. In addition, some museums contain examples of early guitars, and some local authorities provide guitar concerts for schools that may be linked to specific topics.

Project 4: Accompaniment

As we have seen, it is important to place the guitar's capabilities as an instrument of accompaniment in proper perspective. The popular image of the guitar in the classroom is that of the instrument being strummed by the teacher as an accompaniment to the children's singing. From the children's point of view, this has the major disadvantage that it is not they who get to play the guitar. In order to involve children in accompanying it will initially be necessary for the teacher to provide sufficiently simple parts. In this connection the reader is referred to Chapter 6 where there is a consideration of open string song accompaniment. In summary, the open strings of the guitar provide the tonic, subdominant, and dominant roots of chords in the keys of E, A, and D (major and minor). There are many songs based on these chords and it thus becomes a short exercise for the teacher to arrange even the most up to date material with an accompaniment that is playable by the children. These accompaniments would initially be based on root notes, but the open strings can of course provide other components of common chords.

An intermediate stage of accompaniment can be provided by the use of chord shapes that are easier than those normally found in first position. Chords that require merely one or two fingers of the left hand have not only the advantage of being easier to play but, crucially, facilitate the change from one chord to another. In the classroom the teacher may wish to introduce yet another stage where each child is allocated one chord only, thus avoiding the need for any change. When the stage of chord-changing has been reached, it is essential that a key and chord sequence is chosen that minimizes the difficulties. The chords in Ex. 3.5 require either one or two fingers of the left hand.

When the children have advanced to the stage at which it becomes practicable to introduce the common chord shapes it is vital, once again, to select keys and progressions with care. Of the chords listed

Ex. 3.5

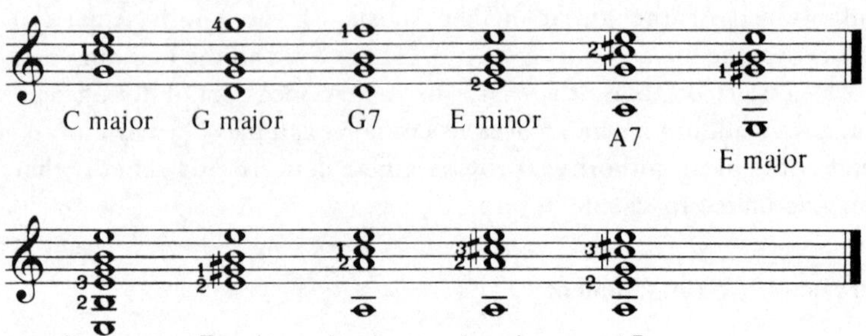

above, the most convenient is E minor because, in using all six strings, it is not possible to introduce by accident open string notes that do not belong to the chord (and it can be strummed). For a detailed account of a chord progression that moves E minor, E major, A minor, A major, B7, and E major, the reader is again referred to Chapter 6. For the purposes of the class teacher who may not be working with notation, these chords and others are set out in Appendix III.

It should be noted that the key of C major, so commonly used in arrangements for other classroom instruments, raises a number of significant problems for the beginner. First, the C major chord itself necessitates wider finger spacing than many chords; secondly, the subdominant (F major) and dominant (G major) chords are both relatively difficult to play; and, thirdly, a finger can rarely remain pressing between two consecutive chords. A chord of F major, in its full form, requires the use of a barré, a technique which involves the pressing down, usually by the first finger, of more than one string and hence the laying of this finger across the strings. Such a chord should not be expected of beginners on the Spanish guitar because of the difficulty of obtaining clear-sounding notes.

However, the technique is referred to here in order to illustrate the advantage of a transposing chord shape, a device that is particularly useful to the electric guitar player. For major barré chords that involve all the six strings, a player should initially press an E major chord. The chord should be re-fingered so that the first finger is left free and the shape moved along one fret to the right. The setting of the first finger across the strings just to the left of the first fret, provides a full F major chord. (A more detailed account of barré technique may be found in Chapter 9.) Movement of this chord one further fret to the right (second position) produces a chord of F♯ major, a similar shift to third position forms a chord of G major, etc. Thus, many (all on an electric guitar) major chords can be derived from this one finger-shape. A similar set of minor chords may be derived in the same way from an E minor chord, although these may also be formed by simply lifting the second finger from the major, barré shape. This process may also be repeated with the shape of A major and minor, and a barré across five strings. It should be noted that other chords, such as sevenths, can be similarly transposed. A diagram of the barré positions for the chords of A major and A minor is shown in Ex. 3.6.

Ex. 3.6

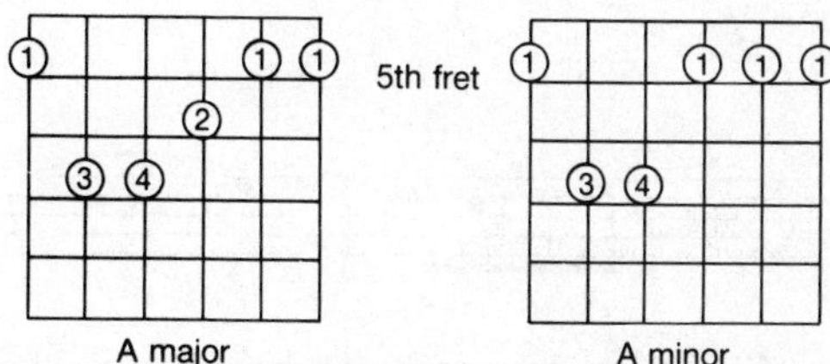

The right hand is, of course, essential to song accompaniment and decisions as to whether it is the flesh of the thumb, the thumb nail, the index finger, the fingers in a pseudo-flamenco style, or a pick that is to be used, will depend on the style and character of the melody. Rhythm is also a vital aspect of accompaniment and some examples of rhythm patterns are set out in Ex. 3.7, each containing an indication of whether an up-stroke (↑) or down-stroke (↓) is to be used.

Ex. 3.7

Project 5: Geography and style

The guitar is used in many different styles of music throughout the world. A survey of some of these styles, together with the provision of some information about the countries concerned, can form the basis of an interesting and open-ended project or series of projects. Here are some examples.

(i) Spain

The country most commonly associated with the acoustic guitar is famous for its dramatic flamenco dancing. Characteristically found in the Andalucían region, flamenco singers and dancers make use of castanets and stamping in order to emphasize the rhythms of the guitar music which accompanies them. Ex. 3.8(a) is a flamenco tune which may be played by beginner guitarists; Ex. 3.8(b) is a short rhythmic sequence.

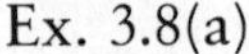

* This chord is formed by shifting the E major shape one fret to the right.

(ii) USA

The guitar is used as the basic accompaniment to country 'n' western songs which stem from the mid-western States. These songs employ diatonic major 'singalong' tunes which are supported by equally diatonic harmonies with a strong emphasis on tonic, subdominant, and dominant chords (chords, I, IV, and V). An example of a country 'n' western tune is shown in Ex. 3.9; it should be played by one group

Ex. 3.9

of guitarists while a second group strums a chordal accompaniment as shown.

(iii) Trinidad and Tobago

Trinidad and Tobago, and indeed many of the eastern Caribbean islands, are famous for their calypsos. These songs with satirical intent, the accompaniments to which make use of guitar in addition to other instruments, are characterized by a 1–2–3, 1–2–3, 1–2, quaver rhythm which can also be found in other Caribbean genres such as Jamaica's mento. Ex. 3.10 is part of a typical calypso bass line which may be played by a small group of guitarists, aided by a bass guitarist if possible.

Ex. 3.10

A harmonic accompaniment may then be provided by a second group of guitarists playing chords so as to emphasize the characteristic rhythm (Ex. 3.11).

Ex. 3.11

Rhythm	4	1 2 3 1 2 3 1 2	1 2 3 1 2 3 1 2	1 2 3 1 2 3 1 2	1 2 3 1 2 3 1 2
Chord	4	G* G G	C C C	D7 D7 D7	G G G

* See simpler chords given earlier.

Project 6: The blues

The guitar lends itself particularly well to a classroom blues project on the grounds (i) of the authentic nature of its contribution to the development of the blues, and (ii) of the comparative ease with which the basic chords of the blues sequence may be played on the instrument in the keys of E, A, and G. The sequence is derived from the tonic, subdominant, and dominant chords in each key, these being most often distributed over twelve common-time bars (Ex. 3.12).

Ex. 3.12

Chord	Number of bars	in E	in A	in D
tonic	4	E	A	D
subdominant	2	A	D	G
tonic	2	E	A	D
dominant 7th	1	B7	E7	A7
subdominant	1	A	D	G
tonic	1	E	A	D
dominant 7th	1	B7	E7	A7
	12			

A blues project for beginners on guitar will involve participants playing a series of notes which together form the fundamental bass line of the blues, that is, the root of each chord in turn. These notes may be played on the beat, or be given a rhythm which, although theoretically posing more complication, actually makes bar-counting easier. Ex. 3.13 shows some suggested rhythms.

More advanced guitarists may then be encouraged to finger and play the blues chord sequence in the chosen key above the bass line provided by the beginners. Rhythms such as those set out below may again be played but it is preferable not to employ the same rhythmic pattern in both bass and chord sections. And, as a third aspect, some classroom guitarists may be encouraged to play brief 'solos' derived from the chord sequence. The essence of blues style lies in the superimposition of minor on major, of a minor melody on the fundamental major chord sequence. So a soloist supported by a classroom band playing the blues in the key of E will tend to play a melody using the E minor (descending melodic) scale, sounding G♮s

against the band's E major chords, C♮s against their A major chords, and D♮s against their B7 chords. (Other commonly used notes in relation to the E major chord are E, B, and D; to the A major chord A, E, and G; and to B7 B, F♯, and A). Example 3.14 is a blues in E for classroom ensemble. It has been set out for three acoustic (classical) guitars and therefore uses treble clefs. It a school is fortunate enough to own a bass guitar then the lower line should be rewritten in bass clef.

Project 7: Reggae

A unique fusion of American rhythm 'n' blues and Jamaican mento, reggae has become a major force within pop music since its inception in Kingston during the late 1960s. True reggae has an elusive quality which can only be attained through lengthy and assiduous listening and practice; for our purposes, however, the music's characteristic bass riffs (repeated melodic patterns) and chord rhythms lend themselves well to imitation in the classroom and can form the basis of instructive and creative project work.

Ex. 3.14

7

9

11

(i) Riff I

This initial project makes use of a simple riff which employs the notes E, A, and B, and a harmonic accompaniment using the chords of E and A major. Section I consists of a riff (Ex. 3.15) which should be played a minimum of four times by perhaps a quartet of acoustic guitarists with the help of a bass guitarist if possible. To accompany this, a second group of children should play off-beat E major chords (Ex. 3.16). If untuned percussion instruments are available they should be judiciously used to accompany these projects. Note, though, that it is best to use light, relatively high-pitched sounds—for example, fingers tapped at the edge of a tom-tom skin—and that the rhythms should point beats one and three by omission (Ex. 3.17).

Ex. 3.15

Ex. 3.16

Ex. 3.17

Section II of the piece uses the riff (Ex. 3.18) (played a minimum of four times) to the accompaniment of off-beat A major chords. Section I will then be repeated in conclusion. Once the material has been practised by the two groups, separately and together, it may then be varied in presentation—for example, the riff group beginning alone, with the chord group entering after four bars—and ultimately used as a basis for individual childrens' extemporizations. Here the children should use notes from the scale of E major for section I and A major for section II.

Ex. 3.18

(ii) Riff II

This (Ex. 3.19) is a longer and more complex example which introduces some bass riff syncopation and a faster off-beat harmonic rhythm.

Project 8: Listening

The vast number of records now available, which between them demonstrate every aspect of guitar playing, gives the teacher more than adequate scope for illustrating specific musical points. Classroom listening can easily set up a degree of boredom and alienation among the children because of its passive nature. Many teachers will themselves remember being unwilling recipients of music lessons which consisted entirely of listening to a whole Beethoven symphony; indeed this form of inflicted 'music appreciation' constituted the be-all and end-all of music education in some schools. It is important, therefore, carefully to relate the length of the musical illustration to the content and overall length of the lesson, to encourage the children to focus their listening on particular elements of the piece and, as far as possible, to link the listening to practical performance. As a general topic, listening to guitar music can, and should, be an adjunct to many of the other subject areas explored in this chapter; projects on music history, for example, would be far too theoretical without the children hearing music from the different periods, preferably played on the authentic instruments. The suggestions for listening made here are presented on a thematic basis, that is, the taking of a particular musical point in relation to the guitar and showing how it has been used in different contexts. (Wherever possible, for reasons of cost, the same record has been recommended to illustrate different points.)

(i) The strum

This is one of the most characteristic sounds of the guitar, and because an increasing number of schools now have a set of guitars for classroom use, the children should be encouraged to imitate the

Ex. 3.19

different sounds that they hear, using either the open strings or a chord of E minor. Note, for example, the short sustain which characterizes chord playing in reggae (Bob Marley) and compare this with the longer, more resonant, chords which open the slow movement of Rodrigo's *Concerto de Aranjuez*. Further distinction may be made between the opening to this concerto and that of *Pinball Wizard*. Five listening examples are shown in Ex. 3.20.

Ex. 3.20

Joaquín Rodrigo, first and second movements from *Concerto de Aranjuez* (John Williams), CBS 73784.

The Who, *Pinball Wizard* from *Tommy*, Track Record 613 013/4.

Bob Marley and the Wailers, *Zion Train* from *Uprising*, Island ILPS 9596.

Bob Dylan, *All along the Watchtower* from *John Wesley Harding*, CBS 63282.

Paco Peña, *The Art of Flamenco Guitar*, Goldcrown Polygram DGSI

These examples may be used to demonstrate aspects of music theory such as chord structure or the rhythm of reggae with its emphasis on the second and fourth beats of the bar.

(ii) Scales

Scale passages of varied lengths and speed provide the basis of many melodies and bass lines (see Ex. 3.21).

Ex. 3.21

Jaco Pastorius, *Come on, Come over* from *Jaco Pastorius*, Epic EPC 81453.

Django Reinhardt, *Swing* from *Djangology*, Vogue VJD 502/1/2.

Paco de Lucia, Al di Meola, and John McLaughlin, *Aspen* from *Passion Grace and Fire*, Philips 811 334–1.

J S Bach, *Allegro* from *Prelude, Fugue, and Allegro BWV 998* (John Williams), CBS 79203.

(iii) Songs and their accompaniments

Here, of course, there are many features to listen for. Note, for example, the varying balance between the voice and guitar, the occasions when the guitar mimics the voice, and when the accompaniment is of a chordal or melodic nature (Ex. 3.22).

Ex. 3.22

Chaka Khan, *Tell Me Something Good* from *Rufus and Chaka Khan Live*, Warner Brothers 92–3679–1.

Blind Willie Johnson, *Dark was the Night*, Folkways FJ 2802.

Benjamin Britten, *Folk Songs*, from *Folk Songs* (Robert Tear and Timothy Walker), Argo ZK39.

John Martyn, *May You Never*, from *Solid Air*, Island ILPS 9226.

(iv) Timbre

The unique contrasts of timbre which are obtainable from the family of guitars provide a fruitful source of listening examples for the teacher. In addition, the recognition and comparison of nuances of playing can offer a more creative means of developing musical awareness than conventional ear tests. Note the contrasts between the mellow and metallic (ponticello) sound in the classical example (Ex. 3.23) (Granados), or the use of distortion by Jimi Hendrix.

Ex. 3.23

Sade, *Fear* from *Promise*, Epic EPC 86318.

Stanley Jordan, *Eleanor Rigby* from *Magic Touch*, Bluenote BT85101.

Enrique Granados, *Oriental (Danza Española No. 2)* from *Music for the Classic Guitar* (Ida Presti and Alexandre Lagoya), Nonesuch H—71161.

Jimi Hendrix, *Voodoo Chile* from *Electric Ladyland*, Track Records/Polydor 613 008/9.

Project 9: Harmonic riffs and extemporizing

Pop music and jazz make much use of repeated chord patterns (usually termed riffs) which can provide the basis for creative work in the classroom. These patterns are often purely diatonic or modal, or a combination of the two, and the reproduction of such patterns, suitably transposed where necessary, can also help to equip children with some knowledge of diatonic and modal scales in the process of playing them. Here are some characteristic examples suitable for use with middle and lower secondary age-ranges in particular. The examples are for playing on both acoustic and electric instruments and for use with either three solo guitarists or two groups of guitarists supporting a solo extemporizer. Untuned percussion and/or a drum machine may also be included.

(i) Extemporization I

This example makes use of the Dorian mode (the white note D scale on the keyboard) but the sequence has been transposed up a tone so as to make for easier playing and the inclusion of an open string bass line for beginners. The chord pattern is shown in Ex. 3.24. Beginners should play a bass line made up of the root note of each chord in turn. More experienced guitarists should play the chords either strummed or arpeggiated with right-hand fingering to a specific rhythmic pattern (such as Ex. 3.25(a)) or Ex. 3.25(b) or the reggae extension of the latter Ex. 3.25(c).

Ex. 3.24

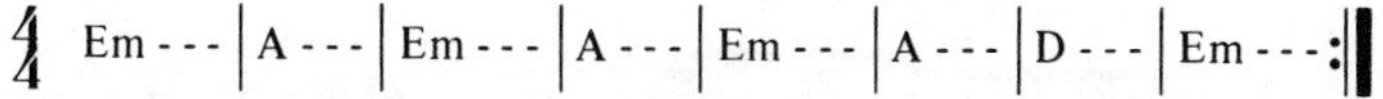

Ex. 3.25

Ex. 3.26

Melodies may then be extemporized above the sequence by individuals using notes chosen from the scale shown in Ex. 3.26. Clearly, not all notes will 'work' equally well above all the chords in the sequence, but repetition of the sequence and aural experimentation by the extemporizer will develop greater musical awareness on the part of both supporting and extemporizing performers. Some melodic fragments which may be used as starting-points for extemporization are set out in Ex. 3.27.

(ii) Extemporization II

This diatonic chord sequence which is a little more difficult to play than *Extemporization (I)* has formed the basis of many a pop song. It should be treated in the same way as the previous sequence, with a C major scale constituting the nucleus of material for extemporization (Ex. 3.28).

Ex. 3.28

4/4 C - - - | Em - - - | Dm - - - | G - - - :||

(iii) Extemporization III

This sequence is in the Aeolian (or white note A) mode (Ex. 3.29). It should be played in the same way as the earlier examples, with the notes shown in Ex. 3.30 forming the nucleus for extemporization.

Ex. 3.29

4/4 Am - - Dm | Em - - G | Am - - Dm | Em - - - :||

Ex. 3.30

Project 10: Pitch, scales, and acoustics

The acoustic guitar has a number of uses in the classroom as a visual aid in the teaching and demonstration of musical and acoustic facts. The following topics for discussion are suitable for middle and secondary age-ranges.

(i) Pitch and scales

An instrument with a fretted finger-board has obvious advantages in terms of its capability to demonstrate visually (on one string at a time) the logic of both intervals and of those consecutive combinations of intervals which together constitute scale patterns. The concept of pitch, of what we mean when we say high or low, up or down in relation to sounds, is a difficult one to explain or demonstrate in relation to any instrument. For children the terminology used in connection with pitch is both confusing and contradictory; for example, the piano keyboard, or set of bars on a glockenspiel, do not actually go up physically as pitch rises. Rather, low notes are to the left of the player on a level with the high notes which are to the player's right. Our understanding, as musicians, that notes progress upwards in pitch from left to right is therefore not demonstrated visually. On the guitar, of course, the situation is further complicated by the fact that, in most of the normal playing positions, the player's fingers actually move downwards along the finger-board as pitch goes up. So we suggest, as a starting point when exploring the concept of pitch contrast, that the guitar be up-ended so as to enable the children to see the frets as, in effect, constituting the rungs of a ladder up which the fingers and corresponding pitches ascend. Untuned percussion instruments may (with some circumspection) be up-ended so as to enable the bars to act as an equivalent pitch ladder. Once an understanding of broad pitch relationships has been established in this way, the guitar should be held in normal playing position (depending on style) and interval concepts explored in more detail. (A move from one fret to the next constitutes a semitone change in pitch.) Then scale and mode patterns may be established, starting on any of the open strings and working along that string. (Remember the guitar is being used here to demonstrate the theory of scale patterns in general terms and that we are not concerned with conventional guitar scale fingering.) A diatonic major scale (tone, tone, semitone, tone, tone, tone, semitone, in ascending order) may, for example, be compared with the standard pentatonic scale (t, t, t + s, t, t + s), a harmonic minor scale (t, s, t, t, s, t + s, s) with the Dorian mode (t, s, t, t, t, s, t), and so on, all the time using the frets, or rungs of the ladder, as a means of indicating the relative sizes of the pitch movements.

(ii) Acoustics

Here the guitar may be used to demonstrate facts both of a general nature and also in relation to its design as an instrument. For example, once the concept of relative high and low pitch has been established by the means outlined above, a correlation between the tension of a string and its pitch may be demonstrated simply by adjusting the tuning peg of one of the guitar's strings. The link between the tightening of the string and the raising of pitch, and the converse, may be appreciated by the children both visually if a chalk mark is placed across string and finger-board (ensure the string is well slackened initially so as to make certain that the movement of the chalk mark can be large enough to be conspicuous without danger of breaking the string), and physically if one of the class places a finger on the string, pressing it against a fret as the string is tightened.

The vibration of the guitar strings caused when they are plucked may also be readily seen and basic facts concerning the behaviour of stretched strings may be demonstrated (stopping a string half-way along its length produces a note an octave above open-string pitch, a third of the way along gives a fifth above). Other general principles concerning string instruments may also be explained, these including the use of a hollow wooden box to amplify and enhance the sounds produced by the strings. (A cloth inserted into the body of the instrument will effectively damp the sounds.) In connection with this aspect of string instruments it will be helpful to draw attention to the bridge over which the strings are stretched and the sound-hole cut into the table, or front, of the guitar. The table's important function in distributing the string vibrations can be shown by sprinkling salt or chalk dust on the table beneath the strings and watching the lively movements of the particles as the strings are sounded. This may be repeated on the back and sides of the guitar, where the vibration-induced movements will be less or not at all obvious. (A comparison with the solid-bodied electric guitar—without amplifier—will also prove helpful in demonstrating the lack of carrying power of strings sounded without the enhancement of a sound-box.) This initial exploration of the principles of acoustics as applied to the guitar could well lead to more broadly based projects in acoustics, perhaps undertaken with the help of the science teacher.

4 Arranging for the Guitar and Other Instruments

Michael Burnett

INITIAL fascination with the guitar often stems from the comparative ease with which it is possible to strum certain basic chords and chord patterns. A common line of subsequent development then tends to be concerned with a gradual extension of chord repertoire, the instrument's role being seen as that of a harmonic prop to another, more important, musical activity such as classroom singing. Such a use of the guitar is, of course, a valid and musically effective one as far as it goes; indeed, as one aspect of the instrument's harmonic capability, it has proved a fundamental strength and an important contributory factor to the growth in popularity of the guitar during the last half-century. However, this overemphasis on the strummed-chord technique has led to a dearth of ensemble publications in which the instrument's monodic and plucked-arpeggio capabilities are explored and developed. This situation is unsatisfactory in a number of respects and has certainly militated against the involvement of guitar students in ensemble work in which their instrument's role is conceived as equivalent in its technical demands to other instruments.

Beyond the musical content of an arrangement lies the wider role that the visiting teacher is on occasion called upon to play. Involvement in the classroom and the need to integrate an individual student into ensemble work, often results in the visiting guitar teacher requiring a knowledge of ensemble repertoire and an awareness of instruments other than the guitar. The purpose of this chapter is, therefore, to offer guidance both to guitar specialists and non-guitar-playing class teachers who wish to make more varied ensemble arrangements which will be closer to the needs of their own particular pupils.

The need for a closer co-operation between class teachers and visiting instrumental teachers must necessarily form the starting-point for the provision of guitar parts; it will be essential for the class teacher to establish the relative abilities of the children for whom the parts are to be written and to act in concert with the visiting teacher in relation to their allocation and teaching. There are a number of occasions when ensemble arrangements involving guitarists in the way proposed, can prove of value. An initial need is for ensemble material which may be played by groups of those children learning the guitar itself. Some guitar ensemble arrangements are available on publishers' lists, but these may well not match the specific requirements of a particular school or, indeed, be suitable in terms of musical content. It is ironic, for example, that given the guitar's contribution within the pop music field, there is little notated music of a pop or jazz nature available for the ensemble; so the class teacher may well find a valuable role here both in terms of choosing and framing material which will prove stimulating and enjoyable to young guitarists in school.

Secondly, mixed ensemble arrangements for the classroom. Many teachers make use of such arrangements in connection with listening and topic-related work. However, as these rarely provide notated parts for guitarists, there is plenty of scope for teachers to write additional parts for those children in their classes who are being provided with guitar tuition. And then there are those occasions when parts will be needed in connection with larger, mixed ensembles which meet outside lesson time. Here again, published material regularly provides for those children who play, for example, the descant recorder, the clarinet or violin, and, of course, percussion of various kinds; but notated parts for guitarists are generally omitted.

Consideration will be given here to the question of arranging for the guitar and guitar ensemble, and subsequently to that of arranging for a variety of instruments commonly found in the school situation. But first, a few points of a general nature about arranging.

(i) *Transposition.* Fundamental to any arrangement is a choice of key which is appropriate to the majority of instruments involved. This will frequently result in the transposition of the original music, be it a melody for harmonization or an extant piece.

(ii) *Part-writing.* It is essential to make parts as interesting and well-shaped as possible. This does not mean that the parts need necessarily be technically demanding but that, however simple to play, they should have a sense of purpose of their own. For example, it is commonly supposed that the basis of simplicity in part-writing is repetition, both rhythmic and melodic. However, to allocate a large number of consecutive minims, perhaps all at the same pitch, to an inexperienced player is likely to prove counterproductive as boredom sets in or the player loses count of the notes. Better, say, to introduce an occasional dotted minim and crotchet and to introduce changes of pitch sufficient to give the part some melodic shape.

(iii) *Scoring.* Avoid the tendency to allocate the 'tune' to the topmost instrumental part in a score when instruments placed lower down may have equivalent range capabilities and the parts may be designed with similar technical demands in mind. If, for example, there are two descant recorder parts of equal levels of difficulty, then the second recorder player should be given a chance to play the 'tune' on occasion; and the arranger should always be aware that it is possible to allocate the melody to a tenor- or bass-pitched instrument in a given mixed ensemble context, provided the higher-pitched parts can be made compatible harmonically.

(iv) *Thrift in arranging.* There is a common tendency to over-write for instruments in an ensemble. Thrift, with a view to the judicious use of contrasts of timbre, is preferable to the kind of onslaught by all available instruments to which many inexperienced arrangers are prone. Of course, there will be times when a 'tutti' is effective in any arrangement, but its effectiveness, as with other combinations of instrumental timbres, is progressively diminished by repetition; and in any case, the louder instruments in the ensemble will simply swamp the contribution made by the quieter ones. Balanced timbre development should be seen as an integral component of any arrangement, assisting in the pointing of phrases, sections, and, consequently, the form of the piece of music which is to be performed. (We tend to forget that, for the listener, an arrangement is purely an aural experience, as opposed to the combined aural and visual experience which it constitutes for the arranger, conductor, and performer. The dots and tails, bars and bar-lines present on paper, provide, in effect, a map of the music, a tangible guide to the intangible intricacies of form and shape. The resultant tendency is for notated arrangements to become over-complex, sometimes too clever by half, and in the process emphasize the arranger's role to the detriment both of the music and its relationship to the listener.) For example, a repeated eight-bar recorder phrase might be accompanied initially by a slow-moving glockenspiel line and relatively faster-moving bass line for a guitar. To help delineate phrase shape, a simple tambourine rhythm might be brought in at bar 5, and an unobtrusive, but rhythmic, part from the xylophone at the commencement of the repeat of the melody.

At this stage the glockenspiel, or guitar, might drop out temporarily, joining in once more at bar 13, perhaps in conjunction with a few pointed strokes from the triangle, the whole helping to provide the listener with a sense of balance and cohesion. Such an approach on the part of the arranger will assist the listener in the process of grasping the music's phrase shape and gives a sense of timbre development through contrast and combination.

(v) *The arranger's role in relation to the development of a sense of rhythmic discipline.* An important aspect of ensemble-playing in general, and one which makes it such a valuable experience for young musicians, is that it can make a vital contribution to the player's sense of rhythmic discipline and control. In isolation, all musicians are prone to rhythmic inaccuracies and poor beat sense. Playing with others will inevitably bring such faults to light, thus facilitating their correction and, with perseverence, their total eradication from, in this case, a child's playing. Rhythmic faults commonly relate to the counting of longer, and dotted, notes which even more advanced performers all too readily shorten when playing solo. Triplets, too, are often rushed and rests miscounted, and an arranger should bear such points in mind when writing elementary instrumental parts. These may be constructed so as to highlight a specific rhythmic problem and thus give the player practice at coping with its solution in the disciplined co-operative context of ensemble performance.

Similarly, an arranger can help pupils to develop a sensitivity to dynamic contrasts and other nuances through ensemble performance. Dynamics should, therefore, be viewed as integral to scoring, with the arranger perhaps focusing attention on one particular device—loud/soft contrast, a crescendo or diminuendo, and so on—in each arrangement or section of an arrangement.

The guitar

The guitar is a transposing instrument which sounds an octave lower than the pitch at which its part is written. The treble clef (sometimes with an appended octave sign in modern publications) is, with the exception of the bass guitar, always used for the instrument and this may result in what may seem, for non-guitarists, copious leger lines. The compass of the instrument is shown in Ex. 4.1.

At the most elementary level of learning, the range of notes offered by the open strings of the guitar (Appendix I) is quite sufficient to

Ex. 4.1

enable beginners to participate in some ensemble work with more advanced players. The strings can provide the roots of tonic, subdominant, and dominant chords in the keys of E, A, and D; of tonic and dominant in G; and of tonic and subdominant in B; in addition, of course, they constitute thirds or fifths of other chords. Thus, a simple, open-string, monodic line may potentially be contributed to a guitar ensemble performance by the least experienced player.

As the beginner progresses and learns to finger a number of scales then, of course, less restricted melodic lines will prove manageable. Scales taught in these early stages include (one octave) C major, starting on written middle C or an octave above, and G major, starting a fourth below middle C or a fifth above. Here, a judiciously chosen key can assist in the development of scale-playing expertise in beginners through the medium of ensemble performance.

Plucked arpeggios—as opposed to strummed chords—are usually taught in the early stages too, and an awareness on the part of the arranger of elementary chord changes can also contribute to the development of guitar pupils' expertise through ensemble work. Some examples of relatively easy chord change patterns are:

E minor, E major, A minor, A major, B7, E major

A major, D major, E7, A major

C major, A minor, D minor, G7, C major

Writing for guitar ensemble, as opposed to mixed, has certain built-in advantages for the arranger. Problems of balance, for example, will be reduced although care should be taken with the number of players per part. Choice of key will be relatively more straightforward as it will not be necessary to effect the sort of compromise usually needed when dealing with a range of instruments. It will not be so difficult for the arranger to bear in mind contrasting range possibilities and in some respects, those of timbre. However, the ground rules of good arranging will still apply, and the reader's attention is drawn once again to the danger of allowing one part to dominate in terms of interest. Similarly, although the ensemble arrangement may be, for example, for six guitars, there is no reason why all six instruments should be asked to play all the time. Sections utilizing groups of, say, three or four instruments will form an effective contrast to the 'tutti' sound.

Another problem which is likely to arise relates to scoring. It is all too easy to assume that a score corresponds, in effect, to a vocal score, with the upper part being the equivalent of a soprano line and the lowest a bass part. It is vital to be aware of, and counteract, this assumption because otherwise the guitar parts are liable to end up unnecessarily restricted in compass and vocally rather than instrumentally conceived. It is worth adding, too, that writing for a group of equal instruments tends to induce an excessive interest in counterpoint in the arranger. Busy, finicky parts can be as lacking in sense of purpose as those one-rhythm, one-note beginner's parts which were mentioned earlier. They are also prone to detract from those elements of the music which the composer, and therefore the arranger, would wish to receive proper emphasis.

The range of a guitar ensemble may be increased. For the guitars likely to be available in school, this will be confined to a lowering of the sixth string to D. More experienced ensembles may wish to draw on the use of a requinto (plays a fourth higher) or the guitars that contain more strings and may go below that D.

The arranger must, of course, take into account what is difficult on an instrument and as far as the guitar is concerned, chords will of course be harder to play and read than single notes. In addition, many players will be reluctant to move along the finger-board to the higher positions. The arranger may, therefore, wish to encourage a player to overcome such a difficulty.

Timbre, as was mentioned earlier, is an important feature of an arrangement and the arranger should be aware of the considerable capacity of a guitarist to introduce such a change. Thus, a phrase may be marked ponticello to make it sound more 'metallic' or for more experienced players, pizzicato or harmonics may be included.

Many of the aspects apply equally to the electric guitars and the reader is referred to a later section of this chapter for further mention.

Recorder and melodica

Of classroom instruments, the most commonly found are the descant recorder and melodica, together with percussion, both tuned (glockenspiel, xylophone, chime bars) and untuned (tambourine, drum, triangle, shaker, for example). The timbre of the guitar forms an effective foil to those of melodic wind instruments such as recorder and melodica, and its lower pitching can help counteract the often shrill and top-heavy effect of these instruments, particularly when they are combined with tuned percussion.

A working compass for the descant recorder is shown in Ex. 4.2. (sounding an octave higher). Accidentals, other than F♯, C♯, and B♭, should be avoided (giving the major keys of G, D, F and, of course, C, together with D minor and most of the notes of the minor scales of E, G, and A), and it is advisable to avoid chromaticisms when writing for the instrument. The melodica is, in effect, a miniature keyboard instrument in terms of playing technique—providing a somewhat greater overall range than the descant recorder—so chromaticisms are more readily available, at least in theory. However, a good rule of thumb in this context is 'If you don't need it, don't use it'; for example, if a piece, or section of a piece, is in G major don't introduce F♮s into those instrumental parts which include F♯s, unless absolutely necessary.

Ex. 4.2

As with other wind instruments, the arranger should ensure that the player's breathing needs are adequately catered for from the outset. Young recorder and melodica players, in particular, need regular and frequent opportunities to replenish their air supplies; melodic lines should, therefore, include breathing indications together with a good sprinkling of rests. (Indeed, the arranger should not regard any given melody as necessarily inviolate as it stands. Very often, more precision and better breath control will be obtained from young wind players if rests are introduced, judiciously of course, so as to emphasize phrase length and shape. For example, a semibreve may sometimes be shortened to a dotted minim and even a minim to a crotchet, depending on speed and context, when circumstances require it.)

Tuned percussion

Although posing problems of a different kind, the tuned percussion instruments can prove highly effective when their capabilities are properly assessed and they are well arranged for. Fundamental here is a real understanding of the contrasting roles of metal (glockenspiels, chime bars) and wooden (xylophones) instruments. Slow moving lines are well suited to the former because of the instrument's sustaining quality, while faster, more rhythmic, writing is appropriate for the xylophone as a result of its lack of capability in this respect. Parts for tuned percussion are written in the treble clef and arrangers can rely on the instruments providing at least the overall range shown in Ex. 4.3. Soprano and bass instruments will sound an octave higher or lower respectively, and it is unwise to rely on the availability of accidentals other than F♯ and B♭. With most instruments, the use of even these accidentals necessitates the removal of the respective natural bars, so parts should avoid alternation of accidentals and naturals.

Ex. 4.3

And then, of course, it is as well to bear in mind that instruments played with beaters do not lend themselves to the kind of stepwise and scale movement which suits other instruments. The arranger should aim at an alternating beater technique, keeping the two hands as static in relation to the bars as possible (the use of implied pedal points, with one beater remaining completely static while the other moves by step on alternate beats, is an effective and sensible approach here), and avoiding beater overlap. For example Ex. 4.4 is better xylophone writing than Ex. 4.5, although the harmonic implications are the same.

Ex. 4.4

Ex. 4.5

Untuned percussion

There are several means of scoring these parts. However, given manuscript paper already complete with staves, then probably the most efficient system is to ink in the second and fourth lines down so that they stand out from the stave, and then to write one untuned part on each of them. Of the two parts, the upper should be allocated to the higher-pitched of the two instruments (triangle, for example) with the stems of the notes pointing upwards, and the lower line to the lower-pitched instrument (tambourine, for example). Dynamic and other indications should be placed equivalently; rests will appear on, or adjacent to, the line, with minim and semibreve rests immediately above and below the line respectively. In the case of a single percussion part being allocated to a stave, the *middle* line should be inked in and the part written with stems of notes either consistently up or down.

Since a number of untuned instruments may be played in several different ways (a pair of cymbals may be clashed together, or a single one suspended and hit with a brush or stick; a tambourine may be struck and/or shaken, for example) it is vital that the arranger takes decisions concerning the manner of performance, and places specific indications in the score and part.

Vocal writing

Since classroom and general school ensembles may be used in conjunction with voices, a word or two about vocal writing is relevant here. A basic working range for girls' voices, and boys' unbroken is as shown in Ex. 4.6. Adolescent boys with broken voices can usually manage the

Ex. 4.6

range set out in Ex. 4.7. In both cases, notes immediately above or below those shown may of course be employed if absolutely necessary, but they will pose something of a strain for the average, non-choir trained pupil. In any case, song melodies should ideally be transposed so as to avoid too much emphasis upon either higher or lower parameters. (This may sometimes involve the arranger in difficult decisions relative to the ensemble as a whole, as good pitching for voices may well not be appropriate, say, for recorders. Usually, though, some reasonable compromise proves possible, given a thoughtful and flexible approach on the part of the arranger.)

Ex. 4.7

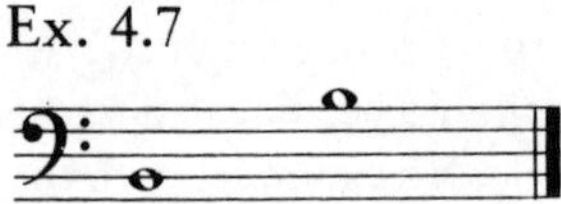

If it is the teacher's intention to introduce some elementary part-singing, then the most obvious and immediately effective formula is to add a vocal line which follows the original tune, as far as possible a third or a sixth below, using the same rhythms as in the original. (Writing in a similar fashion, but at the distance of a tenth or a thirteenth below, works well for broken voices.) Ex. 4.8 is an

Ex. 4.8

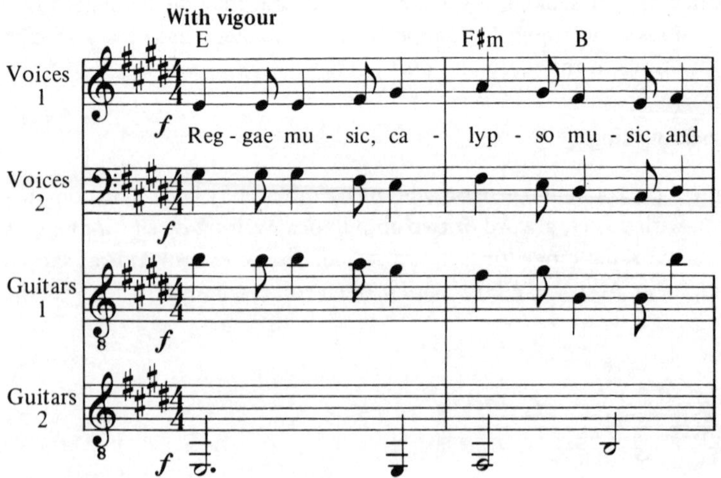

arrangement of part of *In the Caribbean* (from Pearle Christian and Michael Burnett's *Reggae Schooldays*, EMI/IMP) for two voices (girls' and boys' unbroken, and boys' broken) and two guitar groups (one at elementary level), The original melody and chord sequence have been transposed down a minor third; all other parts have been added.

Orchestral instruments

Orchestral instruments most commonly found in schools include the violin, cello, clarinet, and trumpet. However, some information is included here on the following additional instruments, on the basis that arrangers may well come across them: viola, double-bass, flute, oboe, bassoon, saxophone, French horn, and trombone.

The open strings of violin, viola, cello, and double-bass, respectively, are given in Ex. 4.9. As with the guitar, the range of notes offered by the open strings of each of these instruments is sufficient to enable beginners to participate in some ensemble work at an early stage. Keys and scales commonly employed in the teaching of beginners correspond with the three lower strings in each case: G, D, and A major for violin; C, G, and D major for viola; C, G, and D major for cello; and E, A, and D major for double-bass. The latter sounds an octave lower than written, and the viola uses the alto (C) clef.

Ex. 4.9

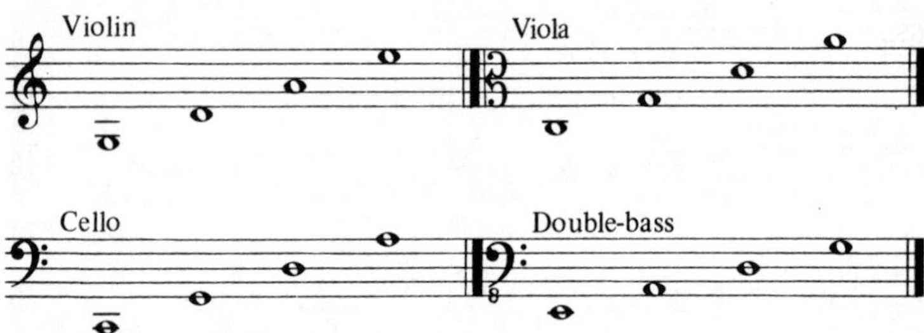

Clarinet and trumpet pose problems of transposition for the arranger as the instruments normally available to the teacher in school will be in B♭; that is, when the note C is written, the player will actually sound the note B♭, a tone *below* (see Ex. 4.10). The corollary of this is that the arranger will need to pitch the part for each B♭ instrument in the key *one tone higher* than for other instruments in the ensemble. Thus, for a piece of music in D, the clarinet and trumpet

Ex. 4.10

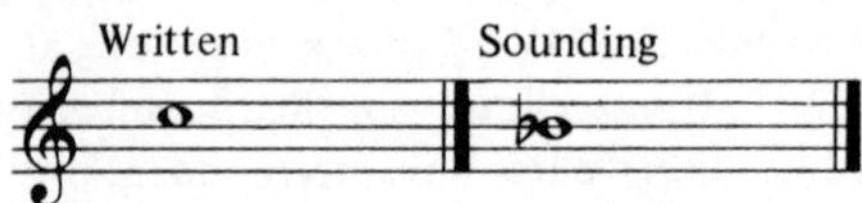

will each be provided with a part in the key of E, complete with key signature of four sharps; for a piece in A minor with a part in B minor, and so on. Both instruments use the treble clef throughout their respective ranges, although the clarinet is capable of playing well below middle C (in the 'chalumeau' register) when leger lines are used rather than bass clef. Among the first scales learned on the clarinet are those major scales going downwards from the notes in Ex. 4.11 (i.e. scales *sounding* E♭ and F major respectively). Crossing the break from the 'chalumeau' to the 'clarion' register of the clarinet (moving from written A to B in the middle of the stave) poses real problems for beginners, so arrangers should avoid writing melodic lines which pass through this area and pitch their clarinet parts either consistently below or above the break. (Incidentally, crossing the break is actually easier going *downwards*.)

Ex. 4.11

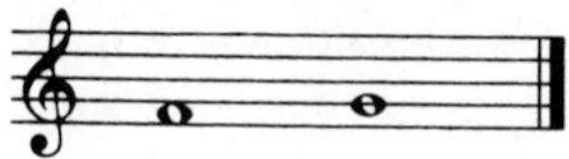

Among the first scales learned on the trumpet are those commencing on the notes in Ex. 4.12 (majors going upwards).

Ex. 4.12

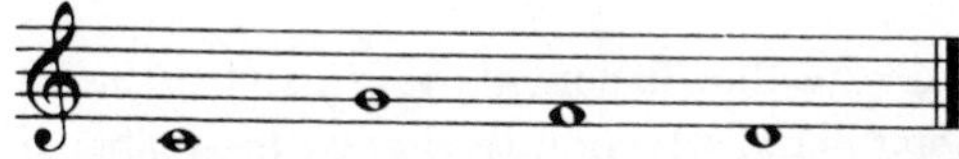

Other transposing instruments include the saxophone and French horn. The saxophone family has seven members, but those most likely to be met by the arranger are the alto (in E♭) and tenor (in B♭). Saxophone parts are written in the treble clef, a written C producing a sounding E♭ (major sixth below) on the alto instrument, and B♭ (a major *ninth* below) on the tenor instrument. Reed adjustment often causes problems, especially for beginners on the saxophone; the notes in Ex. 4.13 indicate scales with which they will be familiar at an early stage (majors going up).

The French horn is most often the one pitched in F (i.e. it sounds a perfect fifth lower than written) and the bass clef is used for the lowest

Ex. 4.13

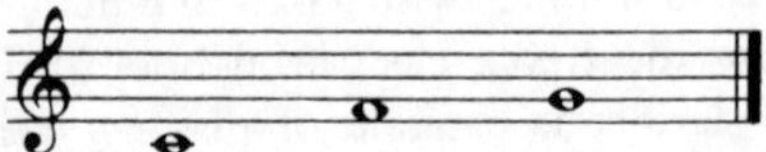

notes of its range. Early scales include those beginning on the notes in Ex. 4.14) (majors going up).

Ex. 4.14

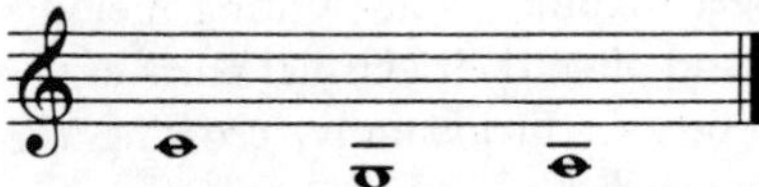

Initial scales on the flute (majors going upwards) begin on the notes in Ex. 4.15. Notes below the F above middle C should be avoided for beginners and the bottom sixth or so of a flute's range in any case lacks carrying power in the context of ensemble playing, although it has a distinctive mellowness which may be used to good effect with some circumspection.

Ex. 4.15

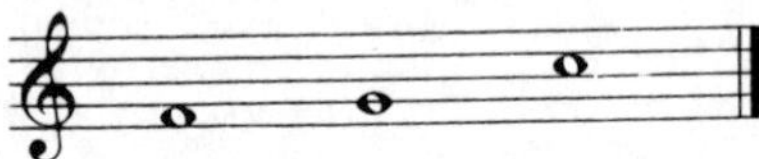

The first scales learned on the oboe include those in Ex. 4.16. In the case of the bassoon, the notes in Ex. 4.17 indicate the starting-points of scales learned initially (majors going upwards).

Ex. 4.16

Ex. 4.17

A tenor trombone with slide in first position will produce the series of notes shown in Ex. 4.18. Second position gives the corresponding series of notes a semitone lower, third a semitone lower still, and so on down to the seventh position. The first three scales usually learned (majors going upwards) are shown in Ex. 4.19.

Ex. 4.18

Ex. 4.19

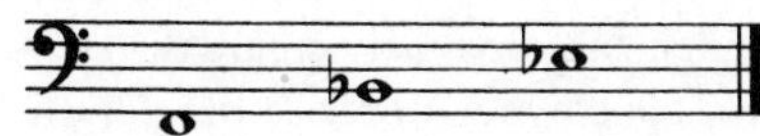

Ex. 4.20

Working compasses of orchestral instruments mentioned, in the hands of competent players. Upper limits are approximate.

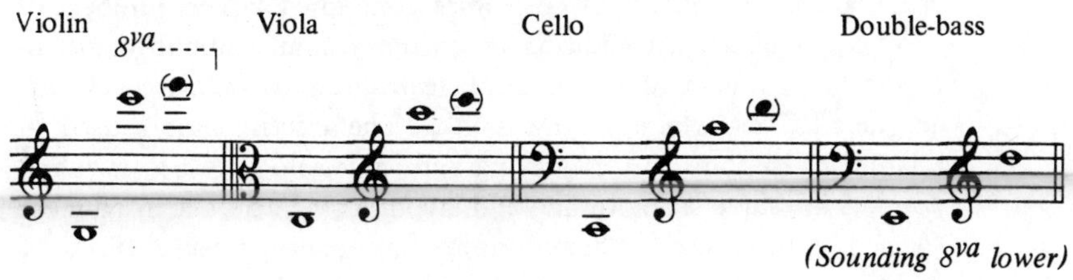

(a) Written notes

(b) The top three fundamental/pedal notes are of good quality at any dynamic level if used sparingly.

Electric guitar

Orchestral instruments, with their relatively greater dynamic and pitch range than classroom instruments, can obviously create disparities of balance when involved in ensemble playing, not least in relation to the guitar. In fact, it may well prove necessary to employ several guitarists on one part so as to provide a satisfactory balance between the guitar (or, indeed, glockenspiel or recorder) line and, say, an only moderately loud clarinet part.

As an alternative, of course, the electric guitar can solve problems of balance in relation to orchestral instruments, and may even prove essential in the context of ensembles containing larger numbers of these instruments. (In addition to greater volume, amplified instruments do, of course, offer a range of electronic and other effects which are detailed elsewhere in this book.) The electric guitar used in relation to rhythm (chord) playing and lead (solo) work in jazz and pop has the same string tuning and layout as the acoustic instrument (Appendix I). However, the bass guitar has only four strings (E, A, D, and G going upwards, Appendix I) which are pitched an octave lower than the equivalent strings on the rhythm and lead instruments. (As with the double-bass, the bass guitar part may be written ottava.) Elementary writing for electric guitars employs the principles already outlined in relation to acoustic instruments.

Finally, a brief word about an instrument often associated with guitars in the jazz, pop and folk fields, the harmonica. Most commonly a diatonic instrument in C, the harmonica has a range of at least two octaves going upwards from middle C, although some instruments do extend to a fourth below that note and a fourth above the topmost C.

Writing for piano

A simple piano accompaniment can act as a useful harmonic and/or rhythmic 'filler' in an arrangement. However, arrangers should always be aware of the danger of the piano, with its large volume and range capabilities, becoming the dominant instrument in an ensemble, thus detracting from the contributions of other, less powerful instruments. For these reasons, arrangers should use the octavo doubling of left-hand notes judiciously, rather than consistently, as so often happens. Consecutive octave doublings do not, in any case, contribute to ease of playing in whichever hand they appear. Indeed, simple writing using merely two or three notes in fairly close position distributed between the hands is often quite sufficient in relation to the piano, and it is advisable to avoid the natural tendency to use lots of notes simply because they are theoretically available. Busy, difficult, and unrewarding piano parts usually result from this sort of approach.

Arrangers should, in general, limit the range of the two parts to within two octaves (up and down respectively) of middle C (this is likely to prove the maximum range of some electronic instruments), and avoid large leaps unless preceded by a rest. Rhythmic complexity should be kept to a minimum, with a useful guideline being that of 'boxing and coxing' rhythmic interest between the two hands; so that, in effect, the left hand will remain relatively static rhythmically when the right hand is busy, and the converse. Octava transposition of an entire section of piano part, corresponding to the repetition of a piece, or section of a piece, is an effective device. The change of timbre which results can add a sense of purpose to an arrangement and, provided the player is given the time needed through the use of rests to make the jump, the device can be an aid to economy of learning. As in choral harmonization, it is important to bear in mind the voicing of chords; for example, the third of a chord in root position on the keyboard is best placed in the middle of the harmonic texture rather than, say, low down in the left-hand part where its effect will be muddied. Remember, too, that harmonic flow can be implied more straightforwardly by repetition of notes than by changing them. Thus (Ex. 4.21) is easier and indeed arguably better than (Ex. 4.22) although the harmonic implications are the same.

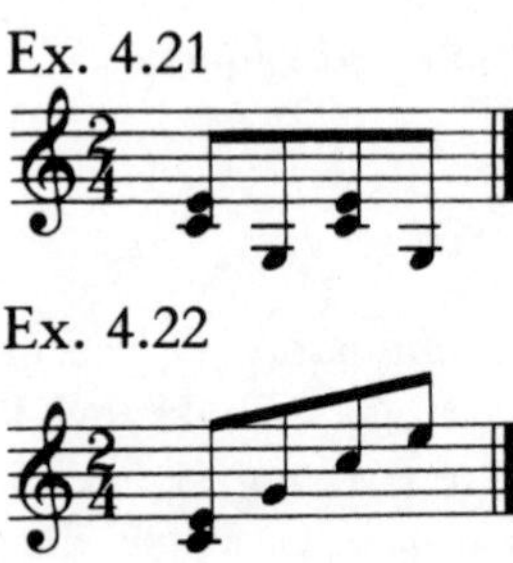
Ex. 4.21

Ex. 4.22

Laying out a score

Here, accuracy and ease of reading are paramount, and it will be necessary to take careful account of the underlaying of parts, together with the placing of bar-lines, so as to allow space to accommodate those instrumental lines containing the maximum number of notes. (Incidentally, bar-lines should not be drawn continuously from top to bottom of the score but separately for each instrumental group (woodwind, brass, etc.) other than for piano in which case the two staves are linked by the bar-lines and bracketed at the beginning of each line of the score.) Since transposition poses a problem for most of us, it would seem advisable to place B♭ parts, for example, at sounding pitch in the score, although the individual parts will, of course, need to be transposed. Bar numbers placed at least every ten bars, or perhaps at the beginning of each line, should be incorporated in the score and parts, together with letters which can helpfully be used to indicate sections of the piece of music which has been arranged. Bowing for string instruments (⊓ indicates a down-bow, V an up-bow) and breathing points (√) for wind instruments should, of course, also be included in the score and parts, together with dynamics, speed indications, and so on. In the case of a large ensemble, one possible procedure in terms of layout would be for the arranger to place woodwind instruments at the top of the score and orchestral strings at the bottom, with brass, recorders and melodicas, tuned and untuned percussion, guitar, voice, and piano in descending order in between. However, layout will obviously vary according to the precise nature of the instruments available and the needs of conductor and arranger. In relation to the former, it will often be found helpful if specific instrumental parts, or groups of parts, are colour-coded in the score by the arranger. One possible method is to place a bracket at the beginning of each line of the respective part(s) so as to assist in identification.

5 Examinations

Martin Teale

THE various but similar systems of progressive practical examinations which were established and developed by the principal music colleges in the United Kingdom over the last hundred years or so, have become an indispensable part of our music education and heritage. They provide a well-defined scheme of graded tests and examinations against which students, at all stages of development, can measure their progress and work, and improve their standard of performance. The success of these examinations may be judged not only by the large number of candidates who enter for them in the United Kingdom, but also by the increasing number of candidates from other countries who now apply to take them.

It was not, however, until the 1960s that examinations for classical guitar were first introduced. This perhaps reflected some initial reluctance on the part of the music colleges to recognize the guitar as an instrument of equal standing with the established orchestral instruments, for which courses and examinations had long been available. As a matter of historical interest and record, it was both the Guildhall School of Music and Drama and the London College of Music who first introduced examinations for guitar in 1960/1. This was followed somewhat later, in 1967, by the Associated Board of the Royal Schools of Music (the examination body which now represents the four music colleges comprising the Royal Academy of Music, the Royal College of Music, the Royal Northern College of Music, and the Royal Scottish Academy of Music and Drama) and in 1968, by Trinity College of Music London, who also introduced the first ever examinations for guitar duet in 1986.

Although the classical guitar has now gained its deserved place as an established examination subject alongside the other instruments, no universally available examinations have as yet been set up to cater for the other styles and idioms with which the guitar is closely associated (rock, jazz, folk, or flamenco). This chapter is, therefore, necessarily confined to outlining the examinations exclusively intended for the classical guitar.

Practical performance examinations as such may be broadly divided into three main categories, dependent on the stage of achievement reached on an instrument or the purpose for which the examination is designed:

(i) Grade examinations which fit into a scheme of eight progressive grades that cover an elementary level at Grade 1 up to an advanced stage by Grade 8.

(ii) Entrance examinations for candidates applying for a place on a full-time course at a music college, the required standard of performance being at least that of Grade 8 on the instrument chosen for principal study.

(iii) Diploma examinations (Teachers' or Performers') which are generally taken by students who have completed a full-time course, normally of three years' duration at a music college, or by external candidates who consider that they have achieved a similar standard.

Grade examinations

Grade examinations for guitar are currently offered by all four music examination Boards in the United Kingdom, namely the Associated Board, Guildhall, London College, and Trinity. They are broadly similar schemes, although Guildhall and London College offer an additional Preliminary Grade that may be taken before Grade 1, and Trinity offers, unlike the other Boards, examinations for guitar duet in Grades 2, 4, 6, and 8. It should be stressed that the four Boards operate entirely independently of each other, and their individual standards and examination requirements may therefore vary to some degree. As may be seen from Table 5.1, there is also some variation in the possible marks awarded under each constitutent section of their respective examinations, as well as in the marks required to obtain a pass, a pass with merit (first class pass), and a pass with distinction (honours). Thus, a slightly different emphasis is placed on certain abilities.

The basic entry regulations, however, for all four Boards, are broadly similar in that their grade examinations are open to all candidates irrespective of age. They are not conditional on a candidate having to obtain a pass in any previous grade, other than a pass in a written paper of Grade 5 standard when taking certain higher practical grades (Table 5.1). In general, the syllabuses comprise of scales, arpeggios, the performance of three contrasting pieces and studies, playing at sight, and aural tests. Prospective candidates and

	Examining Board:						
	Associated Board		*Guildhall*	*London*		*Trinity*	
Grades offered:	2–8		Preliminary and 1–8	Preliminary and 1–8		Solo 1–8	Duet 2, 4, 6, and 8
Pass in Theory Grade 5 required in Grades:	6–8		8	6–8		8[a]	—
Maximum marks in Grades:	2–8	(%)	Prelim.–8	Prelim.	1–8	1–8	2/4/6/8
Scales and Arpeggios:	21	(14)	15[b]	25[c]	15[d]	15	—
Pieces: 1	30	(20)	18	20	20	20	28
2	30	(20)	18	20	20	20	28
3	30	(20)	18	20 (Study)	20	20	28
Sight-Reading:	21	(14)	12	—	10	10	16
General Musicianship/ Viva Voce questions:	—	—	9	15	7	5	—
Aural/Ear Tests:	18	(12)	10	—	8[e]	10	—
Total:	150	(100)	100	100	100	100	100
Attainment Marks:	100 (67) Pass 120 (80) Merit 130 (87) Distinction		66 Pass 75 Merit 85 Honours	65 Pass 75 First Class 85 Honours[f]		65 Pass 75 Merit 85 Honours	

[a] A pass in Grade 5 Musicianship is alternatively accepted.
[b] Cadences are also included in this section for Grades 3–8.
[c] Exercises are also included in this section of the Preliminary grade.
[d] The marks are allocated separately in this section in Grades 3–8, 10 for scales and 5 for arpeggios.
[e] Improvisation tests may be alternatively offered.
[f] Honours not awarded for Preliminary grade.

teachers would be first advised to study and become conversant with the current syllabuses and regulations issued by each of the Boards before deciding which best serves their needs, and which grade best suits their abilities. Syllabuses and entry forms may be obtained by sending a request and stamped addressed envelope (measuring at least 6 in. × 9 in.) direct to Boards at the addresses given at the end of this chapter.

Preliminaries

One or two practical matters first require mention concerning the instrument to be used, any other equipment which will be required at an examination, the question of music editions set or suggested in the syllabuses, and the observance of published fingering, metronome, and other expression marks. All candidates are expected to supply their own footstools, and music stands if required. It is understood that candidates will use the standard classical instrument, and that it will be appropriately strung with the usual nylon and metal-wound strings (all-metal strings would definitely not be advised), though only the Associated Board and Trinity College make any reference to this matter in their syllabuses. Tuning or re-tuning (as may be required by some pieces where scordatura is indicated) is expected to be carried out by candidates themselves. The use of a capotasto (capo) is permitted by Guildhall in their Preliminary and Grade 1 examinations, presumably as a concession to younger candidates whose fingers cannot yet achieve the wider stretches required at the lower positions of the finger-board. Generally, candidates are permitted to use any available editions of the set pieces and studies, the one exception being the albums of pieces published for the Trinity examinations in all grades which must be used. In practice, candidates will find that all the copyright pieces and arrangements are only available in the editions specified in the syllabuses, and that choice of alternative editions is more or less limited to standard works from the sixteenth to nineteenth centuries. On the more subjective question of indicated metronome marks, fingering, phrasing, dynamics, and other marks of expression, their strict observance is not a compulsory and inflexible matter, but one in which teachers and candidates can exercise their discretion, within reason, in deciding what is musically convincing and appropriate to the style and period of the piece.

On the matter of the use of vibrato, only two Boards mention this subject in their syllabuses: the Associated Board specifies that candidates should have acquired some use of this skill by Grade 6; Guildhall specifies some use of the skill by Grade 5. Once again, it is a matter for the candidate's discretion as to where this means of expressive effect may be used to best advantage (in order to give certain notes a warmer and more vibrant tone). Clearly, its use would be expected to be more prevalent in the higher grades of all four Boards, and its speed carefully judged and matched to the pitch and length of note.

Finally, a word or two about examiners and the examination day itself. As has no doubt been pointed out before by others, examiners are indeed human and not devoid of sensitivity or understanding. Their common aim is simply to assess what candidates can do, rather than catch them out on what they cannot do, in as fair and objective a way as possible on the work as it is presented to them in the examination room. In addition to being highly qualified and experienced teachers who are chosen and trained in examination standards and procedures, the vast majority also become widely experienced in dealing with candidates of all ages. Whilst they will endeavour to be sympathetic to all candidates, including those who may have special difficulties of some kind, they are required to be impartial as far as marking is concerned and not make any special allowances for 'exam nerves', age, faulty instruments, or, for instance, broken nails. In short, they are duty bound to assess the work presented entirely on its merits and without regard to any other consideration.

Most candidates inevitably suffer from some nervous tension before entering the examination room, but provided they have been adequately prepared in all sections of the syllabus requirements and have done sufficient work to give them confidence in the technical control of their instrument, they should find they are better able to focus their attention on their playing and away from any tension they may be experiencing.

Candidates are advised to check that their instruments are in proper working order before entering the examination room, and that the required music is all ready to hand. Tuning of strings should also be checked beforehand so that only fine adjustments need to be done during the examination. Examiners will normally follow the order of sections as they are set out in the syllabus, though in some cases, such as the examinations of the Associated Board, candidates are free to present the pieces and studies in any order of their choice. All candidates should of course know and be prepared to tell the examiner which pieces they have chosen to present. The examiner may get up and stand behind a candidate in order to look at the music, or he or she may stop the performance of a certain piece, particularly if it is lengthy or contains repeated sections, once enough has been heard to form a judgement. Neither of these occurrences need to be taken by candidates to indicate anything unfavourable, and are certainly not cause for any alarm or distraction. Page turns are best done by the candidate. In the case of a specially awkward turn, a manuscript copy or a photocopy of the few bars from the top of the following page may be licitly made to overcome the problem and enable a more convenient turning-place to be made.

Scales and arpeggios

Still considered by a large majority of teachers as a basic and essential part of every music student's technical training and development of key awareness, scales and arpeggios can account for up to 15 per cent of the total marks to be gained in a grade examination. Whilst scales and arpeggios are required in all of the grades of three Boards, arpeggios are excluded from the early stages of the London College syllabus until Grade 3. Cadences have now been introduced in the Guildhall syllabus as an additional requirement from Grade 3 onwards, no doubt in consideration of the guitar's role as an instrument of accompaniment. All scale and arpeggio requirements are invariably expected to be played from memory. The Associated Board, Guildhall, and Trinity publish their own scale manuals to cover their specific requirements in all grades. The Associated Board's manual refrains from laying down any specific tempi at which scales must be played, the question of pace being a reasonably flexible matter, and the syllabus simply makes the observation that pace should be 'appropriate to the technical demands of the Grade'. Tempi are, however, indicated in Guildhall's scale manual, but in common with the other Boards, no absolutely strict adherence to suggested speeds is necessarily expected. What is perhaps more important is that scales should sound confident, correct, fluent, rhythmical (but without undue accentuation), and be played at a consistent tempo.

Any practical and systematic left-hand fingerings will be accepted by the Associated Board, those indicated in their scale manual being given simply for guidance. The same case applies with London College and Trinity, whereas Guildhall stipulates that up to and including Grade 5, left-hand fingerings for scales, arpeggios, and cadences 'must be followed with respect to their location on the instrument, although different fingers may be used to stop the notes'. From Grade 6 upwards, however, Guildhall also accepts any practical and systematic left-hand fingering.

The right-hand fingering combinations for scales are introduced in a progressive order and are therefore specified by the examiner when he or she selects the scales to be played from the syllabus. All Boards require the basic combination of index and middle (i,m.) fingers for Grades 1 and 2, adding the next combination of middle and ring (m,a.) fingers in Grade 3. The third combination, using all three fingers in any regular sequence, is then introduced in Grade 4 by London College, Grade 5 by the Associated Board, Grade 6 by Guildhall, and Grade 7 by Trinity. The Associated Board additionally sets the index and ring (i,a.) finger combination from Grade 4 onwards, and Trinity from Grade 5 onwards. Right-hand fingerings for arpeggios are not of course specified, and once again these are left to the candidate's discretion to decide what is practical, based on suggestions given in the scale manuals. The use of rest stroke (apoyando) is normally recommended for the playing of all scales in order to achieve a firm, clear, and sonorous tone, combined with maximum legato, though this is not actually specified. London College, however, states that 'all candidates should be prepared to play scales either apoyando or tirando (free stroke)'. The Associated Board's manual also recommends that arpeggios be played using apoyando, though candidates are free to choose; London College specifies that arpeggios are to be played tirando only. It should perhaps be mentioned at this point that full arpeggios in root position are required by all four examination Boards, as opposed to the type of broken chord which falls easily under the left hand and could be described as idiomatic to the instrument. The required arpeggios are in fact more technically demanding in that they involve left-hand shifts, and therefore much more study and practice, if the performer is to achieve a truly fluent and legato effect.

The order and range in which keys are introduced, as well as the number set for each grade, varies considerably between Boards, as does the introduction of chromatic scales, dominant and diminished sevenths, and double-stop scales in thirds, sixths, octaves, and tenths. The Associated Board's requirements, without doubt, cover the most ground by Grade 6, when candidates will be expected to play scales in all the major and minor keys, arpeggios in seven keys, chromatic scales (first introduced in Grade 3) starting on four different notes, dominant sevenths (also first introduced in Grade 3) in three keys, diminished sevenths (first introduced in Grade 5) starting on two different notes, and double-stop scales, one in thirds, one in sixths, and one in octaves. Guildhall's syllabus introduces fewer keys up to and including Grade 5, though from Grade 6 onwards all major and minor keys are expected to be known. On the other hand, a chromatic scale is introduced as early as Grade 1, a scale in tenths (for a range of a fourth only) in Grade 2, and a one octave scale 'in paired slurs' (every second note played by the left hand), and an A minor cadence, in Grade 3. London College obviously places less emphasis on the range of keys covered, even by Grade 8 when candidates are only required to offer six keys, and dominant sevenths are only introduced for the first time. No chromatic scales, diminished sevenths, or double-stop scales, appear throughout their guitar syllabus. Trinity has recently revised its scale requirements to provide a scheme where candidates work through the scales in all major and minor keys in the first four grades, though they are not called upon to prepare all keys in one session until Grade 8. Chromatic scales are introduced at Grade 2, 'slurred' scales and dominant sevenths at Grade 3, diminished sevenths at Grade 5, and double-stop scales in thirds and sixths as well as scales in contrary motion (a new innovation) at Grade 6.

As has been mentioned before, examiners will just choose a selection of scales and arpeggios they wish to hear candidates play. Examination time in each grade has to be strictly kept within the examiner's schedule, and it is therefore impossible to hear all the set requirements in their various permutations. Nevertheless, candidates are expected to have prepared them all fluently for the examination.

Pieces and studies

With the ever-growing range of new guitar publications and editions covering early, rediscovered, and modern music now available, the guitar selector's task in choosing music which can be appropriately set for an examination syllabus has become reasonably wide and diverse. Many composers today are increasingly writing pieces for the guitar owing to the widening interest in the instrument and its instant appeal in terms of attractive sound quality combined with harmonic potential and flexibility of role. Doubtless the many types of music for which the guitar is effectively used and extensively adapted, particularly pop music, have all helped in some way to focus attention on its classical repertoire and potential.

The major part of any examination rightly centres on the performance of pieces and studies, allowing candidates to display the more important aspects of their interpretative skills and musicianship. This, therefore, accounts for over half the available marks to be gained. Candidates are normally expected to play three contrasted pieces, one from each of three lists containing a choice of three to five items. London College has arranged its lists so that two of them contain pieces and the third contains studies only. All the other Boards, however, intersperse studies with pieces in their lists. Fortunately for guitarists, many of the so-called studies (*études* or *estudios*) are of a high musical quality (especially those by Sor and Villa-Lobos and some of those by Carcassi, Aguado, Coste, Tárrega, and Brouwer) and may be considered as pieces in their own right. Trinity, in a recent revision of its syllabus, has established a new departure in Grade 8 by requiring candidates to include a concerto movement, accompanied on the piano, as the first of the three items in their programme.

The selection of suitable pieces to conform technically and musically to a particular grade can never hope to be an exact science, but will always be very much a subjective matter on which any two specialists may not necessarily agree in every respect. The standard within a grade should not be regarded as a precise point on a scale, but rather as a fairly broad range of difficulty which may slightly overlap in some respects with that in the grade above or below it. The grade standards between the Boards may therefore be found to vary to some degree with each other on certain pieces but agree on others. For instance, in the syllabuses set at the present time of writing, it is interesting to note that the Associated Board has set the *Bourrée* from Bach's *Lute Suite No. 1 in E minor* in Grade 6, whereas London College has set this movement in Grade 4. Conversely, the Associated Board has set Mudarra's *Fantasía que contrahaze la harpa en la manera de Luduvico* in Grade 7, whilst both London College and Trinity (in a recent syllabus) place this piece in Grade 8. Other examples of grading differences occur, though there are indeed a fair number of pieces on which there is a general consensus of opinion; for example Dowland's popular *Queen Elizabeth's Galliard*, which is presently set for Grade 6 by the Associated Board, Guildhall, and Trinity. For whatever grade a piece may happen to be selected, it is the level and quality of performance normally expected in that grade by which candidates will be assessed. In the lower grades, up to about

Grade 5, a candidate will achieve a pass if the pieces are played with accuracy of note and time, and some attempt is made at phrasing. In the higher grades there must be an increasingly greater appreciation and demonstration of style and shape, with evident understanding for expression and interpretation of the composer's intentions. The degree to which candidates may use their discretion in interpreting tempi, dynamics, phrasing, and ornaments must be guided by what sounds musically convincing and appropriate to the style, mood, and period of the piece. Examiners will not expect them to conform to any prescribed model of interpretation, for it is generally understood that there is no one right or completely definitive way in which a piece can be performed in order for it to sound musically convincing. Both the Associated Board and Trinity state that strict adherence to metronome marks is not required, Trinity's syllabus adding that candidates should rather be guided by the Italian tempi markings heading movements and pieces, and that 'accuracy, evenness, and distinctness should be the aim, rather than mere rapidity for its own sake'.

Playing one or more of the pieces from memory is optional though, as mentioned in the Associated Board syllabus, candidates who do so should bring copies of the music to the examination room for the examiner to refer to if necessary. It is important that candidates prepare the whole of a specified piece, for failure to do so might possibly make them liable to disqualification, at least in so far as the Associated Board's regulations are concerned. Examiners may, however, use their discretion in stopping the performance of any piece once they have heard enough to form a judgement, particularly in some of the longer items set for the higher grades. Both the Associated Board and Trinity state in their syllabuses that repeats should be omitted in the examination unless the examiner asks for them, though they should always observe da capo, and in the Associated Board's examinations, dal segno indications. In omitting repeats, candidates should omit any '1st time' bars and just play '2nd time' bars only.

On the rather tricky and possibly contentious subject of ornaments, only the Associated Board syllabus mentions that candidates may use their discretion in how they are realized, with the provision that any alternative renderings to those written out in a published edition are appropriate to the style of the music. It may be taken that this also applies to any ornaments additionally inserted in a piece, or indeed the omission of editorial ornaments, if they are considered inessential.

The use of prescribed, suggested, or alternative editions has already been covered in the 'Preliminaries' section of this chapter. The use of photocopied music which is copyright (and this includes the three separate or interrelated copyrights of the composer, arranger or editor, and publisher) is obviously illegal and should not be considered in any circumstances without the clear and express permission of the copyright owner in writing. Whilst the Associated Board reminds teachers and candidates on this matter in their syllabus and cautions anyone infringing the law in this respect, Guildhall forbids the use of all photocopies and points out that their use will lead to disqualification.

Sight-reading

This is the skill that most guitar students find difficult to acquire with any proficiency, partly due to the number of possible alternatives in locating any given note on the finger-board, and the necessity of fingering a passage of music within the context of what precedes or follows it. The candidate who can achieve a musical performance of the sight-reading passage can earn 10–14 per cent of the total marks in the examination. It is, therefore, worth devoting ample study and practice time to develop this skill, quite apart from the benefits to be gained in all the other aspects of playing and musicianship. The small number of guitar publications specifically devised to help students improve their sight-reading abilities, such as Stephen Dodgson and Hector Quine's *Progressive Reading for Guitarists* (Ricordi) will undoubtedly prove useful here. The Associated Board, Guildhall, and Trinity all publish their own books of specimen or sample tests in order to indicate the standard relevant to each grade.

Sight-reading is, for the most part, a test of speed of reaction to an unprepared passage of music, and candidates will therefore only be given a very brief time to look at the test and establish the salient points, such as key and time signature etc., before beginning to play. In Grades 2–4 of the Associated Board examinations, candidates will first be asked some questions covering these points, as well as pitch and time-values of notes, rests, dynamics, and other marks of expression. This is in order to aid the reading and give them a little extra time in which to concentrate on the essential details and problems in the test. In the early grades the candidate will be assessed essentially on the correctness of time-values and notes, and the ability to keep going with a steady pulse. In the later grades the candidate will also be expected to pay attention to dynamics, phrasing, and any indicated marks of expression. Continuity is above all the most important feature of good sight-reading, and the cultivation and practice of observation, judicious selection of a manageable pace, basic interval and chord recognition, maintaining a steady beat, counting so that rests are also accurate in value, and thinking ahead to the next couple of bars or so will all help in mastering it.

General musicianship/viva voce questions

This section is included in all the grade examinations of Guildhall (but not overseas), London College, and Trinity. It is not included in the Associated Board's practical examinations as such, the rudiments and theoretical aspects being confined to a separate written examination which all candidates in Grade 6 and above are required to pass at Grade 5 level (or an accepted equivalent such as GCE 'O' level Music).

The General Musicianship viva voce questions in the Guildhall examinations apply solely to the pieces and studies in the Preliminary Grade, and may also apply to them in Grades 1–7. In Grade 8, the questions will be directed to testing the general knowledge of candidates with regard to the instrument and its music. Up to and including Grade 7, the purpose of the questions is to ensure that candidates have a basic and progressive rudimentary knowledge of notation, terms, and signs related in part to the pieces and studies set for the grade under examination. Grade 7 candidates will additionally be asked simple questions on the structure of the guitar and its standard classical repertoire. The viva voce questions for the London College and Trinity examinations largely follow a similar pattern and purpose as Guildhall's, and are based on the pieces played. In the Preliminary Grade of London College, as many as 15 marks may be gained in this section towards the total result; in all other grades the maximum is 7 marks. Trinity awards a maximum of 5 marks for this section in all grades and in Grade 8 candidates will be asked to give background details of the pieces and their composers.

Aural tests

All the examination Boards include aural tests as an integral part of their practical examination syllabuses in all grades, and these are designed to test a candidate's musical ear and perception of rhythm and pitch. Books of sample and practice aural tests are also published by each Board and their study is to be recommended. The Associated Board's tests range from simple ones such as reproducing a note played by the examiner, identifying an interval as a 2nd, 3rd, 4th, or 5th, of a major scale, clapping the rhythm-pattern of a short melody, and beating the time of a harmonized passage in 2 or 3 time, in Grade 1, to singing or playing the lower part of a two-part passage previously played by the examiner, recognition and description of intervals up to an octave, clapping the rhythm-pattern and describing the time-values of notes of part of a harmonized melody, recognition of chords of the tonic, subdominant, or submediant, in a major or minor phrase, and identifying whether a short passage starting in a major or minor key modulates to the dominant, subdominant, or relative minor/major, in Grade 8. In Grades 6–8 candidates may choose to do keyboard harmony tests in place of most of the aural tests. These tests include harmonization of a given melody and cadences, and improvisation of a short answering phrase (they are obviously intended for candidates who have some knowledge and ability on the keyboard). It is pointed out in the Associated Board syllabus that for aural tests requiring a 'sung' response, pitch rather than vocal quality is the object.

The aural tests of Guildhall, London College, and Trinity are devised very much on the same lines, though there are of course differences in detail and level. Recognition of whether triads are augmented or diminished and whether they are in first or second inversion, feature in the higher grades of Guildhall and Trinity's tests, while London College candidates may opt to do improvisation tests, strict and free, in place of the aural tests in Grades 1–8. These improvisation tests may include such things as harmonization of a written melody with and without guitar chord symbols, improvisation of one or two short answering phrases to a given phrase, and free improvisation of a short fragment or piece in a style of the candidate's own choice—all played on the guitar.

The candidate's speed of reaction, similar to that required in sight-reading, is an important part of aural perception. A well-trained musical memory, ear, and an ability to concentrate, will gain maximum marks in this section if the responses to the tests are immediate as well as correct.

Theory requirement and links between Grade Examinations and General Certificate of Education examinations

Both the Associated Board and London College require candidates to have passed a written theory examination of Grade 5 standard or above, before entering for a practical examination of Grade 6 or above. Guildhall and Trinity also make this stipulation, but only for candidates wishing to take the Grade 8 examination. Candidates who have already gained an Ordinary or Advanced Level in Music from one of the General Certificate of Education Boards or the Scottish Certificate of Education Ordinary or Higher Grade or the Intermediate or Leaving Certificate examination of Eire, may be able to claim exemption from this requirement, but precise details should first be checked in the regulations of the relevant Board. Certain of the four Board's practical examinations in Grades 6–8 are linked with the Advanced Level examinations of some of the General Certificate of Education examination bodies (whose regulations should be consulted). It is not possible to give more concise detail about this at the present time because they are under review and liable to change.

Entrance examinations

The entrance examinations or auditions which all students applying for a place on a full-time course at a music college in the United Kingdom are required to take, are based on a minimum required standard equal to a very good pass in Grade 8 on the instrument chosen for first or principal study. Bearing in mind that places on most courses are necessarily limited and that admission to the leading music colleges is therefore decided on a competitive basis, it follows that entrance standards are bound to be high. As pointed out in the Associated Board's regulation booklet 'whilst indicating a high standard, a distinction in Grade 8 does not necessarily imply suitability for a professional career in music or for admission to one of the Royal Schools of Music'.

Dependent on which college and undergraduate course a guitar student may decide will best suit his or her aptitudes, needs, interests, and aspirations, and provided they are able to fulfil the basic age, musical, and academic requirements (normally a minimum age of 17 or 18 in the year in which studies commence, a good Grade 8 pass on the principal instrument as well as, for many courses, a Grade 6 pass on the instrument chosen for second study, and at least five GCE passes, two of which should preferably be at Advanced level, in specified subjects), the requirements of most entrance examinations consist of the performance of one piece on their second study instrument, tests in sight-reading and general musicianship, and a written examination covering elementary harmony and counterpoint. Overseas students will also normally be required to submit tape-recordings or cassettes of their performances before being invited to attend an entrance examination or audition.

Precise details of the examination content will normally be found in the current prospectus issued by each college, and intending students would be well advised to obtain copies of these and application forms from the addresses given at the end of this chapter, at least 15–18 months in advance of when they hope to commence their studies.

Diploma examinations

The range of Diploma examinations now available to both full-time students in music colleges and to external candidates is indeed wide and possibly somewhat bewildering. The following brief synopsis has therefore been limited to those Diplomas which are available to external guitar candidates, since it is these which are likely to be of more immediate interest to guitar teachers generally. The two basic types of Diploma, described as 'Teachers' and 'Performers', are both universally recognized as professional qualifications of competence, though the Teachers' Diploma in itself does not confer qualified teacher status in the United Kingdom as recognized by the Department of Education and Science, unless in certain cases holders pursue a further course of teacher-training or also hold a Graduate Diploma following the completion of the appropriate course at one of the music colleges. A very high standard of performance is expected in the Performers' Diploma examination and this standard is invariably defined in most syllabuses as of a level that would be expected at a public concert or recital. It is normally required that candidates take all sections of the examination within the same session. Those who fail in just some sections may re-take them in subsequent sessions within a set period of three years or so of their first partial success. Failing this, the entire examination must be taken again on re-entry. Diploma syllabuses are issued by each of the boards and colleges listed at the end of this chapter.

Associated Board of the Royal Schools of Music

The following Diplomas are only available to overseas candidates, including those in Northern Ireland and Eire:

(i) LRSM (teaching)

Prerequisites: Minimum age limit of 18 and a pass in both Theory Grade 8 within the previous five years and a General Paper within the

previous two years. The latter is a three-hour written paper covering general knowledge of music history and relevant aspects of teaching, technique, interpretation, and repertory.
Practical work: Performance of three set pieces, one chosen from each of three contrasted lists; viva voce questions on works performed and musical form; sight-reading test; aural tests.

(ii) LRSM (performing)
Prerequisites: A pass in Theory Grade 8.
Practical work: Performance of three set pieces in a programme of about 45 minutes length, one chosen from each of three contrasted lists and one of which must be played from memory; viva voce questions on repertoire, composers, style, form, and modulations; sight-reading test; aural tests.

Birmingham School of Music

(i) ABSM (teaching)
Prerequisites: Minimum age limit of 18.
Written work: A 1½-hour aural examination including questions on form, and a 2-hour paper on advanced rudiments and harmony.
Practical work: Performance of three contrasted pieces in a 20–25-minute programme chosen entirely by the candidate; sight-reading test; viva voce questions on interpretation, teaching practice, and history of the instrument.

(ii) ABSM (performing)
Prerequisites: None.
Written work: As for Teaching Diploma.
Practical work: Performance of three works or groups of pieces, two of which must be played from memory, in a varied and well balanced programme lasting between 25 and 35 minutes and chosen entirely by the candidate to reflect the different styles of music for the instrument; sight-reading test.

(iii) ABSM (recital)
Prerequisites: A pass in Theory Grade 5.
Practical work: Performance of a recital programme lasting between 40 and 60 minutes chosen entirely by the candidate and played from

memory; viva voce questions on the instrument, its repertoire, and the works performed.

Guildhall School of Music and Drama

(i) LGSM (teachers)
Prerequisites: Minimum age limit of 18.
Written work: A 3-hour paper containing questions and exercises on melodic composition, harmony, musical form, repertoire, and general musical knowledge.
Practical work: Aural tests; scales and arpeggios in all keys; performance of one of three set programmes consisting of two contrasted pieces and a study; sight-reading test of moderate difficulty; viva voce questions on technique, interpretation, and teaching methods and material.

(ii) LGSM (performers)
Prerequisites: None.
Written work: As for Teachers' Diploma.
Practical work: Aural tests; performance of a recital programme lasting between 35 and 45 minutes and consisting of four set works, one chosen from each of four contrasted lists divided into contrapuntal music, sonatas, variation form, and suites; two sight-reading tests.

London College of Music

(i) ALCM
The Associate Diploma is a first professional examination for performers.
Prerequisites: None.
Written work: A 3-hour theoretical paper.
Practical work: Performance of three set pieces, one chosen from each of three contrasted lists; scales and arpeggios in all keys played from memory; sight-reading test; ear tests or improvisation (strict and free).

(ii) LLCM
The full professional Licentiate Diploma examination for performers.
Prerequisites: None.
Written work: A 3-hour theoretical paper.

Practical work: Performance of three set pieces, one chosen from each of three contrasted lists, with one piece played from memory; sight-reading test.

(iii) LLCMTD

The full professional Licentiate Diploma examination for teachers.
Prerequisites: Minimum age limit of 18.
Written work: Two 3-hour theoretical papers.
Practical work: Performance of three set pieces, one chosen from each of three contrasted lists; sight-reading test; viva voce questions on technique, phrasing, interpretation, and other matters relating to teaching, practising, performing, and explanation with demonstration of the teaching and performing of scales and arpeggios. Candidates may also optionally submit a section on extemporization.

(iv) FLCM

The Fellowship Diploma is a qualification for performers of recital standard.
Prerequisites: Minimum age limit of 18. Candidates must already hold an LLCM, LLCMTD, or an acceptable equivalent.
Practical work: Performance of a recital programme not exceeding 50 minutes in length and consisting of four works chosen entirely by the candidate, one from each of the Baroque, Classical, Romantic, and Modern periods. At least two of the works must be played from memory.

Royal Academy of Music

(i) LRAM (teachers)

Prerequisites: Minimum age limit of 18.
Written work: A 3-hour General Musicianship paper covering rudiments of music, harmony, counterpoint, harmonic analysis, musical structure and design, and a general history of music.
Practical work: Aural tests; performance of one set study and two set pieces, each chosen from three contrasted lists; viva voce questions on technique, teaching practice, and repertoire; quick study test on the right- and left-hand fingering of a piece studied immediately before the practical examination; sight-reading test; scales and arpeggios in all keys played from memory.

(ii) LRAM (performers)
Prerequisites: None.
Written work: As for Teachers' Diploma.
Practical work: Aural tests; performance of three set pieces played from memory, one chosen from each of three contrasted lists; sight-reading test.

Royal College of Music

(i) ARCM (teaching)
Prerequisites: Minimum age limit of 18.
Written work: A 3-hour paper covering general knowledge of music history, principles of teaching, interpretation, style, repertory, and history and development of the instrument.
Practical work: Ear tests; performance of approximately 20 minutes duration of five set works, one chosen from each of five contrasted lists, and one of which must be played from memory; sight-reading test; viva voce questions on the principles of teaching with particular reference to the works performed; scales and arpeggios in all keys played from memory. Candidates may also be required to give a demonstration lesson.

(ii) ARCM (performing)
Prerequisites: None.
Practical work: Performance of five set works from memory, one chosen from each of five contrasted lists; sight-reading test; scales and arpeggios in all keys played from memory; viva voce questions, most of which are likely to relate to the music performed, on repertory, style, musical structure and form, and general musical matters.

Trinity College of Music London

(i) ATCL (teachers)
Prerequisites: Minimum age limit of 17.
Written work: A 3-hour Musical Knowledge paper covering counterpoint, rudiments of music, musical form, harmony, and composers and their works; a 3-hour Principles of Teaching paper covering the teaching of notation and time, aural training, psychology applied to the teaching of music, technique of teaching the instrument, and repertoire.

Practical work: Ear tests; performance of two set pieces and one set study, each chosen from three contrasted lists; sight-reading test; scales and arpeggios in all keys played from memory; viva voce questions on methods of teaching, technique, repertoire, musical form, and general knowledge on the pieces performed.

(ii) LTCL (teachers)
Prerequisites: Minimum age limits of 18.
Written works: As for ATCL. The Principles of Teaching paper will additionally contain questions on the development of musicianship, elementary educational psychology, and the nature and characteristic features of the instrument.
Practical work: Ear tests; performance of two set pieces and one set study, each chosen from three contrasted lists; sight-reading test; scales and arpeggios in all keys played from memory; viva voce questions on methods of teaching, technique, repertoire, musical form, and general knowledge on the pieces performed.

(iii) ATCL and LTCL (performers)
Prerequisites: None.
Written work: A 3-hour Musical Knowledge paper.
Practical work: Ear tests; performance of three set pieces, one chosen from each of three contrasted lists; sight-reading test.

(iv) FTCL
Prerequisites: Candidates must already hold LTCL or equivalent Performers' Diploma from certain other colleges in the same subject.
Practical work: Performance of a programme lasting 35–45 minutes and comprising four works chosen entirely by the candidate, two of which are from the pre-1900 repertoire and two from the twentieth-century repertoire. Credit will be given for the quality of interest and design of the programme as a whole.

Music college and examination board addresses

Associated Board of the Royal Schools of Music: 14 Bedford Square, London WC1B 3JG. Tel. 01-636 5400.
Birmingham School of Music: Paradise Circus, Birmingham B3 3HG. Tel. 021-359 6721.

Guildhall School of Music and Drama: Silk Street, Barbican, London EC2Y 8DT. Tel. 01-628 2571.

London College of Music: 47 Great Marlborough Street, London W1V 2AS. Tel. 01-437 6120 and 01-734 8921.

Royal Academy of Music: Marylebone Road, London NW1 5HT. Tel. 01-935 5461.

Royal College of Music: Prince Consort Road, South Kensington, London SW7 2BS. Tel. 01-589 3643.

Royal Northern College of Music: 124 Oxford Road, Manchester M13 9RD. Tel. 061-273 6283.

Royal Scottish Academy of Music and Drama: 100 Renfrew Street, Glasgow G2 3DB. Tel. 041-332 4101.

Trinity College of Music: 11–13 Mandeville Place, London W1M 6AQ. Tel. 01-935 5773.

Note

Regulations and *some* other information given in this chapter are liable to change and the current syllabus(es) should always be consulted. (Ed).

6 Classical Repertoire—Elementary

Michael Stimpson

THE classical guitarist who decides that teaching is to form part of his or her professional work is likely at some time to face the problems that surround the teaching of beginners. This level of teaching is one which requires the most carefully thought-out strategies, and is made all the more difficult by the wide variety of circumstances that may surround its introduction. While the more 'advanced' levels of tuition are likely to be to an older pupil on a one-to-one basis, the teaching of a beginner may involve, for example, a seven-year-old who is learning individually, small groups of older schoolchildren, students undergoing courses of varying lengths and complexity in higher education, trained class music teachers studying on a short in-service course, or other adults learning the guitar either privately or at an adult education institute. Whatever the situation, the guitar teacher is expected to respond to the different requirements with a sensitivity and pacing of tuition that allows for a successful outcome.

The complexity of this task is added to, not only by the need for collaboration within an educational establishment, but by the different images in which the guitar may be held. Indeed, the contribution of the guitar to many different fields is so considerable that the classical guitarist may find himself or herself working under a totally false premiss, i.e. although their work may be set under a label of 'classical guitar', the 1980s often warrant a more varied and integrated response. Some schoolchildren learning the classical guitar, for example, will certainly wish to experience rock music. In order to respond to some or all of these factors a particular approach is required, not a dogma, but something more flexible. For this, it is essential for the teacher not only to possess an extensive knowledge of the repertoire but be continually aware of the technique required to play a given piece of music. At any one time, therefore, it is vital that the teacher be absolutely clear about three concepts; that of why the instrument is being studied, where the pupil is being taken, and by what means.

Once these are established, the choice of musical example (era, style, etc.) may become much more of an arrangement between the pupil and teacher. Thus, although this chapter is concerned with classical guitar, the principles involved are somewhat broader.

The aforementioned difficulties associated with commencing a study of the guitar relate as much to the structuring of this chapter as they do to the varied situations in which guitarists may find themselves teaching. The learning of the guitar will therefore be set out under five fundamental principles of technique. These principles summarize the essential skills that must be acquired in order to play guitar music of any level of difficulty. Much of the subtlety of a guitar teacher's work is based on the skill with which he or she interweaves the learning of these fundamentals to produce a coherent, interesting, and sympathetic programme. The principles are:

(i) The ability to sound a single string using either the thumb, index, middle, or ring fingers of the right hand (or a pick if the style necessitates it).

(ii) The ability to press and release a single string with the fingers of the left hand and to co-ordinate this with skill (i).

(iii) The ability to shift the left hand along the finger-board of the guitar and to co-ordinate this with skills (i) and (ii).

(iv) The ability to sound two or more strings simultaneously with the fingers and/or thumb of the right hand (or a pick).

(v) The ability to press and release two or more strings with the fingers of the left hand and to co-ordinate this with skill (iv).

The examples of the repertoire that are to be discussed under each of these divisions will not of course be appropriate for all pupils. It is not, therefore, the example itself that is important, but what it is setting out to achieve. Adjustments must be made for the age and learning capacity of a pupil, musical taste or preference, and the many factors that motivate a pupil at any given moment. Furthermore, it is essential that the teacher be sensitive to the length of time for which an example should be studied; thus, what may be a major task for a very young player, for example, may be an untroubled, transient stage for the adult. Of prime concern here is not the ease with which these elementary stages are passed, but that their existence is recognized, particularly a so-called pre-Grade 1 level. Too often publications have adapted the cover and titles for this level rather than the music (generally, by the way, relating 'easy' with the very young—it is difficult for a seventeen-year-old to relate to a piece called *Gobstoppers*) and the word 'easy' is one which the teacher or new player should approach with caution.

The initial lessons

A number of issues will immediately face the new guitar teacher in school, college, or adult institute. These may range from the difficulties that surround the releasing of children from lessons to the acceptance of footstools and the correct chairs as essential equipment for the classical guitarist. In an adult institute, the reasons for a student having enrolled for classical guitar tuition may not be entirely straightforward. Other social reasons may predominate, as will the difficulty for some students (and children) of affording the necessary music or a playable instrument.

Once the lessons have been organized, however, it will be necessary for the teacher to make some important policy decisions. Amongst these, two of the most crucial are concerned with the study of notation and the introduction of tuning. A full discussion of the teaching of notation and working without it, is beyond the scope of this chapter, but the reader is referred to Chapter 1, together with the references to Brocklehurst, Paynter, and Swanwick and Taylor given at the end of this chapter.

Tuning and pitch recognition in children also warrants further reference and the reader is referred to Backus, Davies, and Brocklehurst in 'Further Reading'. It should be noted that many of the common methods of tuning do require some technique, i.e. the guitar must at least be held and a string sounded. In addition, if the 'fifth fret' method of tuning is to be employed, some degree of left-hand technique will be necessary. The formative lessons are, of course, vital in establishing the correct technical habits and it is quite common for less desirable aspects of technique to be unwittingly acquired during tuning. It is clear, therefore, that during these early stages, some compromise will have to be made between the different needs of the pupil. Any arrangements that can be made by the teacher to help the pupil practise with a guitar that is in tune would be of considerable importance. Anyone who has contact with the child over the larger part of the week, a class teacher or parent for example, may be able to provide the required assistance. A tape that contains a recording of the open strings, or a set of pitch pipes, may be considered as being better than having no help at all. Equally, the older student must see tuning as a valid part of their practice-schedule, and anyone who is working with a group (class teacher or instrumental teacher) must recognize the importance of keeping all members of that group involved in the process of tuning rather than concentrate on a complete tuning of one guitar, then another, etc. Time is, however, of the essence in any lesson, and anyone who is responsible for tuning must be continually aware of what else they are hoping to achieve—thus, some compromise will again be necessary.

The shortage of time in the initial lessons, particularly when groups are being taught, necessitates compromise in areas other than tuning. Of major concern is the establishment of certain facets of classical guitar technique (or other), and of these, the sitting position, support of the guitar, the position of the right arm, and the angle at which the right-hand fingers approach the strings are all features that are difficult to ignore. It should be stressed here, however, that the dangers of a pronounced dogma in these early stages are considerable, particularly if it completely overrides the musical experience that a pupil is expecting. Every child who takes up the guitar in junior school must not be looked upon as a potential music college student and in short courses, those for in-service class teachers for example, the degree of technique will have to be matched appropriately to the overall aims of the course. Therefore, as with tuning, technique must form only a carefully-gauged part of the lesson. It is a difficult balance to achieve because with each pupil and group it is a continually changing element. In addition, it must be clear that the success of a task is closely related to the degree to which the technique for that task has been established.

Sitting and holding the guitar will form the initial technical concern. The reader is referred to the comments in Chapter 9, as well as the accounts in the many published tutors. In the context of this chapter, it is just appropriate to remind the new teacher to argue for the correct chairs in any educational establishment and to make arrangements for footstools to be available. The necessary equipment will, of course, be expected if tuition is private and individual.

Principle 1: The sounding of a string

The aspects of technique listed above do assume that, for reasons of sound production, work should begin with the right hand. Before commencing with any exercises, however, a means of communication must be set up. The naming of the right-hand fingers and string numbers is the minimum amount of information that must be given, note names and notation also being given where the circumstances permit. This information is to be found in Appendices I and II, as well as in the published tutors that are available.

Tutors are worthy of some comment. These publications are generally intended to cover all the essential areas for the prospective guitarist. All have their strong and weak points and the degree of detail and repertoire varies considerably, as does the way in which they move from stage to stage. Technical contradictions may often arise when the tutor moves along a strictly notational pathway. Conversely, if the approach is purely technical, a degree of musical knowledge or teaching must be assumed. The latter is a vital consideration when recommending a given tutor, as is the age range of those for whom the tutor is intended. It is likely, therefore, that the guitar teacher will have to draw information and exercises from a number of different sources.

A clearly set-out account of the rudiments of music (plus, of course, other material) may be found in Segovia: *My Book of the Guitar* (Andrés Segovia and George Mendoza, Ariel Publications). *Enjoy Playing the Guitar* (Debbie Cracknell, OUP) is for the younger pupil, and takes the introduction of one note at a time as its theme. *The John Mills Classical Guitar Tutor* (John Mills, Musical New Services) and *Solo Guitar Playing* (Frederick Noad, Omnibus Press) are for the older pupil or perhaps the class music teacher who is not a specialist in guitar. They contain a large number of pieces of varying difficulty, the Noad having the advantage of some excellent exercises written in the form of duets for teacher and pupil. The exercise/duets take a notational approach, concentrating on, for example, the open string notes or E, F, and G, first string notes in first position. *Introduction to the Guitar* (Hector Quine, OUP) is predominantly concerned with technique, repertoire being confined to a small number of studies from the Classical/Romantic era. The explanations are clear and concise and the exercises contained may provide the basis of a sound technique and a course for any age.

At this point, an important decision must be made on the use of the two basic methods of sounding open strings, rest stroke (apoyando) and free stroke (tirando). While the choice and emphasis on each method will be directed by the teacher's opinion on tone production and security of movement, it is important that a clear pathway of study be envisaged which allows for the full exploitation of both techniques. Exercises for rest stroke and free stroke are to be found in all of the aforementioned tutors, although the reader is particularly referred to the sections 'Crossing the Strings' and 'Arpeggio Exercises' in *Introduction to the Guitar*. These rest stroke exercises and right-hand movements may be approached at many different levels, but the important point to make here is the link that is envisaged to the first repertoire example for younger children and examples from the classical repertoire, referred to later in this chapter. The arpeggio exercise for the former is shown in Ex. 6.1, here thought of as an exercise for free stroke.

Ex. 6.1

If disguised with an appropriate title, this exercise may be a convenient first 'solo' for a young player. It is, perhaps, more difficult than the playing of a single string with rest stroke and the alternate use of fingers, but it is the author's preference for establishing the basic hand position. Ten examples of open string guitar solos, presented as string location exercises, are to be found in *The Contemporary Guitarist* (Arthur Wills and Hector Quine, Ricordi).

Even at this early stage of open string playing, the beginner can be introduced to mediums other than guitar solo. The duets for pupil and teacher found in *Solo Guitar Playing* require the minimum of arrangement to expand them to trios and quartets with two and three parts on open strings. In addition, recorders or tuned percussion may be added to give a larger ensemble for the classroom. *Erstes Spielheft für Gitarre* (Holger Clausen, Schott) is a particularly useful publication for this level. Some of the duets use open strings only in both parts; similarly, some of the trios contain two guitar parts on open strings only.

If the six open strings of the guitar are thought of as the roots of certain chords, the elements of the most simple song accompaniment can be further introduced. The open strings provide the tonic, subdominant, and dominant roots in the keys of E, A, and D; the tonic and dominant roots in the key of G; the tonic and subdominant roots in the key of B; and, of course, the tonic roots in the keys of E, A, D, G, B, and E. The very simplest example of open-string song accompaniment is provided by those songs that are based on one chord, examples of which are to be found in *Guitar in the Primary School* (A. H. Green, OUP) and Chapter 12 of this book. Once three or more root notes (open strings) are employed, examples may be drawn from the current hit-parade or publications such as *The Complete Guitar Player Songbook* (Russ Shipton, Wise Publications). The open strings do, of course, provide other chord notes (for example, the open string G could be thought of as the fifth in the chord of C), and this stage of guitar and voice is important for breaking the popular image of the class teacher *performing* a song, i.e. the arrangements may be made easy enough for the child to play the guitar.

Principle 2: The pressing and releasing of a string

Whatever detail is given to the study of the right hand, it will only be a short time before attention is directed towards the left. Once again, it will be necessary to differentiate between the acquisition of a technical skill, that of stopping the string, and the study of notation. All of the tutors listed above will be of assistance, although for a more detailed approach to notation and music theory, the reader is referred to *The Guitarist's ABC of Music* (John W. Duarte, Novello). Initially, the teacher may wish to use an exercise of finger-placing that does not involve the right hand. Concise exercises for stopping the strings and co-ordination with the right-hand fingers are to be found in the sections entitled 'Crossing the Fingerboard' and 'Finger Independence Exercise', in *Introduction to the Guitar.* These provide an effective preliminary to the vital introduction of playing scales, a range of which is published by the various examining Boards. They may, however, be introduced without notation but via the position number, string numbers, and left-hand finger numbers, as shown below.

C major V
③ 1 3
② 1 2 4
① 1 3 4

For exercises that are intended to teach the notes on each string, the previously mentioned *Solo Guitar Playing* may be referred to. For the younger player, *Enjoy Playing the Guitar* takes a more measured approach.

The passing on to repertoire which requires the left hand is a step which will usually be taken quickly. In some circumstances, however, it can expose a considerable gap in the new teacher's knowledge of repertoire, especially where younger children are concerned. Obviously, it will have been quite some years since the teacher had to tackle such pieces, and new music for this level will have been published since then. The development of a teaching style, programmes of work, and a capacity to assess the workability of publications will all take time. However, it will not take long in any school to realize that the very easiest repertoire is often required and that there is relatively little of it available. For the pupil who is new to reading music, the page may appear as a somewhat confusing and unhelpful set of symbols. Layout is, therefore, important at this level, and the page which has fingering, string numbers, position indications, and expression marks reduced to a minimum can be advantageous.

In First Position (Germano Cavazzoli, Ricordi) is one of the few collections that has made such adjustments. The print is slightly larger and left- and right-hand fingering, string numbers, and marks of musical expression are all used sparingly. One main musical idea tends to dominate each piece, making it easier to anticipate the pieces with an appropriate technical exercise. *Sweet Harmonies*, the opening piece, may be related to any exercise which has involved the use of the right-hand thumb in conjunction with the fingers, and a left-hand exercise for stopping single notes. The repeated notes in the second piece, *A Waltz for Tony*, provides a suitable example for fingers that have been trained to alternate. The relationship between technique and repertoire is further developed for the very young in *Playground* (Michael Stimpson, Thames/Novello). This contains eight very easy studies, each of which has been linked to a particular aspect of technique—for example, scale fragments, the use of alternate (i,m) rest stroke, and single notes played with the thumb. Ex. 6.2, for arpeggio playing, *Captain Dazzler's Starship*, illustrates the link between exercise (*Arpeggio Exercises, Introduction to the Guitar*) and repertoire.

Ex. 6.2

Further examples of repertoire that only require the sounding of one note at a time are contained in *Explorations in Guitar Playing*, Vols. I and II (Bryan Lester, Ricordi), *A First Book of Guitar Solos* (arr. John Gavall, OUP), and *Le prime lezioni di chitarra* (Julio Sagreras, Bérben). The aforementioned *Contemporary Guitarist* offers examples in that style, as does a most adventurous publication, *Diversions for David* (Larry Sitsky, Ricordi). For the teacher who is interested in the introduction of avant-garde sounds at this preliminary level, examples such as *Outer Space, Jets*, and *Very High Up* will prove invaluable.

The ability to recognize and stop a single note opens up a range of ensemble music to the beginner. The Dutch composer, Pieter van der Staak, has written a considerable number of pieces that are suitable for this particular technical level. *Lollipops*, one of the easiest duets for the very young, is to be found in *A Bag of Sweets* (Pieter van der Staak, Broekmans and van Poppel). The top line (guitar one) uses the second string notes B, C, and D; the second guitar part is written using two notes of the third string—G and A. The use of alternate rest stroke is therefore required in a duet that can be quickly expanded for larger ensembles by raising or lowering the lines by an octave and adding, for example, tuned percussion. The level of reading facility required for the remaining duets is somewhat varied. Although considerably more advanced, *Birthday Cake* from this publication provides the teacher with a convenient duet for encouraging scale playing. An additional set of duets for the young is available, with other items, in *The Young Person's Way to the Guitar* (John W. Duarte, Novello). These, together with *Easy Two* (Pieter van der Staak, Broekmans and van Poppel) and *Twenty Graded Duets* (arr. John Gavall, OUP), will provide basic material that is a little more difficult than the duet-exercises contained in some of the tutors.

Within the technical limitations so far considered, there are a number of publications that will allow, if appropriate, an early introduction of music for three guitars. Amongst the very easiest material are two publications from Holland, *Seven Easy Guitar Trios* (Henk Hoekema) and *A Set of Sketches* (Pieter van der Staak), both published by Broekmans and van Poppel. It will be common for the teacher to require some classification of rhythmical difficulty as well as technical and notational, the first three examples from *A Set of Sketches* illustrating such a distinction. The first uses crotchets and minims only in all three parts, the second introduces quavers, and in the third, the time signature and rhythms are 6/8. More varied items are available in *Playing Guitars Together* (Debbie Cracknell, OUP) and an example such as *What if a Day or a Moneth or a Year* gives the teacher an ideal link to repertoire that may be introduced at a later stage for the solo guitarist. This theme of early music is continued in the final recommendation at this level, *Early Music for Three Guitars* (arr. John Gavall, OUP).

As the number of guitars increase in an ensemble it becomes far more likely that one of the parts will require a further development in technique, perhaps a change in position or the sounding of more than one string. For the purpose of classification these quartets will be considered later, although it is recognized that some of the individual lines are easier than those in the following examples. Reference should, however, be made to the quartets in the aforementioned *Playing Guitars Together*, as well as in *Nine Easy Guitar Quartets* (Pieter van der Staak, Broekmans and van Poppel), and *Music for 3 and/or 4 Guitars* (selected by Paul Gerrits, Doberman). These all contain examples of single note playing in first position.

Principle 3: Changing position

Moving the left hand along the finger-board, and the subsequent knowledge of the notation, is an aspect of guitar playing that is often viewed with some, or even considerable, reservation. It is, therefore, important that the teacher builds repertoire and exercises that necessitate such changes into programmes of tuition. For a variety of reasons, some may wish to confront this issue at the very earliest of stages and begin work on it before progressing to music that involves the use of chords. The following examples of repertoire thus contain only single notes, but now in different positions.

Work in these areas may not be totally unfamiliar to the beginner because some of the previous exercises were located higher up the finger-board. These were, however, fixed in one position and the difference is, of course, the movement to and from a given position. A two-octave scale that involves one position change only would be a reasonable step to make, anticipating more advanced scales and the many different approaches to their practice.

Clearly, it is advantageous if notes in higher positions are introduced gradually. For this reason the teacher may be referred to *Play Purcell* (ed. Gerald Tolan, Ricordi). The first three pieces introduce second position, but without any changes of position. The fourth example, *Air*, from the *Double Dealer*, a play by William Congreve (1693), requires a change from first to second position and back again. This is shown in Ex. 6.3, not only to illustrate such a change, but to emphasize the level of difficulty that is still under discussion.

For the teacher who wishes to pursue the arpeggio, *Arpeggio Study*, from the aforementioned *Explorations in Guitar Playing for Begin-*

Ex. 6.3

continued

ners, Vol. I, offers a convenient example as a development from the *Air*. The player is required to know the notes A and B on the first string and F♯ on the second. As a development and contrast from the previously mentioned *Captain Dazzler's Starship*, the melody is to be found on the first string as opposed to the sixth. For the very young who have a technique that can use rest stroke on a single string, *F. A. Cup*, from the same publication (*Playground*), requires a shift to fifth position on the first and sixth strings only, i.e. the notes A, B, and C. Also suitable for this age-range is the first guitar solo, *Präludium*, found in the publication *Erstes Spielheft für Gitarre* which was discussed under the section on open string playing. Examples for the older player are to be found in *The Contemporary Guitarist* and *Oriental Guitar* (G. Goorf, Ricordi).

The theme of twentieth-century music can be continued for two guitars in a fine collection entitled *Duos for Two Guitars* (Béla Bartók, arr. Karl Scheit, Universal Edition). Guitar one of *Dance*, the second piece, requires a change to second and sixth position, whereas guitar two remains in first. In addition, the dynamic markings of pianissimo, forte, and pianissimo for the three sections of the piece are a clearly defined example of dynamics for the beginner. Further examples of single note position playing are contained in this collection. Guitar one of the first piece, *Teasing Song*, involves positions three and seven. The pieces are, however, on the outer limit of the level of difficulty being considered here and are therefore more likely to be of use to the teacher who is working with older children and students of all ages. Contrasting in style, and a little easier, are the duets *Handel's Turn* (arr. John W. Duarte, Novello) and *Two Guitars* (arr. John Gavall, OUP).

Examples of guitar trios that move to higher positions are, of course, to be found in some of the collections recommended earlier in this chapter. The final choice of which is most suitable for a situation will lie with the teacher's own assessment of difficulty, cost effectiveness of the publication, and quality of the content. It may, for example, be appropriate to turn to *Erstes Spielheft für Gitarre* on the grounds that it also contains some open string duets and trios as well as a small number of guitar solos. Where the teacher will make more use of a collection made up of trios and quartets only, *Puer natus in Bethlehem* (Michael Praetorius, arr. Elisabeth Bayer, Doblinger) may be recommended. In general, the rhythms are straightforward, only occasionally moving via quavers. The marking of some of the guitar parts with the range of recorder that could be substituted makes it an opportune publication for the early introduction of mixed ensemble. For the teacher who requires a collection that contains only guitar trios, *Easy Pieces by Old Masters* (arr. Werner Kämmerling, Doblinger) should be considered, although these are the most difficult pieces of the three recommendations in this section.

It was noted that the collection of music by Michael Praetorius also contained music for four guitars. *Ten Short Chorales* (Erik Satie, arr. Michael Stimpson, Ricordi) contains guitar quartets of a similar level of difficulty, all parts being single notes with guitar one fingered in higher positions. *Chorale No. 3* (Ex. 6.4), for example, consists of semibreves only in the first section and a mixture of semibreves and minims in the second. Some of the key signatures in the other chorales are, however, a little more advanced and the occasional tuning of the sixth string to D by guitar four directs these quarterts towards older students. Also, the brevity of the chorales warrants some use of repeats. Where the ensemble is made up of players of a similar ability it can be useful to have quartets in which the parts change round. This is a common occurrence in the music of Pieter van der Staak, and two publications, *Nine Easy Guitar Quartets* and *Five Pieces from Tielman Susato's Danserye* (Broekmans and van Poppel) fulfil this criterion and introduce a small number of notes in higher positions.

Principles 4 and 5: The playing of two or more strings

The final step in bringing a pupil to the bulk of the elementary

Ex. 6.4

continued

repertoire involves work on the playing of more than one string. Gradation of difficulty is as vital here as at any other stage and it is preferable to distinguish between the sounding and the stopping of different combinations of strings.

An appropriate exercise for the right hand is to be found in a section in *Introduction to the Guitar* entitled 'Chord Playing—right-hand technique'. This is concerned with the open strings only and is for the index, middle, and ring fingers, each played with the thumb (see Ex. 6.5).

Ex. 6.5

For repertoire, the teacher may be referred to two pieces, *The Old Mandola* and *The Musician*, found in *In First Position*. In the first of these two pieces, the stopped note is varied between the treble and bass strings and is just sufficiently difficult for the introduction of this technique. The rather cramped layout and phrase markings makes *Dance for One* (*Explorations in Guitar Playing for Beginners*, Vol. I) less recommendable, but perhaps one of the easiest examples is *The Dream*, from *A First Book of Guitar Solos* (John Gavall, OUP). The above examples are confined to the sounding of two strings only, still with only one left-hand finger required. Further combinations of three and four right-hand fingers will soon be required, the more common ones being given in Ex. 6.6.

Ex. 6.6

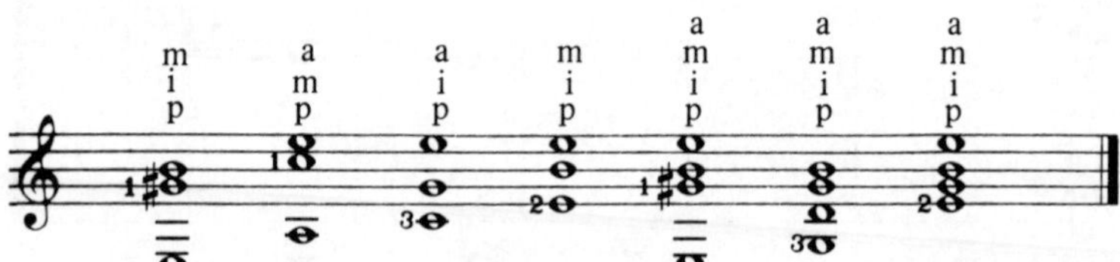

Some reference must, of course, be made to the use of the thumb for playing more than one string (strum) and this can be done via the use of a six-note chord such as E minor. The stopping of two or more strings by the fingers of the left hand leads the teacher into the sensitive area of 'chord' playing. Although a chord is, by definition, two or more notes sounded simultaneously, the word has for guitarists become associated with a series of 'shapes' for the left hand. In recent years, certain areas of music education have placed a severe emphasis on the use of chords, denying not only many other aspects of the instrument's capabilities but also the considerable problems that are brought about by starting with this technical stage. The fatal mistake of assuming that a chord of C major is the most straightforward of chords on the guitar (because there are no sharps or flats in that key) does not take into account that a small hand finds difficulty in stopping the first three frets in first position. Furthermore, the resulting subdominant and dominant chords that are commonly found in song accompaniment, present unnecessary difficulty. It is, therefore, important to distinguish between the relative difficulty of certain chords and the changes between them. There are a number that require only one string to be stopped, but of the chord shapes commonly referred to, a reasonable starting-point is that of E minor. This requires two fingers to press the strings, no stretching, and avoids accidental dissonance by involving all six strings. For the young, the teacher may be referred to *Triffic*, from *Playground*, and the duet *Chewing Gum*, from *A Bag of Sweets*. Both pieces contain, with the exception of the E minor chord, only single notes. The appropriate fingering enables a new chord, E major, to be introduced with the minimum of technical difficulty. This illustrates both the difference between a major and minor chord and a chord that requires three notes to be stopped. The movement to an A minor chord is more difficult because although the shape of the chord is maintained, all the fingers must be released and moved across the strings. The addition of the fourth finger to alter the chord to A major mimics the change in E and allows the first use of this finger in combination with the others. Progression to the dominant seventh, B7, illustrates two principles of left-hand technique, that of using all four fingers and the stopping of a note common to two consecutive chords. The latter was, of course, established during the change from E minor to E major and A minor to A major, and is also to be found as the sequence resolves to an E chord. A similar logic applied to other chords will gradually allow for their smooth incorporation, but it should be stressed that some present major difficulties for the level of player under consideration here. For chord shapes in first position, the reader is referred to Appendix III.

Although strumming is initially the easiest means of sounding chord sequences, previous arpeggio exercises may also be incorporated because this will open up one of the most important technical pathways for further study. Thus, the application to the above sequence of the arpeggio exercise illustrated earlier (p,i,m,a,m,i), gives an efficient exercise for moving left-hand fingers in sequence and may, if wished, be linked with arpeggio patterns of the various examination syllabuses. Different right-hand movements give a pupil sufficient technique to tackle basic arpeggio studies and *Prelude in A minor* (Matteo Carcassi) and *Allegro* (Mauro Giuliani) are among the easiest examples. They exploit the right-hand movements p,i,m,a,m,i, and p,i,m,i,a,i,m,i, respectively. These pieces are found in a number of different publications, for example, *The Guitarist's Hour*, Vol. I (ed. Walter Götze, Schott).

This collection also contains other suitable music, predominantly from the Classical/Romantic era, that will reflect and pursue the present level of technique. Among these are *Étude* (No. 34) by Fernando Sor, a study that explores both scales and arpeggio passages. It is almost invariably made up of single-note playing in the right hand, although in order to create the harmonies of the arpeggio passages, left-hand fingers will need to remain pressing. A similar principle applies to the arpeggio passages in *Allegretto* (No. 8) by Joseph Küffner, a piece which also contains scale passages and the first example referred to under repertoire of three notes sounded simultaneously. It is a relatively small step to move to two-part playing with both hands, and representative of this in the same publication is *Andante* (No. 6) by Fernando Sor. This composer, together with Dionisio Aguado, Matteo Carcassi, Fernando Carulli, and Napoléon Coste wrote a considerable number of studies and some of the most common are to be found in *Études* (ed. Karl Scheit, Universal Edition). The level of difficulty is variable, but nevertheless, there are examples that allow the teacher both to represent this period in a course of study and to assist in the transition through the elementary grades of guitar playing. It should be noted, however, that some of these studies are not in their complete form. After publications such as this, it is likely that a pupil will have sufficient interest to warrant the purchase of collections of studies by a single composer, and a number of the major publishers have these items in their catalogue.

Of equal importance during the early stages of learning the guitar is an awareness of the breadth of the repertoire, and this will have a direct effect on the cultivation of a wide musical interest. English lute music arranged for the guitar is well represented in *Easy Pieces from Shakespeare's Time* (ed. Karl Scheit, Universal Edition). Music by many of the important composers of this period appears in this publication, including John Dowland, Thomas Robinson, and Francis Cutting. *A Toy*, the first piece, is among the easiest pieces in this collection and as well as providing an example of music in 6/8 time, the music has clearly defined phrases that are ideal for developing dynamic and/or tonal contrast. An excellent example for more involved chord work is given by *What if a Day or a Moneth or a Year*, a piece that uses many of the common chord shapes in first position. The harmonies of this piece and the experience of the time signature encountered in *A Toy* make a pupil's progress to the arrangement of *Greensleeves* relatively straightforward. Other titles in this edition that deserve consideration are *Wilson's Wilde*, *Bockington's Pound*, and *Grisse his Delight*, pieces which have often found themselves in examination syllabuses. Additional material from this period may also be found in *Dowland's Dozen* (tr. Chris Kilvington, Ricordi) and *Renaissance Dances* (ed. Karl Scheit, Universal Edition). *Eight Easy Pieces* by Gaspar Sanz (ed. John W. Duarte, Universal Edition) has some technically manageable music by this composer for the baroque guitar. Taken from the 1697 edition of *Libro Terca de Musica*, the music is predominantly two-part, and is useful material for taking the elementary player to higher positions on the finger-board.

One of the major strengths of the modern-day classical guitar is the quality of music that has been written for it in the twentieth century. The bulk of this is, of course, for the concert player, but where possible, the teacher must take the opportunity to prepare a pupil for the new sounds. Excellent for the player who has acquired some facility are the *Études Simples* (Leo Brouwer, Eschig). Although these pieces have been considered to fall within the intermediate classification, the teacher may be referred to *Studies No. 2* and 3 of Volume I. *Study No. 3* requires a bass line to be sounded with the thumb while a repeated note in the treble is played by alternating right-hand fingers. The left-hand fingers must stop either one or two notes at a time. It is approximately the level of difficulty of the *Allegro* (Guiliani) and *What if a Day or a Moneth or a Year*, making possible an early introduction of twentieth-century music. Further music that may be considered includes *Within Easy Reach* (John W. Duarte, Ricordi), ten pieces that have been written to avoid any difficult stretches for the left hand, and *Divertissements pour Guitar* (Gerard Montreuil, Doberman), fourteen pieces in a lighter style.

Many of the publications for two or more guitars listed earlier

7 Classical Repertoire—Intermediate

Charles Ramirez

AN ideal intermediate student is one who can read music fluently and has a working knowledge of at least the basic guitar techniques—rest stroke (apoyando) and free stroke (tirando), right-hand arpeggios and chords, and left-hand chord shapes that include the use of the barré. During further development, it would be expected that the student would be taken through work that is not only varied in its historical context, but introduces what have become standard techniques for the classical guitarist—harmonics, glissando, pizzicato, tremolo, ornaments, and *rasgueados*, etc. The implication of this is that we are therefore considering here a student who is receiving regular, individual lessons of at least a half-hour duration. Time permitting, the lessons should cover technical revision, the new piece and pieces already in the students repertoire, sight-reading, theory, and aural training. *Elementary Training for Musicians* (Hindemith, Schott) and *Aural Tests* and *Questions and Exercises on Theory of Music* (The Associated Board of the Royal Schools of Music) are excellent aids for both student and teacher.

Progressive Reading for Guitarists (Stephen Dodgson and Hector Quine, Ricordi) is a well-ordered and effective way of teaching sight-reading, which is too often neglected. Clearly different approaches should be insisted on when learning and sight-reading. In my view, learning a piece means learning it for life; sight-reading is only a tool for getting to know a piece, for deciding on fingerings etc., and even to find out quickly if one wishes to learn a piece or not. Memorizing a piece should not be the only goal of practice. Furthermore, practice does not end when a piece has been memorized. The maxim is 'practise *after* memorizing' and not 'practise *to* memorize'. To achieve this, a student must decide how much he or she can cope with comfortably in one session—so much the better if this is allied to actual musical phrases. Once the fingering has been decided on and notes, rhythms, etc. are secure in the pupil's mind, the phrase is memorized, and should now be practised until it is second nature. This means that almost at once, full attention will be given to hand positions, legato, etc., with the added benefit of consolidating the memory.

Interpretation will need to be encouraged from the start. In the earliest stages it may be shown how and where a change of colour (tasto or ponticello) can be made, where a change of dynamic is effective, or where vibrato may be used—devices which encourage projection, appreciation, and a sense of performance. It is most important to show how these effects are achieved; it should not be simply stated, for example, 'it needs to be more expressive', but shown how, where, and why it should be more expressive. Explanation allied with demonstration is a very powerful tool. A teacher will need to be particularly sensitive to whether it is better to correct a misconception or mistake, or whether it is preferable to move on. Perhaps the best guideline to follow at these moments is that if the pupil is doing his or her best within the limits of present knowledge and experience, it is probably preferable to move on. However, incorrect technical habits must not be allowed to override. In general, the teacher should introduce new techniques in a few, well-chosen, precise, and direct sentences—a 'treatise' is not necessarily required.

Exercises will have to be given, not only for general technique but so as to overcome particular problems. For example, should a chord shape or stretch cause difficulty, it could be taken up the finger-board as far as is comfortable (where the frets are closer together) and then moved down finger by finger and fret by fret (see Ex. 7.1).

Ex. 7.1

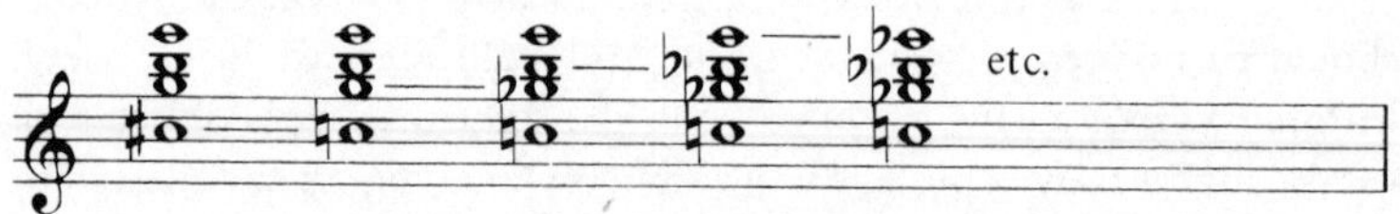

Of all exercises, scales will play a crucial role in the development of an intermediate student. Practising scales to different rhythms can show where the fingering and/or the co-ordination is faulty, but the exercises may be more useful when developing the speed and accuracy of a particular scale (see Ex. 7.2). Building a scale 'note by note' can be most useful. Problems of speed can often be overcome by careful

Ex. 7.2

fingering of the right hand. For example, the use of the ring, middle, and index fingers (a, m, i, in that order) when three or six notes are played on the same string, and the middle and index fingers (m, i, in that order) when two or four notes are played on the same string. Five notes would therefore be played a,m,i,m,i. (At times, it may be better to re-finger the left hand so that this is possible.) (See Ex. 7.3.)

Ex. 7.3

General scale practice can also be used to develop speed by taking a scale pattern and repeating it part or all of the way up and down the finger-board, getting gradually faster (for example, B major to C major, C♯ major, etc.). If maximum speed is achieved too soon and is impossible to maintain, the speed should be relaxed and then built up gradually again.

The Renaissance

Early music now forms an important part of the guitarist's repertoire, and pieces are available at all levels for the intermediate player. Among the most widely played have been the *Pavanes* by Luis Milan.* There are a number of editions that differ in presentation of the notation and textual detail, and I have found the Ruggero Chiesa edition (Suvini Zerboni) of *El Maestro*, in which they are contained, a good text to work from. In some editions the facsimile is included, for example *Six Pavanas* (ed. Karl Scheit, Universal Edition), making it possible to refer to the original. Published arrangements and transcriptions should always be compared with the original source where possible (including later composers). Many of the standard editions, the Bruger and Hofmeister of Bach for example, are unclear at times as to where the editor has intervened—they are a curious half-way stage between original and transcription. Clearly, the teacher's skill in transcribing should be developed.

A glance at the original version and the transcriptions of the music of Robert de Visée shows a similar difficulty. It must be said, however, that the original requires the pupil to be fluent in ornamentation, which will take some pieces out of the early–intermediate stage. Teachers may wish to consult publications containing detailed references on ornamentation etc., such as *Keyboard Interpretation* (H. Ferguson, OUP). The recommended edition of de Visée's work, *Oeuvres complètes pour Guitare* (Ed. Strizich, Heugel), follows the original tuning; the fifth string was tuned to the equivalent of the A found at the second fret of the third string, with no low sixth string E. A short, relatively easy movement from one of the *Suites* will provide an effective introduction to music of this period. (It may be instructive to remove the sixth string and replace the fifth with a second string tuned to A.) It must be further recognized, however, that due to convenience, price, availability, and the fact that examining Boards invariably recommend specific editions, a teacher may continually have to work with a range of less desirable editions.

Another difficult decision for the teacher and pupil is the re-tuning of the third string to F♯. For example, in *Diferencias sobre 'Guárdame las vacas'* by Luys de Naraváez (Hispanae Citharae Ars Viva, arr. Emilio Pujol, Schott), I do not find it necessary. In this and many other instances, there tends to be little technical or tonal advantage to be gained; but teachers will develop their own opinions on the subject. Two other factors that must be taken into account are whether the string will remain in tune and the fact that re-tuning is a requirement for some examining Boards. The variations in *Guárdame las vacas* are not only very attractive, but make an excellent study for right-hand finger alternation using free stroke. A decision must be made on the need for changes in tempo. It can be most instructive if the teacher accompanies the pupil with the melody (and/or the bass line) on which these variations are built.

Much early music is of an intermediate standard and there are many composers who may be considered: Dowland, Cutting, Robinson, Batchelor, Mudarra, Milan, Narváez, Valderrábano, and da Milano. Gaspar Sanz's attractive music offers a good opportunity to practise and experiment with ornamentation in a relatively easy context.

The Baroque

The music of J. S. Bach offers the most stimulating study. Although there are many published transcriptions, the teacher may wish to refer to the *Neue Ausgabe Sämtlicher Werke. Serie V: Band 10* (Bärenreiter Kassel). This is a portion of the complete edition of Bach's music and is thus written on two staves (actual pitch) and in the original keys.

Despite the beguiling beauty of the enigmatic figures in the *Sarabande* of *Lute Suite No. 3* (J. S. Bach, BWV 995), the piece will sound disjointed and be misunderstood unless an overall view of the phrase structure is taken. The piece opens with a short idea that appears to waver between arpeggio and melody and which seems incomplete and in need of resolution. The phrase is repeated, heightening this need. This takes place in the third and fourth bars which must be treated as one longer phrase. Similarity and contrast in the structure of the phrases which follow should be noted, as should the extension in bar 16, which creates the climax of the piece. A variety of left-hand fingerings are possible and the player will need to decide whether it is preferable to achieve an arpeggio effect with notes ringing on, or a clearly defined single line.

There are, of course, many other movements in the Suites of Bach which are of an intermediate level of difficulty, and the student is referred to, for example: *Allemande, Courante, Sarabande*, and *Bourrée* (*Suite No. 1*, BWV 996); *Sarabande* (*Suite No. 2*, BWV 997); *Allemande* (*Suite No. 3*, BWV 995); *Loure and Minuets* (*Suite No. 4*, BWV 1006A).

The *Cello Suites* and *Violin Sonatas* and *Partitas* also provide material. Somewhat more difficult than the *Sarabande* referred to above, but nevertheless often played, is the *Prelude* from *Cello Suite No. 1* (BWV 1007). Unlike the *Preludes* of Villa-Lobos for example, this is a prelude which actually precedes more music. It is, therefore, important for the student to recognize that the interpretation of a piece must be related to its context. The *Prelude* has a sectional structure in the foreground and this gives it its introductory character, the overall movement being carried by the background harmony. The arpeggio figure must be carefully shaped towards its focal point at the second beat, and the weaker notes thought of as a means of moving to the stronger notes rather than being purely static (see Ex. 7.4). The scales should have a similar momentum because they provide an important function, that of linking and giving variety. The teacher here may wish to offer comparison with the *Prelude in D minor* (*'Little' Prelude*, BWV 999) which is also based on an arpeggio, but does not contain contrasting scale sections. Further comparison should be made with the *Allemande* which follows in *Cello Suite No. 1*. The *Allemande* avoids the sectional structure, the lines are fluent and repeats are absent—this is a genuine compositional contrast as opposed to merely a change in tempo.

Ex. 7.4

For the teacher who wishes to give an example of Baroque music in the French style, the *Courante* from the *Lute Suite No. 1* (BWV 996) should be considered. Some alteration of the rhythms may be necessary, and it is common to apply double dotting to such pieces. The tensions of discord and resolution are important and could be crucial when deciding how to play *notes inégales*. Note also the changing metre (dotted lines) (see Ex. 7.5).

The Classical and Romantic eras

The acquiring of technique by a pupil is a factor with which any teacher will be continually concerned. The studies of Fernando Sor have therefore often found themselves in a prominent position in a teacher's programme and they provide an excellent bridge between exercises and repertoire. It is a small number of them, found for

Ex. 7.5

example in the commonly available 'Segovia Edition' (*Twenty Studies for the Guitar*, ed. Andrés Segovia, Belwin Mills) which will be considered here.

Study No. 1 is a fine piece for working on the problems of chord playing and 'legato', and, like many of the pieces referred to in this chapter, has often found itself in the intermediate grades of various examining Boards. The most difficult chords and changes should be taken out and practised in a particular way, a principle that will of course be invaluable elsewhere. Initially, it is important to isolate exactly where the error or problem is, because it is more time-efficient to work on a small fragment that is causing a problem rather than something larger, the bulk of which contains no difficulty. Thus, only one change should be practised at a time. As much preparation of the fingers as is possible must be made, and a finger may therefore be placed on a string before it is needed. If this is not musically possible, it should be positioned above the string. Much of this type of work should be carried out by the left hand only, for it is the analysis of where a finger is at any given time that is crucial to an accurate shift. It will not matter how slowly a change is practised. To be truly effective, only when difficult changes have been thoroughly practised in this way, should the right hand be incorporated—this adds the problem of co-ordination. Both hands should work at exactly the same moment. It is a common fault, and at times a misconception, that the left hand should move before the right hand, in an effort to prepare a new chord shape—this causes problems of legato. Needless to say, left-hand preparation is often possible, but in pieces such as Sor's *Study No. 1*, the left hand should move simultaneously with the right hand and not before. Arpeggiating (spreading) chords is often done quite unconsciously to mask the above problem. This is an abuse of what should be a delightfully effective interpretative device, when used appropriately, as a result of a musical decision. In this piece, as with many others, there are many occasions where the left-hand fingering must be reconsidered. This is a convenient point to underline the importance of this for both teacher and pupil because an unnecessarily difficult fingering often causes a problem, either technical or musical. For example, the middle note of the first chord, C (bar 1), may be fingered on the third string with the fourth finger. This enables the player to keep it in place for bar 2, and the difficult legato change is then made easier (see Ex. 7.6).

Ex. 7.6

These two bars also allow other general points to be made that will commonly be applicable. The strength of a chord, and its relationship with its neighbours, must always be taken into account. Thus, the dynamic of the opening chord of bar 2 must be carefully gauged, as should its resolution. Phrasing is, of course, vital, and these two-bar phrases should be separated from each other and the rest of the piece, just as a singer would take a breath at the end of a phrase. The balance of parts is an aspect of guitar playing that often requires attention, particularly in chordal pieces such as this. For example, each part from bars 10–13 must sing out separately. The bass line in particular must not be held up by the entry of the middle voice, G (see Ex. 7.7). Overall shaping of a piece is clearly worthy of consideration, and it is often difficult for a relatively inexperienced player to take a larger perspective when the detail can be claiming so much attention. In this piece the phrases should grow towards bar 19 and the C major chord, and the upward then downward sequences should be made obvious to the listener as the piece moves to the final section. Thus, the music must always move towards certain points and never be allowed to become static. The realization that each phrase has a focal point or centre of

Ex. 7.7

gravity is most useful for achieving direction and flow, and must be cultivated at all levels.

Study No. 2 may be used as a study in the use of rest stroke over a free stroke arpeggiated accompaniment. This study, as with *Study No. 3* and *Study No. 5*, may be considered by a teacher as a suitable example for the treatment of a melody (see Ex. 7.8). Balance and tone are crucial and it is common for rest stroke to be used. The opening melody notes, E and C, form a unit—motif, would be too strong a word. The C is quite weak and has little up beat power towards the following G. The G to E in bar 2 further reflects this; thus the following C is a light up-beat to the remainder of the phrase, which concludes with the rhythm and lilt of the opening figure. The pedal C should support this delicate structure and not drown it—rather simply re-affirm its presence with a light and varied pulsation. The change of harmony in bar 3 must be helped by a controlled swell of the dynamics. The Es that are played on the fourth string produce a rhythm that adds a delightful urgency, lifting the semiquavers from the ordinary. This should be followed through to give a quasi-contrapuntal effect in the inner voices.

Ex. 7.8

Study No. 3 pursues this work as well as being an excellent study for the fourth finger of the left hand. A pupil should be encouraged to free the melody and let the accompaniment follow, always highlighting the moments when the latter has chromatic interest and divides to become a low bass.

Many factors will contribute to an interpretation that reflects the romantic nature of *Study No. 5*. For example, the pedal F♯ on the fourth string needs a small 'push-accent', delivered with the tiniest of delays. This pointing of the pedal makes the opening phrases more expectant and the eventual change to G all the more effective. Realizing that the inner voice mostly shadows the melody in thirds should encourage greater freedom. A more dramatic response, perhaps an increase in dynamics or flow, should be encouraged in the modulations which occur later, and the final climactic phrase.

Apart from one or two pieces, Francisco Tárrega's music seems to be too often ignored. His *Preludes* offer a variety of short, contrasting pieces, some of which are suitable for the earlier intermediate stages (see also Miguel Llobet's *Ten Catalan Folk Songs*). The greatest help in interpreting a piece such as *Lagrima* (Francisco Tárrega) is to sing the melody out loud and then play the first two bars without the open string B, trying to imitate the way in which it was sung. The technical difficulties involve the changes in the left hand. These must be done quite quickly, with each chord held down until the split second before the next notes are needed, i.e. long after the open B is played (see section on *Study No. 1* by Sor). The accompaniment must be slightly softer than the melody and this opening, like the remainder of the piece, must not be played either too stiffly or over expressively. As the phrase is repeated exactly in bars 3 and 4, it is necessary to make the second one different in some way—perhaps more emphatic or more pleading. The barré often presents problems and excessive force should not be used to try to obtain clean sounds. This is not conducive to good practice and can easily lead to bad hand positions. This may be an occasion where a mirror could be useful for a different viewpoint on a technical difficulty. The second section, in E minor, is a beautiful contrast to the first. The six quavers in bar 9 must lead evenly to the two open Es, and the opportunity should be taken on the fourth quaver (E on the first string) to move down to the second position. There is a golden opportunity on the high E, as there is on the high D of bar 14, to use vibrato and show off the sound of the guitar.

Spain and the twentieth century

Spanish music, whether original or transcribed, seems to be the most popular in guitar literature. Many students will feel they have 'arrived' when they tackle their first Iberian-flavoured piece. Many transcriptions or arrangements of composers like Granados and Albéniz require considerable technical skill, but *Spanish Dance No. 5* (Enrique Granados) and *Malagueña* from *Rumores de la Caleta* (Isaac Albéniz) are possibilities in the later intermediate stages (see also Manuel de Falla's *Recit du Pêcheur*, arr. Emilio Pujol, *Chanson du Feu Follet*, arr. Emilio Pujol, and Joaquín Turina's *Soleares* from *Hommage à Tárrega*).

It is a piece specifically written for the guitar by Fedrico Moreno Torroba that will be considered here, a non-guitarist composer whose music is particularly suited to the instrument—indeed, on being interviewed he displayed great pride in not having written an unplayable chord for the guitar. His *Suite Castellana* and *Preambulo* and *Albada* from *Pièces Charactéristiques* are also suitable at this level.

The opening phrase of Nocturno (Federico Moreno Torroba, Schott) should not be distorted by facile rubato, unrestrained dynamics, and accentuation, in an effort to capture attention—restraint is more effective. The point of arrival in this phrase is shown in Ex. 7.9. I like to imagine the echo of this rhythm when playing the rests and chords because this makes them seem more organic to the piece. It also forms a connecting idea with the underlying swing of the next section which is marked 'moderatamente animato', and must not be played

Ex. 7.9

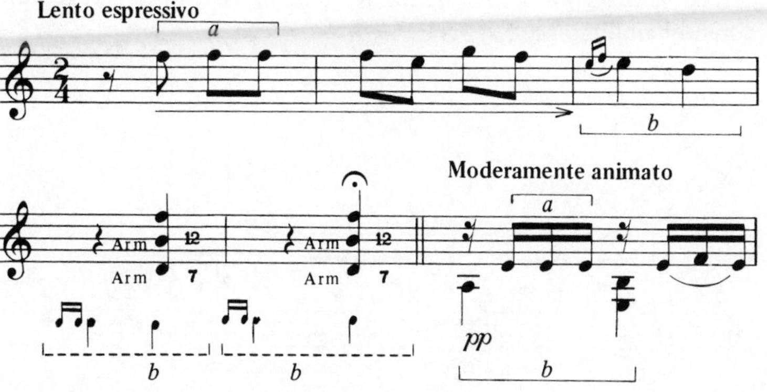

too fast. The repeated E is a motif related to notes of the opening, and clear shaping and articulation is therefore important. The semiquaver configurations are mostly incomplete, that is, they lack rhythmic conclusion. They keep the foreground loose and cloudy and also adorn spiced, unresolved harmonies. This all adds to an evocative, impressionistic effect, and the performer's right-hand articulation must adapt to give a less incisive, more covered sound. The melodic scale fragments should almost break out from this cloud. The use of the swing rhythm in this passage should be noted (see Ex. 7.10). The accompanying figures are akin to the rhythm of the opening repeated E and must be shaped by subtle, rhythmic means. This also applies to the open Es in the bass and the accompaniment of the fifth string under the whole tone scale. Relationships of this kind are to be found throughout the first section and it is worthy of more than just a dash through.

Ex. 7.10

The next section is more definite. The melody, however, requires careful handling (see Ex. 7.11).

Ex. 7.11

It is all too easy to distort the rhythm at the point of arrival by making the first quaver long and quickening the following triplet. This seems facile and tasteless, and stems from misunderstanding this climax. The whole figure is the climax and therefore must not be divided into 'expressive' notes followed by a Spanish-style appendage. The repeated notes at the start of the melody should create a sense of suspense without obvious forward movement other than that demanded by the fact that they need to be joined together. This momentum should be released when the melody notes move. The chords between the phrases should be carefully balanced so that the discords have their full effect. Their role should change from harmonizing the cadence note to introducing the next phrase. This means that the first chord should blend with the last melody note and not be over-articulated.

The first two phrases are followed by two shorter ones on the third string providing a chance to exploit the fullness of tone through the use of rest stroke and vibrato. The following phrase in the bass answers and balances this section and does not start a new section. The continued use of bass register in the following phrases means that the start of the first phrase of these needs to captivate the attention of the listener. This can be done by varying the dynamics, attack, or any combination of means. Care must be taken not to drown the sustained last note of these phrases with the accompanying chords, but to play the chords 'inside' the resonance of these notes (see Ex. 7.12).

Ex. 7.12

This figure holds the movement in abeyance, only to release the climax in the very next phrase with the most positive harmonic progression in the piece. This moment must not be rushed and full sonority must be sought for in both the strum and the chord. The descent, in single bars, soon dissipates the climax and itself wavers uncertainly. The following phrases in the treble round off this section.

But they are interrupted by a chordal passage introducing the coda which consists of two phrases.

The Preludes by Heitor Villa-Lobos have for some years been amongst the most popular music written for the classical guitar. It is, of course, beyond the scope of this chapter to provide a detailed analysis of the pieces, and so comments, as with the discussion of other works, are confined to a few, limited areas.

The open-string accompaniment in *Prelude No. 1* is too often played as if it merely fills in the space between one bass note and the next. A thin tone should be avoided on these open strings, and it should be noticed exactly how the accompaniment is written; if it is played with the open strings damped on the rests and the long notes held, a subtle feel of 6/8 time is introduced above the 3/4 time of the bass melody. The rests are produced by touching these strings with the index, middle, and ring fingers of the right hand at exactly the same time as the melody is played with the thumb. Damping can seem unnatural when first introduced because it involves extra moves. It should be insisted on only when the time is right and the student will not develop other faults as a result (for example, locking the knuckles in an effort to stay near the strings). The teacher should not neglect to point out the overall form of this first section, that is, three long phrases, each one more intense, followed by a coda of three shorter phrases. The C♯ that begins the third of these short phrases must come as a surprise after the preceding two C♮s. In the middle section, the opening arpeggio too often sounds like a semi-strum, i.e. just out of control. Re-fingering will possibly help as it is difficult to control the drag of the thumb across the three bass notes. It is, however, effective to move the thumb across the first two strings when the open B appears, thus using i or m for the intervening notes. The student should be adventurous when strumming the chords of the following bridge passage, possibly varying the speed of the strum and experimenting with different attacks, e.g. flesh or nail etc.

One of the most difficult decisions that the student has to make when playing *Prelude No. 2*, is how long the ritenutos are to be. They can so easily be exaggerated, creating a disjointed impression. An important aspect of this is the 'a tempo' marking which follows each ritenuto. This means that the tempo must be picked up without delay, thereby sustaining the flow. I prefer to play the opening G♯ on the fourth string because the note is then more substantial and forms a good springboard for the following arpeggio. In addition, the note can be held longer, enabling the inner voice (G♯, B, A♯, and A) to be effective. In the middle section, the balance of the voices should surely favour the fifth string. The arpeggio should not sound like a wash of notes, but have its own rhythmic shape. Fingering this so that the thumb is used on the fourth string will help. This use of thumb also introduces a small breath between the melody and the arpeggio.

In *Prelude No. 5*, the achievement of a fluent melodic line must be a player's main concern. This is made awkward by some of the left-hand changes. The rhythm of the accompaniment must be characterized, but not to the extent of interfering with the melody. The rise of the bass line should be noted. The melody of the second section can either be fingered to include glissandi on the fourth string or to avoid them altogether. However, the accompanying chords must be played carefully. The first are quavers only: later, they have the value of a dotted crotchet and damping must reflect these rhythms. When playing the former, care must be taken not to snatch at the strings. There is enough time to follow through with the articulation and still bring the fingers back over the strings to damp them. In the following contrasting section the chords should be substantial and exciting. The differing meters between bass and top must be played effectively.

The *Preludes* by Manuel Ponce provide repertoire from Central America. The atmospheric character of the opening section of *Prelude No. 1* requires the player to use a very smooth right-hand action. This will contribute to the production of an impressionistic sound rather than one which is purely melodic. Waves of dynamic shaping should enhance the feeling of rise and fall. Some re-fingering may be necessary, particularly for those pupils who have difficulty in stretching from the barré to play the slurs (the open E string can be used). Care should also be taken at the end of the piece where a rallentando is uncalled for.

The opening of *Prelude No. 6* can be played either by strumming with the thumb or with a mixture of the thumb and fingers (p,p,i,m,a.). The repeated chords and pedal necessitate a processional pulse, and the player will need to make subtle use of rubato, dynamics, and colour. The discords formed by the inner voices should be clearly sounded, and the piece therefore provides a good example, like the Pavanes of Luis Milan, for chord playing. The effect of the acciaccaturas should be noted, i.e. they force an accent on the notes which have them and make the following note weak. This creates an individual lilt which must nevertheless be subordinate to the general

8 Classical Repertoire—Advanced

Carlos Bonell

THE repertoire of the advanced guitarist contains virtuoso music by the great guitarist-composers of the nineteenth century and the twentieth-century masterpieces that were mostly composed by non-guitarists. This includes music by the Spanish and South American composers and by those writing in a more modern style outside the Spanish tradition. As far as the Renaissance and Baroque eras are concerned, the advanced guitarist can turn to lute and vihuela transcriptions and to arrangements from the so-called lute music by Bach, as well as from the keyboard composers such as Scarlatti.

The teacher should encourage the student to raise the quality of his or her practice in order to tackle advanced repertoire. Whereas before, the student often let things pass as long as they were approximately right, now all things have to be examined, as it were, under a microscope. At this stage, small and even minute adjustments to technique (hand positions, finger movements, and posture, to name but three) can lead to very considerable improvements all round. The same considerations apply to the improvement of the student's musical faculties. In order to effect these improvements, the student will have to become more self-critical and so less tolerant of a standard of playing appropriate only to much easier material.

The Renaissance

The guitar at this time had only four double strings and a compass of little more than two octaves, while the contemporary vihuela and lute had a minimum of six double strings (courses) and a compass of around three octaves. In spite of this, some interesting pieces were composed for it by Mudarra and the French player Adrian Le Roy amongst others, including fantasias and pieces in variation form. In general, the early guitar was overshadowed by the lute and Spanish vihuela, so that the marvellous wealth of music composed for these two instruments has been thoroughly plundered by the modern guitarist. For the vihuela, both Mudarra and Narváez composed outstanding sets of variations on popular tunes of the time, including *Diferencias sobre 'Guárdame las vacas'* and *Diferencias sobre el 'Conde Claros'*.* Luis Milan excelled at a contrapuntal type of fantasia of which more than thirty appeared in his collection *El Maestro*. From the lute repertoire, Dowland's fantasias, pavans, and galliards contain some of the finest music ever conceived for a plucked instrument. Textual amendment is minimal although the lute's greater bass range often necessitates octave transpositions. By re-tuning the third string down by one semitone and transposing the music down by a third, the player reproduces the same interval arrangement between the strings (although not at the same pitch) as the original instrument. In this way the great lute and vihuela pieces lie under the guitarist's fingers in exactly the same way as they were originally conceived.

The advantage of re-tuning is that in certain keys tonic and dominant chords are easier to play because open strings provide a root, third, or fifth of a chord. In this way, a piece transposed to D major on the guitar (originally F major) contains an F♯ open string. Similarly, in the key of E the dominant chord B has the same re-tuned string acting as the fifth of the chord. The disadvantage of re-tuning is that the string slips out of tune very easily, which is disconcerting, to say the least, in performance. This is a key decision the advanced player must make in tackling any transcribed lute and vihuela music since a re-tuned modern guitar does not necessarily make pieces easier to play, and certainly creates new problems of intonation. Take Mudarra's *Fantasía sobre la arpa de Luduvico*: the D major section Ex. 8.1(a) is easier to play with the third string tuned down but the G major arpeggio from the beginning of the piece Ex. 8.1(b) is much more difficult. A further point to consider in re-tuning the guitar in this way is whether the modern guitar sounds any more or less like a lute or vihuela. After all, the pitch is being lowered by a semitone. One could argue that by doing so the guitar acquires an even more sombre sound which makes it sound more different, and not less, than the higher-pitched and lighter-sounding lutes and vihuelas.

Dowland's *Fantasia No. 7*, from the *Varietie of Lute Lessons* has become one of this composer's most frequently performed pieces on the guitar, and illustrates many of the problems discussed above. This piece, like many of Dowland's other fantasias, is composed in a freely-structured contrapuntal style, with apparently unconnected melodic

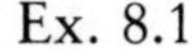

Ex. 8.1

ideas building up to an exciting two-part climax. A more careful examination of the piece reveals thematic links between the various motifs (see Ex. 8.2(a) and Ex. 8.2(b)). Even the upper part in the climax from bar 84 is no more than a slight variation on the original motif in Ex. 8.2(a). It is disguised by appearing in a different rhythm and much slower note values. The musical challenge to the player is in voice-leading with clarity and in articulating the shifting rhythms. As far as voice-leading is concerned, the teacher can recommend to the student that he or she should be able to play (and even sing) each line alone with special attention to phrasing, rhythmic clarity, and expression. When the student can satisfactorily play the single line, a second line

Ex. 8.2

should be studied in a similar manner. I would also recommend that however arduous or novel a task this should prove to be, the student should be able to play one line and sing another (without playing it). The result should be that the student will ultimately feel rewarded by knowing that he or she can truly hear and control all the lines in a contrapuntal web. The teacher can assist the student by playing the other part or parts, so that the student can concentrate on the one line at a time with reference to the aspects I have discussed above. This approach can be used in other less contrapuntal music whenever it appears that the student is not listening to, or cannot hear, the movement of parts in a musical fabric.

The Baroque

This method of learning can be particularly applied to all of Bach's music, especially the fugues. The fugues by Bach most frequently played on the guitar are the *Fugue* from *Prelude, Fugue, and Allegro* BWV 998, the *Fugue in A minor*, BWV 1000 (originally G minor) and the *Fugue in A minor* from the *Partita in A minor*, BWV 997 (originally C minor). All these pieces are generally referred to as lute works, even though there is not always real evidence to support the fact that Bach intended them to be so. The manuscript of the *Prelude, Fugue, and Allegro* is in Bach's hand and is entitled 'for the lute or cembalo'. The *Fugue in A minor*, BWV 1000 exists in several versions, one for violin (which is the second movement of the *Sonata No. 1 in G minor*, BWV 1001), one for the organ in D minor (BWV 539), and one in lute tablature which is not in Bach's own hand and which was freely arranged by a lutenist of the period. The *Partita in C minor* exists in several versions including lute tablature, but none of them are in Bach's own hand. In fact, apart from the *Prelude, Fugue, and Allegro*, only the *Suite in G minor*, BWV 995 is entitled for the lute in Bach's own hand. Even the *Suite in E major*, BWV 1006a, which sounds so appropriate on the guitar (and not only because of the key), is not entitled for the lute, and although it is in Bach's hand it specifies no instrument.

Since so much of Bach's so-called lute music does not appear to have been composed for the instrument, the problems of transcription and arrangement are much more complicated than playing Renaissance lute or vihuela music. The music does not lie under the fingers in an idiomatic way like Renaissance lute and vihuela music. Also, although the spirit and texture of the music may be lute-like (particularly the *Partita in A minor*, BWV 997), it often takes some skilful arranging to make it convincing on the guitar (especially the *Partita*, BWV 997). The problem is compounded by the number of arrangements in publication which offer different solutions. Even with the *Prelude*, BWV 998 which is only in two parts throughout, the player has to choose between a variety of fingerings in high or low positions, slurrings from the beat or on to the beat, or no slurrings at all. At least in this *Prelude*, textual problems do not arise since the only changes required are the occasional octave transposition in the bass.

The teacher would do well to establish certain ground rules for left-hand fingering which should be observed in all Baroque music, especially of a contrapuntal nature:

(i) Playing in position to avoid awkward leaps.

(ii) Changing position between musical phrases or where there is a tiny gap or break.

(iii) The use of open strings (especially between changing positions) to create a smoother effect.

(iv) The avoidance of consecutive movements across the guitar (from the first string to the sixth string) with the same finger. The faster the music, the more difficult and awkward this movement becomes.

Stylistically, the *Prelude, Fugue, and Allegro*, BWV 998 (in D major) presents an interesting contrast with the *Partita in A minor*, BWV 997. Both works contain a fugue using an A B A structure that is very uncommon in Bach's music. The central section of the *Fugue* (D major) consists of two-part writing while the outer sections are clearly in three. The *Fugue* (A minor) is more consistently in three parts, although the central section moves in time values twice as fast. Both *Preludes* are in two parts throughout (a transparent texture very suited to the lute and guitar), although the A minor *Prelude* implies a third part (see Ex. 8.3). Special attention must be paid in such passages to

Ex. 8.3

accent, rhythm, and voicing to project the full richness of the counterpoint. A comparison between the *Allegro* (D major) and the *Gigue* (A minor) shows the Italian influence of fast passages with even rhythms and sequential phrases in the *Allegro*, as opposed to the more nervous, dotted, and syncopated rhythms of the French-style *Gigue*. The principles of *notes inégales* should be familiar enough to the reader. Suffice it to say that in the French style all dotted notes are held for longer than is modern custom, that evenly notated quavers were more often than not played slightly unevenly with a swing and definite lilt, and that mordents and trills were freely employed to spice and decorate the music.

Although Scarlatti was an exact contemporary of Bach, his keyboard sonatas are much less contrapuntal in character. His style is essentially monodic, although it does not exclude contrapuntal interest. The difference between them can be clearly seen by comparing Bach's *Prelude* from the *A minor Partita* discussed above with Scarlatti's *Sonata*, L 483. This sonata consists of a melodic line in the upper part moving in crotchets and quavers supported by a solitary bass line moving in minims. Now this is not dissimilar from the Bach *Prelude*, but the upper part in the Scarlatti has no contrapuntal insinuation or tensions within itself, while the Bach has. In the lower part too, there is less animation in the Scarlatti. Its role is more harmonically supportive than contrapuntal. Both pieces, as all the Bach music referred to or discussed above, need rhythmic impetus and direction in performance. The player needs first to understand and then project the subtle emphasis certain notes must receive to give impetus to the music (see Ex. 8.4).

Ex. 8.4

The Classical and Romantic eras

At some point, difficult to date exactly, something with far-reaching consequences happened to the guitar. A sixth string became a standard feature, and it was strung singly. Various types of guitar, both old and new, are certain to have co-existed for some time, but by 1800 a generation of guitarist-composers were beginning to make their presence felt exclusively on the new instrument. The musical importance of this new instrument was that it added range to the limited compass of the old instrument and that a combination of single strings and new developments in guitar construction led to a louder instrument.

Sor, Giuliani, Carulli, and many of their early nineteenth-century contemporaries were prolific as composers and widely travelled as performers. Although a lot of their music is based on formula-writing, a few works do stand out as being quite superior. Sor's *Marlborough Variations, Fantasia in C minor, Variations on Ye Banks and Braes*, and '*Mozart Variations*' can be counted amongst them as well as Giuliani's *Grande Ouverture*. Diabelli also composed many pieces for guitar, including a duo for guitar and flute. With the possible exception of his *Sonata in A* and his *Sonata in F*, his compositional technique falls some way short of his harmonic ambitions. Julian Bream has edited a *Sonata in A* which brings together the first two movements of the F major *Sonata* (transposed to A) and the last two movements of the A major *Sonata*, thus bringing together some of Diabelli's best music in one extended work. It is a better sonata than Sor's own attempts at this genre (opp. 21 and 25) because on the whole it has more rhythmic vitality and melodic interest, although the *Rondo* from op. 25 is a better piece than Diabelli's last movement. As an introduction to the classical sonata this work is to be recommended to the student.

Amongst the many works that Sor composed there are more sets of variations than anything else, with the exception of miniatures like studies and waltzes. Most of these variations demand an advanced technique; the very essence of these pieces is a cumulative sense of various guitar techniques including the arpeggio, fast scale passages, and passages in parallel thirds and sixths among others. Sor's *Variations on a theme from Mozart's the Magic Flute*, op. 9, contains real invention and variety. As far as a choice of tempo is concerned, the player must be careful not to slow down for the more difficult variations (4 and 5) which will lead to a relaxation of the musical tension at precisely the wrong moment. Similarly, the variations should flow continuously rather than be punctuated with long pauses between them. Sor's *Fantasia*, op. 7 contains a particularly fine set of serious-minded variations, prefaced by a well-shaped and finely judged Largo. This is an outstanding slow movement for it avoids the repetitive two- and four-bar phrase modules characteristic of many of his other slow movements (for example op. 21). Giuliani's *Grande Ouverture*, op. 61 is an extrovert and very appealing work, reminiscent of Rossini, demanding of the advanced player a clear dynamic range in fast arpeggio passages as well as considerable control over the ebb and flow of the music.

Regondi, Coste, and other guitarist-composers of the mid-nineteenth century wrote many difficult pieces in a fluent, flowing style, drawing heavily upon contemporary piano-writing. Rippling arpeggios and quasi-operatic melodies proliferate, but much of their music seems a shade too derivative from the great masters to bear repeated practice or listening.

One aspect of many Romantic composers was their interest in folk music. Lizst's *Hungarian Rhapsody* and *Variations on the Spanish Jota*, Rimsky-Korsakov's *Capriccio Espagnol*, Brahms's *Hungarian Dances*, Lalo's *Symphonie Espagnole* are just some of the many compositions inspired by folk music. The nineteenth-century guitarist-composers were surprisingly reluctant to share this enthusiasm. It is true that Fernando Sor composed a number of *seguidillas* for voice and guitar and a marvellous duo (*Fantasy*, op. 54) but scarcely another phrase in all his considerable output recalls the Spanish style.

Tárrega did compose several pieces in the Spanish idiom including an extended set of virtuoso variations on the *Jota* (the *Gran Jota*) from Aragón. He devoted a lot of his energy to dozens of transcriptions, including the piano music of Albéniz and Granados. These two composers gave an unmistakeable Spanish identity to Romantic music, and much of their piano music has a guitar-like quality: tremolandi, chord-spacings, and harmonic progressions are a continuous reminder of the guitar. Albéniz's *Suite Española* and Granados's *Spanish Dances*, originally composed for the piano, have been arranged and rearranged since the time of Tárrega and now occupy a central part of the advanced repertoire.

The twentieth century

The Romantic tradition continued

The early part of the century continued the Romantic tradition associated with Tárrega who died in 1909. Llobet, who was a pupil of Tárrega, and the leading Spanish guitarist of that time, composed a handful of exquisite miniatures including *Scherzo-Vals, Mazurka, and Romanza*, full of harmonic adventure and character. These are difficult pieces with some big left-hand stretches but well worth the attention of the advanced guitarist. Meanwhile, Barrios, who was a contemporary of Llobet, continued the Romantic tradition, composing waltzes, mazurkas, and preludes. Born in Paraguay, Barrios was a brilliant player himself who succeeded in making these pieces, which were so strongly identified with the European Romantic tradition, totally convincing as guitar music, an accomplishment which had proved elusive to so many Romantic guitarist-composers before him. A Romantic style is still detectable in the colourful and impressionistic music of the Brazilian composer Villa-Lobos. Almost all of his guitar music is difficult to play, but the clear influences of Brazilian folk music, of the music of Bach, and of the Romantic impressionism of Chopin and Debussy make it unique and irresistible.

The Spanish composers

The Spanish composers Rodrigo, Turina, and Torroba, who wrote in a strongly nationalistic style, provided some colourful, idiomatic, and well-crafted music. Rodrigo's *Tres Piezas Españolas* and *Invocation and Dance*, Torroba's *Sonatina*, and Turina's *Fandanguillo* and *Sonata* contain some striking and beautiful music, and require very considerable technical and musical accomplishments from the advanced player—this is all virtuoso music mostly composed for Segovia.

Rodrigo's *Tres Piezas Españolas* (Three Spanish Pieces) are entitled *Fandango, Passacaglia*, and *Zapateado*. The *Passacaglia* is in some ways the most original movement; it takes as its model the Baroque chaconne and passacaglia which is in effect a set of variations on a continuously repeated bass line. Rodrigo follows the established pattern of rhythmic progression from long note values to triplet quaver and semiquaver passages over the bass line, even incorporating a bolero-like sequence of *rasgueado* chords in the middle (see Ex. 8.5). Rodrigo's style is immediately apparent in the first bar of the

Ex. 8.5

Fandango, the major seventh and semitone dissonances are very much his hall-mark. The *Zapateado* is an exhilarating and extraordinarily difficult climax to the work. This is a moto perpetuo with a vengeance; fast arpeggio and scale patterns as well as chordal strummings all figure in the piece.

Ponce's *Sonata Meridional* is a three-movement work entitled *Campo, Copla, and Fiesta*, and has a strong Spanish influence apparent in the languid triplets of the slow movement, as well as the *rasgueado* chords and much faster triplet rhythms of the finale. The first movement is a model of concise sonata form. The attention of the student should be drawn to clear articulation of the opening rhythms of the work and to the profusion of dynamic marks which strongly indicate the expression of the music.

Turina's *Fandanguillo* is a slower one-movement work with a brief introduction which distils the essence of a typically Spanish progression over a pedal E (see Ex. 8.6). The main melodic part of the piece is in fact derived from this progression. The pacing and development of the piece is perfectly judged by Turina, as are most of his works for guitar. The *Fandanguillo* is also a very convincing piece of guitar writing, exploiting the tonal resources of all parts of the guitar from the lowest octave to the highest. Fast scale passages, *rasgueados*, and tambour effects complete the impression of a haunting Spanish piece.

Ex. 8.6

For the player with an advanced technique this is an ideal piece to draw out the best tone in the lyrical moments, and to develop a sense of bravura in the fast passages towards the end.

Other notable works by these same composers include Rodrigo's *Invocation and Dance*, composed in homage to Falla, whose influence can be felt in much of Rodrigo's music. In this piece, Rodrigo strikes a more introspective and at the same time more intense note. The result is a more tightly-drawn work which avoids completely the superficial glitter and facile dissonances that often disguise his much richer musical personality. Ponce's *Variations on la folia de Espana and Fugue* are this composer's most ambitious works for the instrument, and must stand out as a pinnacle of achievement for the ambitious player. It is a shame that Turina's *Sonata*, in three movements, has been overshadowed by his shorter pieces, since the work is a model of concise, well-contrasted ideas and is technically less demanding than the *Fandanguillo*.

Three Spanish composers not drawn into Segovia's orbit were Falla, Gerhard, and Ohana. Falla and Gerhard composed only one piece each for solo guitar. A brooding Spanish temperament underpins both of them, a far cry from the foot-tapping dance rhythms of so much music by Turina and Rodrigo. Falla's piece, *Homenaje: Tombeau de Claude Debussy*, quotes directly from Debussy's *Soirée dans Grenade* for solo piano. The work is composed in the rhythm of an habanera and the many ritenuto signs give the work a halting, improvisatory style. The player has to reconcile two apparently contradictory interpretative demands; on the one hand the piece has the lilt of the habanera dance and on the other it must have the restraint implied by a tombeau and by Falla's own expression marks. Harmonically, Falla builds the work on a pivotal semitone figure, first heard at the beginning and which recurs many times in various modulations (see Ex. 8.7).

Ex. 8.7

This Phrygian cadence, which is unmistakeably Spanish, or more precisely Moorish Spanish, pervades so much flamenco music and for Falla this was clearly associated with the guitar. Gerhard's *Fantasia* is also clearly Spanish in context and inspiration. The same Phrygian figure pervades the opening and the ending but the much faster central section reveals another Spanish characteristic, the juxtaposition of 3 beats against 2 (for example 3:8 followed by 6:16). Dynamic marks in both pieces give very clear indications to the player as to accents, volume, tempo, and phrasing. The teacher could usefully encourage the student to compare the style, harmonic content, and development of these pieces with a view to understanding both the similarities and differences between them.

Maurice Ohana (b. 1914) has composed a *Tiento* for solo six-string guitar which takes its name and inspiration from its Renaissance counterpart, and a cycle *Si le Jour se Parait* for ten-string guitar. Ohana's music shows the influence of Falla and Stravinsky, but he has a clear vitality and personality of his own. Falla, Gerhard, and Ohana pushed the frontiers of music influenced by Spanish folk music beyond the tonal edge, and have provided the advanced player with some first class music.

The European tradition

A clean break with the Spanish tradition occurred with Frank Martin's *Quatre Pièces Brèves* published in 1933. They are a twentieth century re-creation of the form and spirit of a Baroque suite. The outer movements are entitled *Prelude* and *Comme une Gigue* and the inner movements are *Aria*, which is reminiscent of a sarabande and is the most tonal in its musical language of all the pieces, and *Plainte* (lament), which was surely inspired by the grand tombeau of the Baroque era composed in memory of a departed soul. The *Prelude* and *Gigue* are composed in a quasi-serial technique. In its strictest sense serial technique treats each semitone of the scale absolutely equally, with no repetitions before each has made at least one appearance. This, Martin does not do, although the only repeated note in the beginning of the *Gigue* is the B, which acts as a pedal note and tonal centre throughout the work. Martin's pieces share the distinction with Falla's *Tombeau* and Walton's *Bagatelles* of having been composed for the guitar and subsequently orchestrated by the composer himself. In Martin's orchestral version the pieces are called *Guitare*, as is yet another version for the piano.

Martin was not alone in returning to an earlier age to give a different impetus to the creative effort in composing for the guitar. Henze's first work for solo guitar, *Drei Tentos* (1956), like Ohana's *Tiento*, takes its name from the Renaissance *Tiento*, a prelude in contrapuntal style, alternating running passages with block chords.

Benjamin Britten used Dowland's song *Come Heavy Sleep* as the basis for a series of variations which he called *Nocturnal after John Dowland*, op. 70. The variations are based on fragments of the Dowland original, and describe various states of sleep: *Meditative*, *Very agitated*, *Restless*, *Uneasy*, *March-like*, *Dreaming*, *Gently rocking*, building up to a *Passacaglia* based on a falling diatonic figure, which rather than acting as a harmonic underpinning is treated as an obsessive interruption to the upper part. This conflict is finally resolved in a magical confluence of both parts which ushers in a partial statement of the Dowland song at the end of the work. In effect, this is a set of variations where the theme is heard at the end rather than the beginning. The entire range of guitar techniques is employed, including an extended use of pizzicato in the *Passacaglia* and of double octaves in the fifth variation. The work was dedicated to Julian Bream who described it as the greatest work composed for the guitar. Few would quarrel with that assertion. For the advanced guitarist, a familiarity with this work should be irresistible, if only because there are many passages where this great music does not demand a virtuoso technique.

The South American folk and jazz connection has provided some excellent music outside (or at least only partly derived from) the Spanish tradition. I have already referred to Barrios continuing the Romantic tradition, but an equally vital part of his musical personality is manifested in the many pieces he composed in a style derived from popular songs and dances. Many of them are difficult to play with big stretches for the left hand, but are immensely attractive for the advanced player. Villa-Lobos also showed folkloric influences in his *Suite Populaire Brasilienne* where he attempted to imbue various European dances with the Brazilian flavour of the popular *choros*. In more recent times the guitarist-composer Leo Brouwer has also revealed the strong influence of popular song and dance in his *Elogio de la Danza*. This piece is strongly tonal in character and presents interesting technical and musical challenges to the advanced player. Brouwer has also composed many other works outside the influence of folk music. These include *La Espiral Eterna* (clearly reminiscent of

Ligeti's *Continuum* for solo harpsichord) and *Canticum*, which gives the player a direct opportunity in determining the musical material by providing a choice of unmeasured musical cells.

The Argentinian composer Alberto Ginastera (1916–83) was not a guitarist and by his own admission resisted composing for the guitar for most of his adult life. His one work, the *Sonata*, op. 47 composed in 1976 for the guitarist Carlos Barbosa-Lima, is the most substantial work by any South American composer. Ginastera himself has written about the work: 'The first movement, *Esordio*, is a solemn prelude, followed by a song which was inspired by Kecua music and which finds its conclusion in an abbreviated repetition of these two elements. The second movement, *Scherzo*, which has to be played "il più presto possibile", is an interplay of shadow and light, of nocturnal and magical ambiance, of dynamic contrasts, distant dances, of surrealistic impressions, such as I had used in earlier works. Right through to the end the theme of the laud of Sixtus Beckmesser appears as a phantasmagoria (see Ex. 8.8). The third movement, *Canto*, is lyrical and rhapsodic, expressive and breathless like a love poem. It is connected with the last movement, *Finale*, a quick, spirited *rondeau* which recalls the strong, bold rhythms of the music of the pampas. Combinations of *rasgueados* and *tamboras* percussion effects, varied by other elements of metallic colour or the resounding of strings, give a special tonality to this rapid, violent movement which thereby gains the overall aspect of a toccata.' The work is original, compelling, and communicative in its musical language, and expressive, exciting, and arresting to the ear. Like Walton, he writes with a loving affection for popular styles (in this case the folk music of Argentina) weaving his

Ex. 8.8

way unnerringly along that difficult path between parody and pastiche. Like Falla, who seemed to distil the very essence of Spanish darkness in the *Tombeau*, so too, Ginastera evokes the flashing rhythms of a frantic samba going straight to its core.

Other works of a very individual character which provide a real challenge to the advanced player include Henze's *Royal Winter Music* (1976), a sonata on Shakespearian characters in which, according to Henze, the dramatis personae of this piece enter through the sound of the guitar as if it were a curtain. The composer also describes the guitar as a 'knowing' or 'knowledgeable' instrument, with many limitations, but also many unexplored spaces and depths within these limits.

William Walton's *Five Bagatelles* were composed in 1972, only four years before Henze's *Royal Winter Music*, but their musical language belongs to a much earlier part of this century. Walton's predilection for jazz-like harmonies and robust syncopations is evident throughout, as is his ability to create the tenderest melodies. Their spirit is richly resonant and allusive in a fragmentary way of other styles (No. 3 is called *Alla Cubana*), of a hypnotic stillness (No. 2) and of a sad nostalgia (No. 4). Technically, no. 1 and no. 5 are by far the most difficult and demanding of an advanced technique. All of the *Bagatelles* are profusely marked with expression and dynamic marks, although all the tempi/metronome marks are indicated approximately.

Tristan Murail's *Tellur* (1978) contains some of the most elaborate and extended uses of *rasgueado* techniques of any contemporary piece (see Ex. 8.9). The composer has written that the instrument should sound more like a flamenco guitar than a classical one. Another substantial addition to the modern repertoire, which the advanced player should become familiar with, is Michael Tippett's *The Blue Guitar* (1984), an impressionistic work full of subtle images and an echo-like resonance, for this is music about a poem about a painting. Reading the poem, *The Man with the Blue Guitar* by Wallace Stevens,

Ex. 8.9

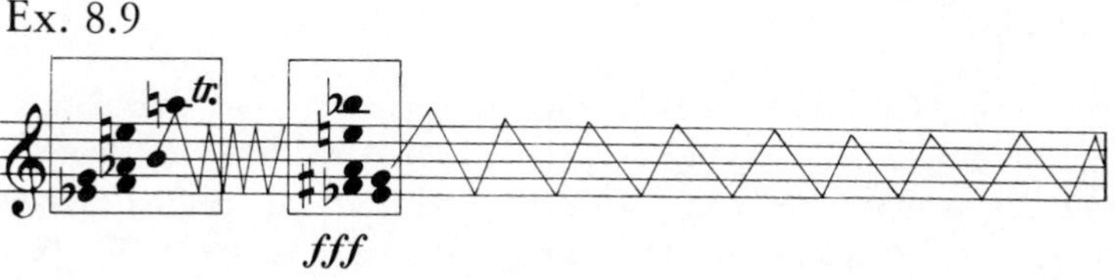

acted for Tippett roughly as the sight of Picasso's picture did for the poet. Tippett has written that all the words and concepts have disappeared and that this piece for guitar is essentially music. It could quite properly be appreciated solely as a short sonata. All that remained from the poem were three moods, or gestures, which suggested titles for the movements: *Transforming*, *Dreaming*, and *Juggling*.

Less extended works worthy of attention include Takemitsu's hypnotic and impressionistic *Folios*, Petrassi's quasi-improvisatory *Nunc*, and all the guitar works by Stephen Dodgson, which include two *Partitas* and two *Fantasy-Divisions*. His writing is angular and full of nervous fragmented phrases which reveal a total grasp of the idiomatic possibilities of dense chord shapes in higher positions using some open strings, as well as confident counterpoint in fast passage work. Lennox Berkeley's *Theme and Variations* is another work more clearly within the grasp of the advanced player without demanding a virtuoso technique.

Twentieth-century composers, apart from Leo Brouwer, who have rekindled an almost extinguished tradition of the guitarist-composer include the Czech, Štěpán Rak, and the Russian, Nikita Koshkin. Koshkin's declared intention in his most celebrated work to date, *The Prince's Toys*, was to incorporate as many novel effects as possible. The work is in six movements and some twenty-seven minutes long, and what it may lack in musical sophistication is (almost) compensated for by an astounding array of innovative effects. Rak's music is often inspired by a strong visual impression as in *Voces de Profundis* where eerie aural effects are invented to project a musical realization of Hitchcock's film *Psycho*. A strong tonal basis underpins most of these composers' music, but it is laced with idiomatic figurations and sequential patterns which are atonal. The sheer novelty of so many percussive effects should be a strong incentive for the advanced player to study their music, provided he or she is not overwhelmed by the profusion of notational symbols used to indicate them.

Studies

The most interesting studies for the advanced player were composed by Villa-Lobos. Even though Segovia has compared them to Chopin's own efforts in this genre they are not as musically compelling as they are technically demanding. Outstanding among them are studies No.

1, 4, 5, 8, 11, and 12. There is a strong bias among them towards arpeggio techniques rather like those in Sor's op. 29 and Giuliani's op. 48 collections. Taken together these collections provide all that the advanced guitarist could reasonably wish for in furthering his or her technique. Stephen Dodgson and Hector Quine in their two collections of studies, endeavoured to fill some of the gaps in the earlier collections by other composers by incorporating the sort of rhythmic complexities and idiomatic figurations more often met in twentieth-century music.

Chamber music

Substantial guitar parts are included in the following works: Schoenberg's *Serenata* (op. 24), Webern's *Dreilieder* (op. 18), Boulez's *Le Marteau sans Maître*, Henze's *El Cimmaron.* The student at a music college or university is ideally placed to take advantage of the presence of fellow musicians to be able to play these works, since opportunities in the world at large are so regrettably rare.

More on the home patch, so to speak, and certainly more practical, are Hindemith's *Rondo* for three guitars, Jolivet's four movement *Serenade* for two guitars (1956), Stephen Dodgson's *Duo Concertante* for harpsichord and guitar and his *Quintet* for guitar and string quartet. The nineteenth-century repertoire includes several outstanding guitar duos by Fernando Sor, *L'Encouragement* (op. 34) and the *Fantasy* (op. 54), and the recently published *Grand Duo* by Napoléon Coste. The song repertoire includes some marvellous music in the *Songs of the Chinese* and the *Folksongs* by Benjamin Britten, Walton's *Anon in Love*, and Gerhard's arrangements of Spanish popular songs.

Note

*The classification of pieces as 'intermediate' or 'advanced' is *at times* arbitrary. Inevitably there is some overlap.

(Ed.)

9 Classical Technique

David Russell

THERE are about as many ways to play the guitar as there are guitarists, although some ways work better than others. Amongst the many wonderful players of today, some use very odd and theoretically inefficient techniques to achieve their musical desires. Others, with the most refined movements, fail to stir us in the concert hall; thus, the reasons for considering technique in its own right must be clarified. Technique has one dominant motive, that is, to produce music of any character with as much beauty and ease as is possible.

In general terms, the movements of the left hand are standard for most of the advanced players. There is some variation within the different fingerings that they may use, either because they reduce the difficulty of a passage or, more usually, because of the varying musical tastes. There is, however, considerable variation in the way in which the right hand is used, and each player commonly ends up with his or her own individual position and technique. For example, there is variation in the side (angle) of the nail that is used to sound a string and there has, of course, been much disagreement between players on the very issue of whether or not nails should be used.

During the last hundred years or so there have been many advances in the construction of the guitar and quality of strings, with the result that it is now possible to produce a little more volume than it was previously. The development of right-hand finger action has also contributed to the louder sound, although it is still important for a player to maintain the intimate quality of the instrument.

Since the advent of recording, many players have been able to hear each other and learn quickly about different styles and techniques. In addition, concert-hall audiences expect a much higher standard of performance because they have often had note-perfect recordings to listen to at home. All of this is very serious for the professional player, and it is therefore vital not only to maintain a sense of perspective about technique, but also not to forget the original reason for playing the guitar—that is, because we like it and it gives us pleasure.

Sitting and holding the guitar

My own preference is for an armless chair with a flat seat (no ridge around the edge) and no backward incline. I also prefer a small amount of padding or a thin cushion for longer hours of practice. The suitable height of the chair will depend on the height and proportions of the player, and the angle at which he or she wishes to hold the guitar. In general, a chair between 40 cm. and 50 cm. high should suffice. An adjustable piano stool makes the life of a concert performer far easier, and it is of course most suitable for the teacher who will have a number of different pupils visiting for lessons.

When sitting, the left leg should be raised approximately 15 cm. by a footstool that is placed about 15 cm. in front of the left chair leg. The guitar should rest between the legs, mostly on the left, but with the lower bout touching the inside of the right thigh. The upper bout should rest lightly against the middle of the chest. The head of the guitar should be set at about the height of the left shoulder, and a fourth point of contact is the right arm, the weight of which helps to stabilize the instrument.

Perhaps the most important aspect of the above positioning is the balance of the player and the guitar, together with its relation to ease of movement. In addition, a position should be taken that does not twist the neck of the player too much. It is important that the back be straight from the pelvis and not hunched or rounded. This is sometimes difficult at first because the student will wish to see the hands and thus try to peer over the instrument. It is preferable to sit up straight and look at the hands from a distance, taking a somewhat detached and panoramic view. Care should be taken that when the left foot is raised on the footstool, the lower part of the back remains erect. As a general rule the player should not hunch over the guitar because this tends to restrict the breathing and is not good for the internal organs. These comments reflect the current approach to sitting and holding the guitar, but it should be noted that, for example, during the nineteenth century there were many different ways of holding the instrument, and some players today prefer to use a 'guitar-cushion' rather than a footstool.

The right hand

When setting the right hand, a position is sought that is the optimum for mechanical movement. Any undue twisting will result in a restriction of this movement. The forearm should rest its weight on the lower bout of the guitar. The exact position varies from player to player; some place the instrument in the crack of their elbow, others prefer to place it a little further down in order to avoid an excessive angle of the wrist and the cutting of the circulation to the fingers. The length of the arm is a factor here because the hand must be able to easily reach the normal plucking-points of the strings (between the middle and right-hand edge of the sound-hole).

When setting the normal position of the fingers on the strings, the ring finger should be placed on the first string, middle on the second, index on the third, and thumb on the fifth. The index finger can be thought of as an extension of the forearm and the wrist may then be raised until it is approximately at a height equivalent to the width of four fingers (6–8 cm.). This should give a reasonable wrist elevation in proportion to the hand, although some variation is likely to occur owing to the different dimensions referred to earlier. In addition, the angle of attack will be varied at different times during a performance, but for the beginner the fingers should be thought of as being able to move in and out of the hand, towards and away from the elbow. There are two main ways of sounding individual strings—free stroke (sometimes referred to as tirando) and rest stroke (apoyando). Both of these actions need to be mastered in order to deal with a classical repertoire. Rest stroke generally produces a deeper, more solid tone, and it is usually possible to play louder with this type of stroke. The action and the power comes mostly from the knuckle although I like to use a little action in each of the different joints. I also prefer to keep the finger strong to the tip and nail rather than flex at the last joint. The finger should, after sounding the string, come to rest on the adjacent string—hence the Spanish term apoyando which means leaning. However, most notes that are sounded will be done with free stroke, and so this must be developed to be a powerful action that can produce good quality singing notes, equivalent to those played with rest stroke. One of the reasons why rest stroke sounds the stronger is because the string is vibrated perpendicularly to the soundboard. Thus, the aim should be to try to achieve the same with free stroke. The tip of the finger should move through the string, pushing it toward the soundboard as before, but this time with much more action in the last two finger-joints. Plucking at an angle will help to avoid hitting the adjacent string on the follow-through. The height of the wrist is also important. If it is too low, the fingers will not be able to follow through cleanly, without plucking upwards. If the wrist is too high, the tendons will restrict the movement of the follow-through and a finger will not be able to deflect a string properly. One of the main reasons for emphasizing the follow-through is to avoid 'hand-bounce', i.e. the movement should be made with the finger and not the arm.

It is possible to use both rest stroke and free stroke with the thumb. Because it is such a strong digit, it is preferable to use free stroke in order to avoid giving a bottom-heavy sound. Rest stroke can be used to bring out a bass line such as that found in the *Prelude No. 1* by Heitor Villa-Lobos. For contrapuntal music, such as that found in the *Suites* for lute by Bach, it is preferable to use free stroke, so that the lower notes maintain an appropriate balance with the upper voices. The above discussion has concentrated only on the striking action. Players should remember that all digits must return in order to prepare for the next movement. This 'return' should be made independently of other fingers, especially during alternation (for example, i,m,i,m), as in scale playing. Thus, one finger returns as the other is plucking.

The sounding of more than one string is made almost exclusively with free stroke, the basic finger action being the same as for the individual strings. Care, once again, should be taken not to let the hand jump after each action, although a small amount of movement will not cause too much problem. Attention should be given to the extent to which the fingers touch the strings before sounding them because, as with the playing of single notes, the action should (in the interest of *legato*-playing) begin above the string.

Although tone is a somewhat difficult subject to discuss in print, there are some points that may prove to be helpful. A good tone does not of course guarantee good music, and the converse is equally true. However, high quality notes are certainly a major contributory factor to the listener's enjoyment, whatever music is played. There are sounds that are thin, fat, meaty, and scratchy, etc., and all can be used according to taste and ability. It is a subjective area and opinions on what is good and bad tone vary, but perhaps the main point that should be made is that the sound should be clean. Each player will have to make his or her own judgement on the quality of this sound, and listening to good players and the comparison of the student's own efforts will help. With all of this in mind, it is important for the teacher to prevent a pupil from becoming demoralized by the wonderful tones of a good recording. These will have been made under optimum acoustic conditions.

Almost all professional classical guitarists today use their finger-nails to sound the strings. Sometimes this is not possible for a beginner, but it should be something for the player to aim for as he or she advances. Occasionally, a player may find that the nails are too weak to use. There is, for these people, a range of false nails that can be purchased. Alternatively, small half-moons made from ping-pong ball can be slipped under the nail and shaped to make a very good and strong tone. It is, however, unwise to use large amounts of adhesive to fix them because this will damage the natural finger-nail. The manner in which the nails are filed and polished is crucial. There are a number of very fine sand-papers available on the market and many shops, magazines, and of course, teachers, will be able to give detailed advice on the care of nails. A clean edge should be aimed for and filing, until experienced, should be carried out with the guitar in position so that the progress towards the ideal sound and shape can be continually checked. It is certainly possible to play without nails and most of the principles of finger action will still apply.

Experiments should also be made with the different angles of attack available, using either more of the side of the nail, more in the centre, or an angle that will bring the nail straight across the string. It is usual for the latter to produce a sharper tone, sometimes thin in quality. This is, however, useful for very quiet passages of music in which a degree of clarity may be required. If it is used in a louder section it will tend to sound torn and most probably piercing to the listener. The use of the action that takes the nail across the string at an angle usually produces a warmer tone, one with more of the fundamental note and less upper partials. For general use, it is best to find a tone that lies somewhere between the two alternatives. This will then allow scope for movement either way, according to the musical requirements. When playing loud, it is important to keep the tone fatter, because the notes tend to become thinner when plucked harder. I do this by increasing the angle of attack and also by pushing the string further into the soundboard. The tone may also be changed by altering the position of the finger along the string. As this is moved towards the bridge (sul ponticello), the tone will become sharper. Conversely, when playing over the sound-hole or even further towards the finger-board (sul tasto), the tone will become rounder. As a general rule it is recommended that the arm make the movement rather than the wrist.

The left hand

The tip of the finger (and sometimes the whole of the finger as for a barré) is used to press down the strings against the finger-board. The quality of the note is dependent on the finger pressing just to the left of the fret and with sufficient pressure to avoid an unpleasant buzz. Accuracy should be emphasized more than strength—it is not how hard the string is pressed but where the finger is placed that is important.

The left arm is used to place the hand in the optimum position for reaching chords and single notes. The elbow can swing towards or away from the body, depending on the shape of the group of notes that are to be played. This is because the many different chords necessitate a variety of subtle changes of approach. The arm is also the guide for all position changing along the finger-board. This should be trained well because the effect on the fingers is commonly underestimated. When playing in the highest positions above the twelfth fret, it may sometimes be necessary to lean the whole body downward and over to the left. This should only be done in exceptional circumstances, it being usual to use only the arm and wrist for such adjustments. The left wrist, as with almost all joints, will do the job well if it is in its optimum position. Thus, there should not be too much twist or bend in the wrist—experiment will soon show that it is impossible to close the fist when the wrist is turned right in. Many adjustments of the exact position will be necessary during playing, but in general the wrist should be moved forward when pressing the lower-sounding strings and almost straight for the upper ones.

When pressing a string, a finger should, as far as possible, move on to the string with the tip perpendicular to the finger-board and all the joints bent. The semicircle shape is the most powerful and no joint should be locked straight—all must be able to move. The position of the fingers close behind the fret reduces the pressure that is required and generally results in a much more agile hand. The bulk of the pressure should be exerted between the fingers and thumb, not with the whole of the arm. The height at which fingers are raised above a given string should be reduced to a minimum because this substantially affects the chances of missing a string during the downward movement. Furthermore, accuracy is dependent on the degree to which a finger is prepared, in the air, for a future position. If the left arm is tightened, it will affect the right hand. However, a small degree of pull on the left arm is almost inevitable and this should not be worried about excessively. When releasing a finger, it should move off a string cleanly and perpendicularly, especially from the wound, bass strings. Otherwise, some sound that is unrelated to the note will be produced.

The left-hand thumb acts as the other half of the circle that is formed with the fingers. The normal classical position is for the pad of the thumb to be placed close to the middle of the back of the guitar neck. The exact position will depend on the length of the thumb. There is some variation amongst players as to the exact position of the thumb in relation to the fingers; some prefer the thumb to be placed underneath the first finger, others underneath the second.

When changing position along the finger-board, the left arm should be allowed to do as much of the work as possible. Initially, it is usual to use the eyes to guide the fingers but it is easy to forget that the arm is really doing the work. Thus, the arm should be trained to measure the distances between the various frets and it is particularly useful to practise the shifts from second position to fifth and seventh positions because these are the most common. These should be practised without looking and it should be noted that it is unwise to use guide fingers on the bass strings because they tend to produce string whistle and squeak during the shift. As one's guitar technique develops, it is usually possible to avoid most of the unwanted, extraneous noises. The shift along the finger-board is always easier if the pressure is released during the move. This also avoids unwanted glissandi. For the beginner, the most difficult aspect of changing position is the avoidance of cutting the note before the shift. A sensitive ear is a vital factor, as is the rapidity of the shift itself.

Slurs are the movements that the left-hand fingers may make to sound the strings, without any need for the right hand. They are often used to make two or more notes more legato and because it is one of the more difficult techniques for a guitarist, slurs should be practised often. The ascending slur depends largely on the finger landing accurately and speedily on the desired fret position, so that it produces maximum vibration of the string. If the finger lands flat, on the fleshy part, it will damp the note and little or no sound will come out from the guitar. The independence of movement is as important as it is for the normal stopping of a string. The descending slur is formed by plucking the string with the left-hand finger. It is common for a beginner to use too much strength for this type of slur; it is the speed of the action that will help more than the strength. Care should be taken not to pull the string too much to the side because otherwise the upper note will move out of tune. I sound the descending slur without falling on the adjacent string—a type of left-hand free stroke. This is because there are occasions when the note on the adjacent string will be required to continue vibrating.

There are, of course, many occasions when decisions must be made on whether the slur itself is appropriate musically. This can often be most difficult and the player must rely on good musical knowledge and awareness, as well as taste. The removing of slurs from a given edition does not, of course, lessen the need to master the technique, for there are many cases in which slurs are absolutely essential. A common problem for the player is that the note before the slur may be sounded extra hard. This should be avoided because it clearly makes the following note sound weaker; to assist this, rest stroke should not be used on the preceding note. In addition, the use of rest stroke will encourage an imbalance of tone. All these habits become quickly ingrained and it is common to hear many passages of music where the player has put in slurs to achieve a more legato phrase but ends up with a series of accents and lumps. Once recognized, this very point can be used to emphasize accents if that is what the music requires.

Trills, mordents, acciaccaturas, and appoggiaturas are formed by a combination of ascending and descending slurs. The clarity and audibility of the ornaments is more important than the speed, and it is therefore important to keep the whole arm relaxed throughout the trill. Once again, a good balance of the two alternating notes should be aimed for; they should have the same volume, duration, and have as near equal a tone as is possible. Care should also be taken with the dynamic of the initial note, that which is to be plucked by the right hand. One alternative concerning trills that should be briefly referred to is the playing of trills on adjacent strings. These clearly require the right hand (and will therefore be considered later) and give a totally different effect.

The barré is a technique which involves the pressing of more than one string, almost invariably with the first finger of the left hand. This is laid across the strings, six for a full barré, less for the half-barré. This is a relatively difficult technique and will therefore require some time to be spent on it. The most crucial factor is the extent to which the finger can be kept straight. When some of the notes do not sound clearly, the student should not just try to squeeze harder. The hand is designed for grasping, not for holding barré chords, and so if it is simply squeezed more, the pressure will go only to the notes that are already sounding clearly. Neither is the finger a capo, but a flexible digit. Some concentration will therefore be required in the areas where the strings are not sounding. If the first string is buzzing, for example, then the student will need to direct some weight just there, and not right across the full barré. The usual problem is on the third or fourth string, which will either buzz or give a muffled note. Once again, via a flattening of the first finger or a shifting of the position where the joints lie in relation to the strings, pressure should be applied to these weaker points. Similar principles apply to the half-barré although it is usually found to be easier. The position of the second finger is also important because it should not lean onto the first finger. Once the second finger has become incorporated into the barré, it cannot be used for more intricate work. Similarly, the third and fourth fingers will have been taken away from their respective frets, and so a good clear gap is required between the first and second fingers. Some adjustment may have to be made to the position of the thumb because a stronger squeezing force can be created by placing the thumb opposite the index finger. Also, some players may feel that a small amount of extra finger pressure can be achieved by pulling the neck of the guitar back against the body. Although this may account for a small degree of pressure, it is the hand that should do the work.

Co-ordination and further techniques

It is common for technique to be talked about in terms of which kind of hand position is used, but in reality it is the co-ordination of the many tiny movements which is the basis of guitar technique. All the various sitting and hand positions are only adopted to make the timing of these movements easier and more efficient. For the beginner, co-ordination and the achievement of a legato series of notes is a considerable problem. This is because both the left- and right-hand fingers have the capacity to damp a note before the other has completed its own movement. This, together with the short sustain of a note on the guitar and the difficulty for a beginner to hear whether a passage is smooth or not, makes it a difficult area for the potential player. Whether in a basic exercise for a beginner or a more complex passage for the advanced player, there is much to be gained from initially separating out the action of each hand. Thus, by removing the very music that one is trying to play, the mind can focus on the individual problems that the passage presents. The vital factor in establishing and developing co-ordination is the speed at which a given exercise or passage is practised. This must be slow, although it is not often appreciated how slow this really means. Slow practice, and clarity of thought and purpose, present the most difficult disciplines in any practice session.

Scales are clearly one of the most vital aspects of technique because they concisely contain so many fundamental elements of the facility required for guitar playing. It is the occasion where the teacher or player can, for example, consider in the finest detail, the movement of a particular finger, a refinement of posture, or an improvement in tone. I prefer to do most of my scale practice without using the whole scale, but by playing it in fragments of four or five notes in each position. In this way, it is possible to learn more about the finger-board and it will eventually cover almost every short scale that will be found in the guitar repertoire. Each day a scale in a different key may be selected, perhaps starting with C major. Initially, the notes C,D,E,F, and G, found in first position on the first and second strings, should be played, both ascending and descending. The left hand should then be moved to third position and the notes D,E,F,G, and A be played as before. This can be continued along the finger-board before playing a similar fragment on the second and third strings (in first position, G–D in the key of C, then A–E in second position, etc.). Similar scale fragments should then be played on the remaining, and any other, combinations of adjacent strings. Some attention must of course be given to the right hand and as well as the different finger combinations, some attempt should be made to play musically. For example, a crescendo or diminuendo may be attempted, as can an increase or decrease in tempo, or a change of tone. All should have a sense of direction and it should never be forgotten that the reason for playing scales is so that the music can be improved.

Two images tend to form in a student's mind when considering arpeggios; firstly, the theoretical, broken chords which are required in a guitar examination, and secondly, the right-hand patterns contained in some well-known passages or pieces in the guitar repertoire. For musical reasons, it is advisable to know the arpeggios in every major and minor key. They provide an invaluable source of knowledge of the finger-board and are indispensable for any analysis and interpretation. For technical reasons, the practice of different arpeggio patterns develops the independence and actions of the fingers. Many patterns will arise in the repertoire and this is another occasion where a problem can be extracted from the music and scrutinized on its own. The series of arpeggio patterns referred to in Chapter 6 will provide a useful starting-point, although any player should develop other patterns which expose weaknesses in their technique.

Initially, when practising arpeggios, accuracy and evenness of tone, dynamics, and rhythm will be among the highest priorities. Care should be taken not to sacrifice these elements for an increase in speed; I find that the placing of a cloth down between the strings and the table of the guitar damps the notes sufficiently to hear if the rhythm is absolutely precise.

The spreading of a chord is a form of arpeggio in which a group of notes are played one after the other in quick succession. It is usual for the lowest note to be played first, although the other direction is indicated by an arrow. In preparation for the spreading of a chord, it is common for the left-hand fingers to be placed in readiness for the right-hand action. A decision must be made on whether the right-hand fingers are to start their movement from a position resting on the strings or just above. It should be noted that if two spread chords follow one another, the latter of the two actions (i.e. from above the strings) will be essential for a legato result. There is a small number of cases where a melody note is hidden within a chord that is to be spread. Here, it is necessary to alter the order in which the right-hand fingers sound the strings. The melody note, if played with rest stroke, will then stand out from those notes played with free stroke.

Trills and other ornaments have already been referred to during the discussion of the left hand. There is, however, an alternative method which places the notes in question on adjacent strings—thus, the right hand is required. The following example shows a trill between F on the first string and E on the second. A right-hand pattern is necessary and care should therefore be taken with the balance of the volume and the tone (particularly with the thumb) (see Ex. 9.1). This is a useful technique for playing final cadences, although in many cases it will be

Ex. 9.1

out of style to use such an effect. If this form of trill appears as an oddity in the middle of a phrase or clashes with the musical intentions, it will clearly upset the remainder of the music. Usually I do not mix the two forms of trill in the same piece because they tend to show each other's deficiencies.

One of the most important tasks of a player is to obtain the correct balance between the various voices, particularly when playing chords or melodies with accompaniment. Within a four-note chord, each individual note should be balanced, one by one. For this, it should be remembered that a string that is displaced further in towards the body of the guitar, will produce more volume. Thus, it is possible to simply push a given right-hand finger down further in order to produce an increased dynamic. An alternative method is to give a right-hand finger much more follow-through. The playing of chords tends to be an aspect of technique that is underestimated and little practised. It should therefore be given somewhat greater status, particularly the work on the ring finger of the right hand, because the majority of melodies tend, in chords, to lie under this finger. The guitar, in comparison with many other instruments, has very little volume, and the fine gradation of dynamics is therefore of the utmost importance. When playing counterpoint or several voices moving in different registers, a volume should be chosen for each voice. The player should then try to shape each voice within its own level. The problem is made even more difficult when some of the notes are to be played together and some are to be played alone. This is found in the *Fugue* of the *Prelude, Fugue, and Allegro* by J. S. Bach; accents on the main beats give a vertical aspect to the piece when it should be thought of horizontally.

There are a number of examples of a more straightforward relationship between the melody and accompaniment, for example, *Study No. 5* by Heitor Villa-Lobos. The main priority with this piece should be the melody. This appears a very obvious statement, but it is common for a player to underestimate the extent to which the accompaniment may impinge on the melody. The dynamic of the melody should be set first, and this will then determine the level of the accompaniment. The use of rest stroke for the melody and free stroke for the accompaniment will help to distinguish the two, and because notes on the guitar cannot be long sustained, the tempo is also important. Problems do, however, arise if the quality and strength of the free stroke is weak because this will leave thin areas in a performance of the piece. It will also be noticed that each string has its own tone quality. It is quite common for a melody to move across several strings and it is therefore necessary to make some adjustment to the tone, in order to give the melody a constant tone throughout. I do this mostly by altering the angle of attack of the right-hand fingers. The action may be made a little more perpendicular to the third string and more angled on the second and first. In addition, I always play straight across the wound bass strings with the fingers, so that the scratching sound which commonly precedes a note is removed. Other pieces that should be considered for the development of melody technique (with accompaniments) are *Capriccio Arabe* and *Estudio sobre la Sonatina de Delfin Alard* by Francisco Tárrega, *Study No. 5* (B minor) by Fernando Sor, and *Study No. 3* (A major) by Matteo Carcassi.

Vibrato is the rapid change in the pitch of a note, achieved by moving a left-hand finger while holding a string down. The movement can be either transverse across the finger-board or in a direction that is parallel to the strings. On the classical guitar it is usually the latter that is used. It should be noted that the speed and intensity of the vibrations can be varied considerably and it is not necessary to use one speed for one note. The choice of when vibrato should be used is most difficult and is a subjective decision. In general, the later the music was written the more acceptable vibrato is. Nevertheless, I would not rule it out anywhere if used with discretion. Vibrato can help a melody soar over a large phrase, highlight a motif, or turn a dull passage into a thrilling one. Listening to some of the great violinists and cellists will be invaluable, particularly with regard to the intonation of each note. It will be heard that they play some notes sharper and others flatter. This helps to give more meaning to a phrase and is as important to the music as are, for example, rubato and dynamics. It is possible to measure all the various speeds of vibrato with a metronome, and the practice of vibrato at different tempi can act as a good warm-up exercise for the left-hand fingers.

Tremolo, when well-executed, provides the closest illusion to a continuous note possible on the guitar. It is an odd feature of guitar technique that some people have little difficulty with tremolo while others struggle with it for years. The normal pattern is for the thumb to play the bass notes and the ring, middle, and index fingers to play the same note on an upper string, as shown below. This right-hand pattern is then repeated continually to create the effect (see Ex. 9.2). It

Ex. 9.2

is important that the hand does not bounce up and down on each pluck of a string because this will hamper the speed. It is the speed rather than the evenness that normally interests a player, but this can often make it sound like a gallop instead of a ripple. It is preferable, once again, to concentrate on the quality of note rather than tempo, keeping the notes full and even. Occasionally, the middle finger is pulled on to the string by the action of the ring finger, thus damping the preceding note. In this case the result is a staccato line that again will not help the music. During practice of the tremolo the main beat should be altered, beginning with the above pattern (p,a,m,i), then leading with the ring finger (a,m,i,p), middle finger (m,i,p,a), and index finger (i,p,a,m) respectively. Other patterns such as the flamenco tremolo, in which an extra note is added to each group, should also be attempted (p,i,a,m,i). Once again, a cloth placed between the strings and the table of the guitar can make it easier to hear if the rhythm is even. Examples of tremolo pieces are *Recuerdos de la Alhambra* (Francisco Tárrega), *Una Limosna por el Amor de Dios* (Agustín Barrios), and *Campanas del Alba* (Eduardo Sainz de la Maza).

Pizzicato is usually played by the thumb with the heel of the right hand on the bridge, just touching the beginning of the vibrating part of the strings. The result is a note that is damped. The degree of damping can be altered, depending on the exact position of the hand. For general use, I prefer the mild pizzicato where the attack of the note is taken away, but there still remains a trace of it after. The shorter version is useful in aggressive passages. Examples of pizzicato are to be found in *Nocturnal* (Benjamin Britten) and *Impromptus* (Richard Rodney Bennett).

Two forms of harmonics are possible on the guitar, natural and artificial. Natural harmonics are those found on the open strings at the fifth fret (two octaves above the natural note), seventh fret (an octave and a fifth), twelfth fret (one octave), and nineteenth fret (one octave and a fifth). A harmonic note can also be found at the fourth, ninth, and sixteenth fret (two octaves and a third). An excellent example of the use of natural harmonics is found in *Prelude No. 4* (Heitor Villa-Lobos). The artificial harmonics are produced by pressing a given note on the finger-board and touching the string with the index finger of the right hand, one octave higher than that which is being stopped. The note may then be sounded by the ring finger of the right hand. For artificial harmonics in the bass, I prefer to sound a string with the thumb because this avoids the scratching sound referred to earlier. Two technical points should be noted; first, the touching finger should touch a string immediately over the fret, not just to the left; second, the touching finger should be removed immediately after the note has been played—this will give a little more clarity. Artificial harmonics are to be found in the arrangement of the Catalan folk song, *El Testament de Amelia* (Miguel Llobet).

The technique of glissando provides a guitar player with a means of moving from one note to another without the use of the right hand. To achieve the second note a finger should be slid along the string quickly so that arrival at the new fret produces the desired note. The extent to which the intervening notes are sounded may be varied, and care should be taken, as with previously mentioned techniques, over where glissandi are used. For some styles of music the use of glissandi sounds inappropriate. However, fashion does change, and there was a time, not long ago, when the technique was used extensively. Thus, glissandi should be used with discretion.

Tambour (*Tambora*) is a technique that involves striking the saddle of the bridge with the right hand. The sound produced is a mixture of the strings and the wood, the exact combination depending on the position of the strike. This effect is to be found at the beginning of *Fandanguillo* (Joaquín Turina).

There is an array of further percussive effects, possible by tapping, rapping, or knocking around the body of the guitar. Each guitar has its own best places for these effects and the player should experiment in this field when working on music with these requirements. In addition, there have been many pieces written in the last twenty years or so that ingeniously incorporate percussive and more avant-garde techniques. The latter may include smacking or scraping the strings, or the production of a snare-drum roll by overlapping two bass strings. These may be heard in, for example, *Sonata* (Alberto Ginastera), *The Prince's Toys* (Nikita Koshkin), and *A l'Aube du Dernier Jour* (Francis Kleynjams).

Although it is stretching a definition of technique to its limits, the technique of memory and practice is so vital to progress and performance, that it deserves mention here. A mistake in performance, particularly by players with an advanced technique, often tends to be related to the memory. To prevent this, the more work that can be done on improving the memory and concentration, the better. The student should attempt playing through a short passage of music just in the mind, that is without using the guitar. It will become possible to build up the whole piece in this way, and although each player must eventually find their own solution, I myself will not play anything in concert that I cannot play in my mind. During the learning process of a piece, it is essential to build in as few mistakes as possible. Thus, the more careful and slow these early sessions are, the better. Practice is concerned with achievement, whether it be the removal of a particular mistake or the acquisition of knowledge and musicality. The most important point is that progress must be made, and if long sessions of practice are only serving to reinforce something that is already wrong, then the time should be carefully reconsidered. During the analysis of a problem, an attempt should always be made to isolate the cause and then deal with this on its own. It is the very analysis of the cause that directs the solution to a problem.

One of the most valuable assets of the guitarist is enthusiasm and this should be nurtured, rested, and generally maintained at a high level. In this way, practice sessions should remain stimulating, enjoyable, and successful.

10 Rock Guitar

Brian May

OVER the last thirty years or so a battle has been fought, and perhaps won, for the acceptance of the classical guitar as an instrument worthy of serious study. It is ironic that even in this atmosphere of enlightenment, the electric guitar has suffered from a similar prejudice. Now the situation is changing, and it is the purpose of this chapter to examine the state of the art in 1987 and delve into some of the areas of music that have been regarded as unsuitable for schools.

If true rock guitar-playing is to be taught in school alongside the piano, violin, and even the classical guitar, it requires a very careful approach. There is a real danger of institutionalizing it, robbing it of much of its living character, and worse still, removing its very appeal as a means of personal expression and escape. Rock guitar-playing may be for many young people, not only an escape from formalism, but a symbol of freedom and a physical and mental release from the chains of authority. Even a cursory glance at the lyrics of rock music reveals immediate confirmation of this, and it can be traced from Van Halen and AC/DC, back through Alice Cooper (*School's Out*) and Jimi Hendrix, to the roots of rock music, the negro blues. Why the electric guitar should be singled out for this particular kind of expression is not immediately obvious. The reader of pop commentary of the late sixties and seventies, which intellectualized electric guitar music, found little clue; to make an art form falsely esoteric can be an attempt to make it palatable for the establishment. It is quite possible that one reason for the choice of the guitar is because it is often considered easy—it is not of course easy to be great, but sufficient knowledge to make a personal statement can be acquired relatively quickly. It is also a common observation that an ability to read music is by no means an essential qualification for electric guitar playing. Some rock players are proficient readers, and this opens up the field of studio session work. The innovative guitarists are, however, frequently those who have learned purely by ear, and the attraction of the guitar for them was perhaps that it was one of the few skills and means of expression that could be acquired without reading through pages of formal work. This is not to suggest that a rock guitarist is by nature illiterate—far from it—but an approach to teaching by written example misunderstands the means by which the art is transmitted and may well put off a potentially keen student.

There are other social characteristics which teachers should take into account. Decorously to ignore the sexual side of rock music, for example, is to put it absurdly out of context. It is very often the boy who would blush and stammer if faced with the prospect of making a suggestion to the girl sitting beside him, who will glory in screaming the very same on stage, with a guitar around his neck. The joy of the electric guitar is, furthermore, maintained by picking it up only when one feels the urge to play, never out of obligation, and by self-discipline rather than discipline imposed from above. Thus, it is wise for any teacher of electric guitar to be aware of the different forces that may be spurring a pupil on.

History

Pick-ups were first added to guitars in the days of Les Paul and Django Reinhardt, to enable the guitar to compete in loudness and tone with a live ensemble. It was soon found that a normal acoustic guitar body picked up the vibrations from the amplifier, making an unpleasant feedback sound, something like a fog-horn. The semi-acoustic and totally solid body of early Gibson and Fender guitars greatly reduced the problem, and it is a strange accident of history that these very modifications led to a type of feedback which opened up a completely new avenue for the guitar. By the time white rock 'n' roll was emerging from black blues, these early Gibsons and Fenders were becoming a different instrument in the hands of James Burton, Buddy Holly, and Scotty Moore who appeared on the first records by Elvis Presley, The Everly Brothers, Rick Nelson, and the Crickets. They used a harsh setting on the guitar and drove the amplifiers quite hard; the distortion added a characteristic rasp to the sound. A little later, Hank Marvin of The Shadows was one of the first to use a mechanical guitar tremolo as a part of his style. Their black counterparts, Bo Diddley, B. B. King, Albert King, and other fine blues players were already using their guitars to make sounds which could never have been coaxed from an acoustic guitar, or a slightly amplified guitar. They were using the fact that with a certain (high gain) amplifier setting, and by standing in a particular place near the amplifier, acoustic feedback would make certain notes sustain indefinitely. This new voicing enabled them to play very emotionally charged music. In the music of the Beatles, George Harrison expanded the vocabulary of the electric guitar with many fine solos, mainly using a setting of the amplifier below the distortion point. Meanwhile, Eric Clapton, Jimmy Page, Ritchie Blackmore, Pete Townshend, and especially Jeff Beck followed the black American electric blues tradition and took the style to a new stage in the later sixties. They turned up the amplifier a little more, so that the notes could really sing. They were able to sustain notes and actually have them spontaneously burst into a higher harmonic, and to play whole passages without ever striking a string with the right hand. The arrival of Jimi Hendrix on the scene represents to many people a crowning glory of this period of development of the rock guitar. He was able to fuse all the new elements into a giant style which made the electric guitar 'sound like an orchestra'.

Since that time, the genre has been truly international, the tradition being carried on by brilliant and innovative players such as Neil Schon, Steve Lukather, Edward Van Halen, Randy Rhodes, Steve Morse (USA), Michael Schenker (West Germany), Yngwie Malmsteen (Sweden), Angus Young (Australia), Trevor Rabin (South Africa), and many others. Britain has continued to produce spectacular players, although many had to travel outside to the USA, Japan, and Europe to gain recognition, for example, Mark Knopfler of Dire Straits, Gary Moore, Steve Hackett, and Steve Howe. Mentioning all these names defines a kind of guitar which bears little resemblance in sound or technique to simply an electrified acoustic guitar. The following section examines the physical characteristics of such an instrument, and effectively will be concerned with a solid body guitar.

The guitar and accessory equipment

In choosing a suitable instrument for rock-playing, many of the same considerations apply as for the acoustic guitar. The construction of the neck and body are however a little different, and there are extra items such as pick-ups, tremolo units, and switching which should be taken into account.

The **neck** of a steel-string guitar has to take more strain than that of the nylon-string variety, and, if fitted with a tremolo unit, must withstand frequent, violent changes of tension without bending. This, coupled with the preference of many rock guitarists for a very thin profile, means that a plain wood neck, even with a hard wood insert, is quite inadequate. The neck is usually, therefore, braced with an internal steel rod, which can be tensioned to oppose the bending force of the strings. This truss rod is normally adjusted by means of a nut concealed under a plate on the head of the guitar. There are other ways of dealing with the problem (for example, the English Bond guitar has a rigid graphite neck), but generally a guitar without a truss rod will never hold its tuning well, and may eventually become unplayable owing to a progressive warp. It is essential to check that the neck is straight at the time of purchase and that the octaves are in tune.

Most modern guitars have **bridge pieces** which allow for individual adjustment of the effective string lengths, to bring the octaves into tune. Owing to the differing end corrections for different gauges of strings and the effect of additional stretching produced by fretting the string itself, it will normally be found that the bridge position needs to be different for each string. Many modern bridges are designed to give this individual adjustment. Some people may think this too fussy, but the tuning of a highly amplified guitar is so critical that lack of this kind of bridge adjustment may give serious problems. Many bridges also have a vertical adjustment for changing the action, i.e. the height of the strings above the frets (see Fig. 10.1). Most players prefer a low action for speed and the lessening of tuning problems, but if the action is too low, the fretted notes will begin to buzz, especially when the string is pushed across the finger-board, (string bending). About 3–4 mm. is a good clearance distance for the top strings at the twenty-

Fig. **10.1**

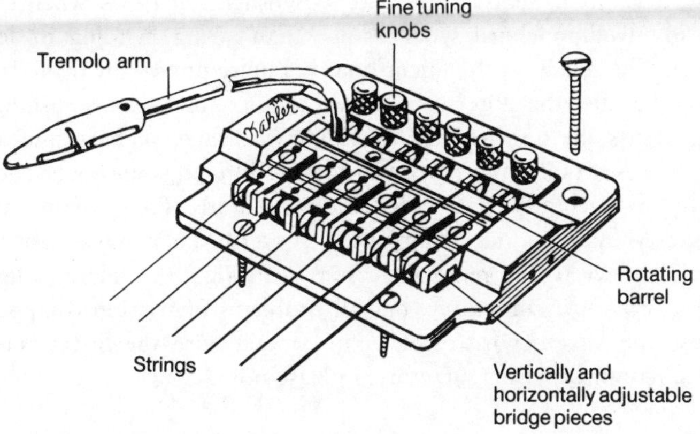

second fret; the low strings normally need a little more. If the action is good to start with, a vertical bridge adjustment may never be necessary; if the action is uncomfortably high, the adjustment will be needed. It is important to try this in the shop because a high action could be the manufacturer's disguise for the fact that the finger-board is not accurate enough to permit a low action without problems of buzzing. If a fret is wrongly positioned, it will usually be obvious to the eye, but even with correctly placed frets, problems may still occur at the first two or three fret positions. Some guitars require a lot of force to press down the string to the fret, and the notes will then sound sharp in relation to the open-string note. This occurs when the nut holds the strings too high. Again this seems to be a fail-safe device adopted by some makers, but it can ruin the feel of the guitar, particularly at the lower frets where the student usually begins. The grooves in the nut can be carefully deepened, but this should be left to the professional craftsman. A much better arrangement is the use of a bottomless nut and a zero fret. In this construction the strings should not touch the bottom of the grooves in the nut at all. The nut locates the strings horizontally only, and the zero fret locates them vertically, in relation to the finger-board. The zero fret should be at exactly the same height as all the other frets, producing a perfectly uniform action and, as a bonus, the open string sound quality now closely matches the fretted sound.

Most rock guitarists use a cambered finger-board; the frets are slightly curved to ease the fingering. Many players prefer a fairly wide neck with a thin profile. If the width across the strings is too narrow, string bending can be awkward. It is noticeable that the narrow necked Rickenbackers, for example, have been used mainly by guitarists such as John Lennon and Pete Townshend at times when they were involved in chord work rather than string bending or lead playing. The finish on the finger-board is quite important if the frets are low because the skin of the fingers is in contact whilst pushing a string across the finger-board. A slippery surface, such as polished ebony or rosewood, can be an advantage. A different solution has been adopted by such guitarists as Ritchie Blackmore, Tony Iommi, and Yngwie Malmsteen, all highly fluid players. They have had the material between the frets routed out as in Fig. 10.2. Here, a light touch is obviously necessary, but all problems of friction disappear because the finger ends are never in contact with the finger-board surface (commercial manufacturers please note!).

Fig. **10.2**

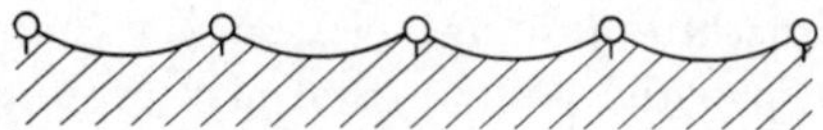

Although the sound of a rock guitar is totally electronically transmitted, the material and shape of the body undoubtedly contribute to the sound of the guitar. A discussion of exactly why and how, is, however beyond the scope of this chapter. This said, it is also true that most shapes have been designed to make the guitarist look good and/or feel good on stage, and the sound qualities have been at least partly accidental.

A **pick-up** is a device which converts the movement of a string into an electrical signal. The signal is processed electronically, amplified, and by means of a loudspeaker, converted back into a sound wave. A pick-up detects the actual movement of the string rather than the sound waves in the air, and the instant advantages of this are that the pick-up will not detect other sounds that are present (for example, the drums), and will not feed back uncontrollably. The pick-up consists of one or more magnets surrounded by a number of turns of very fine copper wire, the assembly sitting underneath and close to the strings. When the steel string vibrates, a voltage is induced across the ends of the wire. A single coil of several thousand turns will give sufficient voltage, and makes a crisp open sound, because it has a relatively low inductance and 'hears' the string at a sharply defined point (for example, Stratocaster and Telecaster). It does, however, have the disadvantage that it will pick up stray radio signals in addition to the guitar notes. The Humbucker was invented to reduce the problem. Two coils are used, wound in such a way that stray electro-magnetic fields are cancelled out, and the wanted signals are preserved. This makes a pick-up almost free of interference noise, but it has a different sound, rounder, with a less pronounced top end, and a kind of 'nasal' coloration (for example, the Gibson Les Paul). Single coils and Humbuckers are both very popular, and some players use a combination of the two. Some modern pick-ups have multiple coils which are switchable for different effects, and the DiMarzio company and others make replacement pick-ups with a variety of sounds which can, for example, give a humbucking effect in a pick-up with a single coil shape.

The sound of a pick-up also depends dramatically on its position along the string length, becoming brighter and more metallic the closer the bridge is approached. Just one pick-up may be placed by a manufacturer in a favourite position, and may procure the perfect sound for the player. Two or three pick-ups may also be used, and they can be wired in many different ways for a wide range of sounds. Normally a selector switch (or switches) will be provided to make use of the different pick-ups, and some models have the facility of using two or more together, increasing the total range of the instrument still further. Some guitars have volume controls for each pick-up, but most players I have met prefer a single master volume control. It is debatable whether any tone control is necessary (for instance Edward Van Halen takes them out), but most models have a variable treble cut which will remove excess harshness if necessary. Simplicity is a cardinal virtue for live work, and in my opinion any fancy controls, such as sliders or electronic touch controls are best avoided.

A **tremolo unit**, or vibrato, is a means of making changes of pitch with the right hand. It does this by making the anchor points of the strings, at the bridge end, movable at the touch of a lever, the tremolo arm. In the normal equilibrium position the strain of the strings is balanced against a spring arrangement; movement of the tremolo arm upsets this balance, changing the tension of the strings and hence the pitch. This is very simple on the face of it, although the factors that govern the sensitivity, range, and feel of these units are complex. When buying a guitar, it is vital to check that the pitch of the strings is precisely restored after movement of the tremolo arm. Nowadays many tremolo units have an integral bridge, using a roller arrangement to reduce friction and loss of pitch. The string movement at the nut end is smaller, but can also make a difference. One solution is to let the strings slide, and reduce friction by making sure that they are not bent through a large angle at the nut, using a material such as graphite. The other solution is to prevent the strings from moving at all, by using a string lock at the nut.

Electric guitar strings are, of course, made of steel or a similar ferromagnetic material, the bottom strings being wound with a wire covering to increase their weight for the low notes. Guitarists' preferences for different gauges are so diverse that strings are more often sold singly than in sets. Any diameter can be bought in 1 thou inch increments from 7 thou to about 50 thou. Very light gauge strings are comfortable for the fingers and make the bending of notes an easy matter. They are, however, prone to tuning problems because, as mentioned earlier, even the fretting itself produces a bending effect. The tuning discrepancies may not be noticed in single-note solo passages which may include bends anyway, but intonation in chords may noticeably suffer. The lighter gauges also give a less powerful signal and slightly inferior tone, which means that the pre-amplifier has to do more work and probably generates more noise. In addition, very light gauge (7, 8, and 9 thou) top strings can frequently break at the most awkward moment. Thus, depending on the strength of the player's fingers, a compromise should be found. For the low strings the windings may be of different cross sections, normally either circular (round wound) or flat (flat wound or tape wound). Tape wound strings greatly reduce the scratching noise in left-hand slides, but give a less brilliant tone, and are not therefore generally favoured by rock players. Some examples of the gauges used are as follows.

1st	2nd	3rd	4th	5th	6th	*string*
7–11	8–13	11–15	16–24	22–30	32–40	*thou*

If the string gauges are changed, an adjustment must be made to the tremolo unit (if fitted) so that the arm will return to the correct position.

The guitar **strap** is important as the liberator of the player from a static sitting position, but needs little comment except to note that the safe suspension of the instrument depends on both the strap itself and the fittings which hold it to the guitar. The modern captive lockable attachment is preferable. The **lead** is the guitarist's umbilical cord. The coiled spring type is a great improvement on the ordinary straight cable, facilitating movement and lessening the possibility of the violent pulls which are the main cause of embarrassing broken contacts in the connecting plugs. Many cheap cables produce a rustling sound if they are moved, owing to an instability of capacitance between the conductors in the cable. They may also muffle the sound due to bad transmission of the high frequencies. A high-quality, low-noise cable of the Belden type, is therefore a wise investment. An alternative is to use a radio link, which gives greater mobility to the player.

The **pick**, usually called a plectrum in circles other than rock music, was formerly often made of tortoiseshell. Nowadays it is widely variable in material, shape, and thickness. A thin, pliable pick gives a speedy right-hand action which is little impeded by contact with the strings. A somewhat pointed corner emphasizes this and produces a wiry sound. Such a pick is often favoured by rhythm (chord) players. The opposite end of the spectrum is a completely rigid object, rounded at the playing end. This type of pick is held more loosely, and all movements associated with the contact, deflection, and release of the string are transmitted directly to the fingers. This gives an intimate feel, preferred by many players, and more variety of tones. One variation used by the author is a small coin which, depending on the angle at which it is held, can produce a smooth tone, or a rasping attack. This is also the cheapest pick on the market! A medium-gauge pick may give something of both worlds and be a good starting-point, although almost anything may be considered such as pieces cut from plastic containers or ball-point refills. It is, of course, possible to play without a pick, usually with the fleshy finger-ends rather than the nails for single notes (for example, Jeff Beck), and the nails for the glancing blows in chord strumming. A combination of both pick and fingers may also be used. Again, there are no rules.

It is convenient to regard a guitar **amplifier** as made of three parts, the pre-amplifier, the power amplifier, and the loudspeaker. The pre-amplifier provides an initial, variable boost to the signal, and embodies the means to change the sound by either emphasizing or cutting various frequencies (treble, bass, middle, at least) or adding effects. A power amplifier further boosts the signal to the level where it can power the last part, the loudspeaker. The speakers are contained in a separate box in many set-ups, but in a 'combo', the pre-amplifier, power amplifier, and speakers are all in the same unit.

The first amplifiers used electronic valves. Later, transistors supplanted the valve in almost every commercial application, but received a cool response from most guitar players because they did not distort in the right way. The next generation of electronics revolved around the integrated circuit chip, and by this time, the point about the superiority of the valve sound had been well taken. Extra circuits were incorporated into the pre-amplifier section to imitate the soft saturation, or compressed sound of an overdriven valve amplifier. Most modern practice amplifiers have this saturation control built in, so that a suitable compression effect can be obtained even at low volumes. The majority of stage amplifiers are still old-style valve (tube) amplifiers whose design has changed little in twenty years (for example Marshall, Vox, Fender). No more than a 10-watt amplifier is needed for practice at home, and although on stage some players use several hundred watts just for guitar amplification, the advent of very powerful monitor and PA systems has made this mostly unnecessary.

Some extra effects are sometimes included in an amplifier. **Reverb** is an attempt to simulate the reverberation of an auditorium and is variable to suit personal preference. **Tremolo**, in an amplifier, usually means a cyclic variation in volume rather than pitch. A **high sensitivity input** brings into play an extra stage of pre-amplification, useful for extra sustain, and the bright channel gives an overall boost to the high frequencies. The **graphic equalizer** is a sophisticated system of variable filters which allows a finer adjustment to the sound spectrum than is possible with the conventional bass and treble controls.

Auxiliary pre-amps, species of which are otherwise known as treble booster, distortion booster, fuzz box, or compressor, are devices that usually take the form of a box with an input socket for the guitar lead, and output socket for connection to the amplifier. They all perform a similar function, which is to provide an extra, often variable boost to the signal, helping the guitar's ability to sustain. They also change the sound to varying degrees, the fuzz box being the most extreme. If the amplifier itself has a very powerful integral pre-amp, no booster may be necessary. With a valve amplifier it is seldom necessary to introduce distortion or fuzz, because the mere fact of overdriving will often produce a good sustained sound. In this case a simple pre-amp is sufficient, perhaps with the option of cutting down the bass frequencies to clean up the sound a little (treble boost). The **wah-wah** is a species of pre-amp which passes only a selected band of frequencies (pitches). The position of the band-pass in the sound spectrum is varied by a foot-operated control. Popular in the sixties, when it was used to create a sound reminiscent of a human voice, it is now less fashionable. Good examples of the use of the wah-wah are to be found in *Voodoo Chile* and *Gypsy Eyes* by Jimi Hendrix (*Electric Ladyland* album) and *Tales of Brave Ulysses* by Cream (*Disraeli Gears* album). There are a number of other effects that the player will wish to consider, such as phasing, delay devices, octave generators, triggered filters, and noise gates. In addition, new devices are constantly appearing.

Safety

Every year deaths and serious accidents occur as a result of inadequate attention to elementary safety requirements in guitar amplification. The first rule is that any metal part of any piece of equipment which may be touched by a human body must be properly earthed at all times. Normally, access to an earth is through the centre socket of a three-pin wall mains outlet where the device is plugged in. Care must be taken in correctly wiring the plug. If there is any doubt that the mains outlet is provided with a good earth connection, it must be checked by a competent electrician. Never use a two-pin connector.

The chassis and exposed metal parts of the amplifier are connected to this earth. The earth is carried to the guitar by the outer conductor of the guitar lead and the outer exposed part of the connector, normally a standard jack-plug and socket. To this, the strings, bridge, tremolo, etc. should be connected, so that when playing the instrument the guitarist is also earthed. The guitarist is not yet out of danger, however, because if he or she touches another metal object which has accidentally become live, such as a microphone or another guitar, the electricity has an easy path through the body to earth. This really means that anything within reach has also to be earthed, including, in a classroom, radios, tape recorders, and even drink machines. There is one additional precaution which removes the risk. An earth-leakage-detector, coupled with a circuit breaker, will instantly sense any current which appears in the earth line, and switch off the equipment. It is a great pity that use of this invaluable device is not required by law, because the cost of installing it is nothing compared with the possible cost of not bothering. Electrical equipment should never be touched with wet hands. Even after all these precautions have been taken, most professionals in a concert situation insist on a check being made with a voltage meter, to ensure that there is no voltage between the guitars and microphones. In the event of a player receiving an electric shock, never try to pull him or her off without first switching off the equipment at the mains. If connection of guitar to amplifier is by a radio link instead of a lead, the guitarist is already fairly safe, especially if wearing shoes with rubber soles.

Setting up

The procedure for setting up will normally be to switch the amplifier on and give it a few seconds to warm up before making any instrument connections. Leads should only be plugged into the amplifier (or removed) with the master volume control at zero, or with the amplifier in stand-by condition, if it has one. This avoids damage to the loudspeakers due to violent transient signals which would otherwise be generated when the input is momentarily short circuited by the jack-plug on its way in. A good starting point is to have the tone controls in an intermediate position (at 5 on most amplifiers) and with reverb or tremolo off. If a pre-amp volume control is fitted as well as the master volume, this can also be set at the half-way position to begin with. At this point the guitar is plugged in, a pick-up selected, the guitar volume and treble controls set to maximum, and the amplifier master volume set to a suitable listening level. It is worth spending time experimenting with the volume controls. The player can confirm that turning the pre-amp volume up and the master volume down (to keep the listening level reasonable) produces increased distortion and sustain, while turning the pre-amp control low and the master volume high produces a clear distinct sound suitable for chords.

To make the maximum range of sounds available, the pre-amp control can be set to a high enough level to drive the amplifier into an overloaded sustained sound. The volume control on the guitar can now be adjusted to produce anything from a clean sound at low levels to various degrees of distortion or compression at higher settings. If, with the pre-amp volume control fully up, the sound is still clean and does not help sustain, a high sensitivity input on the amplifier should be selected if available. Alternatively, an external pre-amp can be connected between the guitar and amplifiers. If the amplifier does not have an overload-sound pre-amp system, a pre-amp with such a circuit may have to be used. Otherwise the amplifier will only produce good sustain at volumes which will annoy the neighbours.

Sound and settings for the guitar

It always takes time to become familiar with the controls of a guitar, and if the manufacturer supplies an instruction booklet, it pays to read it carefully. If there is any doubt as to what is happening with a given switch position, gently scratching the pick-ups will determine which is in use. This technique also easily locates a faulty pick-up. The range of sounds available is extended by the tone controls on the guitar and amplifier, and little comment is needed except that an excessive use of overall treble or bass cut will mask the natural tone variation of the guitar. A classical guitarist plucks the string at different points to obtain tonal variation. The same technique is open to the rock guitarist, but selection of different pick-ups does the same job in a more dramatic way, the finger-board pick-up giving the roundest sound.

A strong rhythm sound, in the Keith Richards style, is the result of a fairly harsh pick-up selection (perhaps the bridge pick-up only), and only moderate distortion. Going further into distortion and continuing to play chords, produces the dirty sound favoured by many players in the punk era. Increasing the level still further, and boosting the high frequencies a little, introduces the incisive sustaining tone of many of today's lead players.

Many factors contribute to the length of sustain obtainable. The natural decay time of the guitar is determined by the quality of the strings, the rigidity of the anchor points, the body of the guitar, and to a lesser extent, the temperature and humidity of the air. As already mentioned, saturation or compression in the amplifier can artificially increase the decay time by lifting the quiet ends of the notes to the same volume as the beginning. This, however, cannot sustain the note indefinitely. Only acoustic feedback can do this; energy is fed back into the string from the sound waves in the air at exactly the right frequency to keep its vibration going. This can only happen if the guitar is close to the loudspeakers and the level is fairly high. So this is the point where the neighbours' problems really begin!

Technique

The technique of rock guitar playing has now grown up over a generation, to such a point that it would be quite possible to lay down a whole system of rules regarding the position of the hands, fingering, etc., and a corresponding set of exercises to develop a stock style. It is quite evident, however, that the most important rock guitarists have developed their style of playing by breaking the rules. They listened to guitarists to whose work they were exposed whilst growing up, but early on in their own development, they found their own ways. Therefore items of rock technique should perhaps be presented as 'this is how many players have produced this effect', rather than 'this is how it ought to be done'.

The position of the hand is largely governed by consideration of comfort. Most rock guitarists find a favourite picking position unobstructed by a pick-up and stick to it for much of the time, except when harmonics are being played. Standardization of the right-hand position helps to promote dexterity in working the controls during playing, so that changes can be made during a phrase if necessary. The angle to the strings at which the pick is held also makes a difference, and this is a matter for experiment. It should be noted, however, that the most attacking sound is not necessarily obtained by the hardest hitting of the strings; many an aggressive solo has been played with the lightest touch, but with an abrasive setting of the guitar and amplifier controls. The hand may also be moved to make damped notes. It is possible to strike the string and cut off the note by bringing back the right hand to touch the strings, or releasing the left-hand pressure so that the strings are no longer in contact with the frets. Another common technique is to rest the side of the hand lightly on the bridge while actually playing the strings. This produces a distinctive, chugging sound which has the feeling of power held back (for example, the author's *Brighton Rock* soloing, and Pete Townshend's *Happy Jack*). The free fingers of the right hand are used to operate the tremolo arm. It should be clarified that movement of the tremolo arm across the strings does not affect pitch, making it possible for the arm to be carried while picking a whole phrase. The most common grip for the pick is between a slightly flexed thumb and a first finger curled around to point back along the direction of the thumb. For a looser grip the pick may be held between the tips of the thumb and first finger. When soloing, movement is mainly from the wrist, the complete forearm usually only being used for aggressive rhythm playing. Special grips have been developed by many players to produce harmonics in fretted notes. To produce the first harmonic (octave) a favourite technique is to move the picking position of the string and incorporate into the picking action a light brushing of the string, with the finger following the impact of the pick. The touch of the finger damps out the fundamental note and leaves the octave harmonic ringing. Applying this technique to different points on the string produces different harmonics, and the power of these notes can be enhanced by using a pick-up combination which picks them up strongly (for example, the finger-board and centre pick-ups switched out of phase, or the bridge pick-up on its own).

The left-hand position is variable from the formal barré position with the thumb in the middle of the back of the neck, to a clutch position with the thumb actually fretting the bottom string. The latter can allow some chords which are not possible in any other way. Many very dextrous players use the former position, many of the expressive blues players use a more relaxed position and tend to ignore the smallest finger much of the time. It is the lightness of the action which allows this latitude in left-hand technique.

The slide (in rock terminology, a glissando or portamento in classical guitar language) is very much a part of rock-playing, and is used for generating excitement when moving from one note to another. Of course, the way of moving to another note which is the forte of the rock guitar, is by bending. For this technique, the string is pulled to one side while it is sounding, it being possible to raise the pitch one or two semitones, or with light strings considerably more. The pitch is infinitely variable, and much expression is therefore possible using bends. Slight sideways rocking of the string produces a vibrato which again is very personal in speed, depth, and point of use, and it is much more effective than rocking the fretting finger parallel to the string. It should be noted that in this kind of vibrato, all movement of pitch is in the upward direction, no matter which way the string is pulled. In contrast, the balanced tremolo unit can be used to create a vibrato which moves above and below the fretted note, giving a more relaxed feel to the notes.

In addition to the left-hand hammer-ons and pull-offs (slurs for the classical guitarist), changes of note can also be made by hammering on the fingers of the picking hand (for example, Jimi Hendrix, *House Burning Down*, and the author's *Its Late*). Initially this was a minority technique, but Edward Van Halen developed it into virtually a new language for the guitar, influencing many young players and providing a good illustration of the power of unorthodoxy in the rock world. The technique uses multiple hammer-ons and pull-offs with the fingers of both hands, treating the finger-board very much like a keyboard. The work of the jazz guitarist Stanley Jordan is also essential listening in this field. Electric-guitar strings normally vibrate parallel to the finger-board since there is very little room in the vertical direction. An exception is in the snap, produced by pulling the string up and letting it go.

Two very important fields of guitar sounds have been omitted so far. Reggae music engenders an entirely different approach to guitar playing which should be taken very seriously because the vocabulary is broad and innovative. The sounds used are usually clean and bright. Rockabilly is the term applied to music directly descended from the early rock 'n' roll era, and again guitar-playing in this field is highly specialized and highly developed. The sounds are typically broad, yet clean and metallic, and the astonishing technique of Albert Lee is a fine example.

Ensemble Playing

If the rock guitarist is playing with other musicians, it should always be borne in mind that the balance of instruments heard by the player may be quite different from that heard by the audience. Of course, the requirements are different too. Most musicians need to hear themselves louder than anyone else, while the audience needs an overall balance, perhaps highlighting certain instruments at certain times. The rock band does not have the natural balance of a symphony orchestra and in a small room, where a PA system is used only for voices (and no monitors are available), audience balance can be achieved by adjustment of the master volume controls and the relative position of the players and speakers. In a large auditorium the problems are separately solved by a monitor mixer for the players and an 'out front' mixer for the audience.

Considerable media coverage has been given from time to time on the subject of damage to ears during rock concerts. Concern in this area has even been used as an excuse to avoid the introduction of rock instruments in education. At extremely high levels of sound there *are* dangers, and any listener who experiences actual pain during loud passages should immediately cover their ears, move away from the speakers, or use medically approved industrial ear plugs. Recently, however, as the problems have become more understood, skilful sound engineers have managed to produce high enough levels of sound to move the body as well as the mind, but with very little risk to the audience's hearing. It is done by attention to the overall sound spectrum issuing from the PA system. The modern sound engineer sets up the system to have a flat response from lows to highs, and the signals during the concert are monitored, using a sound spectrum analyser. With a loud sound which is fairly evenly spread throughout the audible range, our ears make a temporary compensation—a lessening of sensitivity especially at high frequencies. If the sound is concentrated in a narrow frequency range, as for example in many old fashioned, 'tinny' PAs, the ears are unable to compensate and discomfort and potential damage result. Thus it is not wholly realistic to put a numerical limit on the number of decibels allowed. There is, of course, a point where even well-balanced sound becomes a danger, though the duration of exposure is an important factor. In spite of all the alarm, most people who go to rock concerts seem to experience little effect from a two- to three-hour show at very high levels, other than to find their cars very quiet on the way home. Noise is, of course, a factor in any educational institution, and any teacher who is hoping to persuade a school or college to invest in electric guitars must be ready with a timetable and venue that will allay colleagues' fear of disturbance. Practice headphones or the more sophisticated Rockman device, which allow the player to work privately, without a loudspeaker, are also worthwhile for any teaching situation.

Repertoire

Examples in the following discussion of repertoire should be regarded not as essential exercises but as useful study material (which contain various examples of lead lines), particularly for the student who was not around to witness the development of electric guitar style.

Les Paul is, of course, historically the first famous name in electric guitar playing, but his work is now seldom heard. *Little Rock Getaway*, among other early works, used variable tape speeds, multi-tracking, and echo chambers. A fascinating portent for the future.

The Crickets, led by Buddy Holly, have to be considered one of the first rock groups as such. Their early hit records such as *Maybe Baby*, *Oh Boy*, *Think it Over*, and *That'll be the Day* were made with a purely electric-guitar-based small group, without all the customary back-up of a large ensemble. In *Looking for Someone to Love*, the guitar is given solo breaks in which Buddy Holly improvises over the chord changes of a verse, much as a jazz or blues soloist might. This may seem like stating the obvious but pop records of this time were more likely, if they had a solo break at all, to feature a wind instrument or string section merely restating a portion of the melody. Buddy Holly's guitar was not only a back-up instrument, but also a voice; it sounded totally revolutionary at the time. It should be noticed that the playing is rhythmic and closely related to the chord shapes. Lonnie Donegan's early records also featured some fine early soloing (*I'm Just a Rolling Stone*) as did those of his rival, Johnny Duncan (and the Blue Grass Boys), for example, *Footprints in the Snow*. And many early Elvis Presley and Rick Nelson records (especially *Hello Mary Lou*), contain excellent early electric solos. Many young players preferred these solo breaks to the rest of the record, which may have led to the phenomenal success of The Shadows.

The Shadows shifted the emphasis of group music to instrumental rather than vocal. They backed Cliff Richard of course, but are best remembered for *Apache*, *Man of Mystery*, *Wonderful Land*, and many other instrumental hits. On *Apache*, Hank Marvin played with a metallic, yet sustained sound, against a background of Bruce Welch's smooth rhythm sound (usually acoustic on record, electric on stage), plus electric bass and drums. Hank Marvin's use of an electronic echo chamber, mechanical tremolo, and fluid touch, created a sound which countless thousands of budding guitarists tried to imitate. Their first LP, *The Shadows*, is essential listening and is, compared to their many imitators, highly sophisticated (for example, Shadoogie, Blue Star, Nivram, etc.). The Ventures had a similar line-up, and much of their material, such as *Walk Don't Run* and *Rambunkshush*, was also influential.

Eric Clapton provides the next turning-point. His playing relates directly to blues, which, against deceptively simple chord sequences, introduces a style with perhaps less melodic variation but with more rawness, more emotion, more fire and speed, more string bending, and more volume. The *Five Live Yardbirds* album epitomizes the content of countless Clapton-inspired Rhythm and Blues groups of the time. *Got to Hurry* shows off early blues leanings with the Yardbirds, but the classic exposition is on the *Bluesbreakers* album with John Mayall. *The Key to Love* solo is a masterpiece which stands the test of time—it more than talks, it screams. The first Paul Butterfield Blues Band album was also highly influential; and of course Eric Clapton's work through Cream, and many other situations to the present day, is exemplary.

Jeff Beck is widely recognized as one of the most expressive players ever. When he replaced Clapton in the Yardbirds, their first release was the album *Roger the Engineer*. Even when the subject is blues-oriented, as in *The Nazz are Blue*, Beck's soloing is a long way from orthodox blues. He uses a mixture of scales, and this track includes a single note sustained by acoustic feedback for about ten seconds, against a number of chord changes. Again, this was revolutionary playing. The solo in the original Yardbirds' *Shape of Things*, also provides essential material for listening and/or practice. Here, the guitar is bursting with spontaneous feedback, and since hardly any right-hand picking is needed, the guitar is transformed into some strange Indian-sounding instrument.

Against this background of innovation it seemed unlikely that any one player could come along and shock everyone to the core. Yet Jimi Hendrix was able to do just this. It was as if all the nascent elements of guitar technique came together in his hands. The sound was huge, warm, yet biting, and his soloing was lyrical and melodic, yet with the passion of the great blues player. He had full control of acoustic feedback, and used many electronic devices without ever losing the human touch. The first album, *Are You Experienced*, captures some of his style but not his sound. *Axis Bold as Love* and *Electric Ladyland*, are both *tours de force*. Something of his live, improvisational magic is captured in the play-out of the title track, *Bold as Love*. By way of contrast, *Little Wing* is a gem of sensitive picking.

From this point on, choice is difficult with a great variety of material to choose from. For example, the work of the author of this chapter may be heard on Queen albums and the Star Fleet Project. The solo from *Brighton Rock* (from the album, *Sheer Heart Attack*), has been frequently cited as an influence. It uses a single repeat echo and a technique of half muting with the right hand at the bridge to produce a percussive attack and long sustain. A further development of the 'canon' effect appears on the later, *Live Killers* album. *Killer Queen*, also on the *Sheer Heart Attack* album, is an early example of 'orchestral' arrangements for guitar, and the *Night at the Opera* and *Day at the Races* albums include many complex arrangements for guitars in the style of jazz bands, string sections, etc.

At sometime in the seventies, rock music split into distinct subsections, and many of the best technicians found themselves in the 'heavy metal' category. Edward Van Halen is widely regarded as taking the biggest step forward. On the album *Van Halen 1*, he introduces a highly personal technique, using fearsome harmonics of fretted notes in conjunction with tremolo and a new kind of fluidity based on multiple hammer-ons and pull-offs with the fingers of both hands. His work constitutes another significant expansion of the vocabulary.

The country guitar style of Albert Lee is well exemplified by his well-known *Country Boy*. This, among other pieces, is demonstrated on the *Star Licks Master Series* video cassette, which is highly recommended. This series of teaching videos provides the best possible insight into the techniques of many well-known players. There are, of course, a fair number of publications concerned with lead guitar playing. These tend to fall into two major categories, namely tutors and notated examples of a player or band's hits. For an extensive list of these, the reader is referred to, amongst others, the following publishers: Chappell Music; F. D. and H. Music; Music Sales Limited. Sheet music for ensemble is rare, and for this reason reference is made to the *Rockschool* series (video, practice cassette, and publications from the BBC and Boosey and Hawkes).

Above all, enjoy!!

11 Bass Guitar

Alphonso Johnson

IN 1951 a man by the name of Clarence Leo Fender revolutionized the music industry by introducing his Precision Bass. This instrument differed from earlier double-bass viols by its innovative body and pick-up designs. The original instrument had a fretted neck, a single coil pick-up, and a single volume control. In addition, it had an optimum length of 34 in., gut strings were used, and there were $\frac{3}{16}$ in. pole- and percussive-type pick-ups located directly over the polepieces under each string. Today, there are many different types of electric bass guitars, but they all owe their beginnings to Leo Fender. Thirty-six years later the Fender Bass remains a standard.

The electric bass was responsible for a dramatic change in the way bass players thought about performing. With its smaller body design the electric bass gave the bassist more mobility in the band. Also, having a smaller body design gave the player more options when planning for transportation of their equipment. In order to be heard, the electric bassist required an amplifier which allowed better control over how the sound of the instrument would project. These new changes by no way meant that the electric bass was replacing bass viol; instead, it enhanced the role of the bassist in all types of settings. Now the bassists had more options of sounds at their disposal which usually meant an increase in employment. A bassist could take in an orchestra rehearsal in the afternoon with bass viol and in the evening perform with the electric bass at a rock 'n' roll dance. This type of liberation helped the bass-player become part of the orchestra in a broader sense of the word. Through having to devote more time to developing the skills required to play the electric bass, the bassist became even more dedicated. With this resurgence of interest, the art of playing bass was elevated to greater heights and improved the overall musical community in general.

With these differences in the instrument also came a difference in the attitudes of not only the performers but the listeners as well. Recording engineers now had a better electronic signal to work with and so the bass was a little easier to record. The sound has, and always will depend on the quality of the instrument being used, the performer's ability to project a good tone, and the engineer's ability to capture the performance accurately. Yet now the listener was able to detect that recordings sounded different. In the beginning the electric bass was mostly heard in pop music but as it became more popular with musicians it eventually found its way into other musical styles.

One of the first electric bassists to make a significant breakthrough and capture the hearts and imaginations of musicians, was Monk Montgomery. With his brothers Wes (on guitar) and Buddy (on piano), they used their jazz background to extend current ideas beyond the normal realm. Monk Montgomery used the bass guitar in a very fluid manner. When he was not backing a soloist he could adapt to playing lead lines or solos without losing any sense that something different had just taken place—this is a very difficult task for a player in any band. Usually, when a bassist changes from a background supporting role to a lead soloing position, there is a noticeable change in the sound of the band. The bottom to the music always seems to drop out, or the lead seems weak. With a rich, smooth tone that was neither bottom-heavy nor too much like a guitar, Monk's sound seemed to fit any situation at any moment. And not only did it fit, but his sense of timing, dynamics, and choice of notes, made the music swing. There were many other bass-players who followed Monk to make significant contributions to the development of bass styles and techniques. Most musicians would agree, however, that Monk Montgomery was a major influence on their playing.

Another bassist who made a significant contribution to developing styles which influenced other players was Chuck Rainey. Although he was mainly a rhythm 'n' blues player, his unique knowledge of harmony made his playing stand out. He never restricted himself to playing only the root note of a chord and his use of different harmony notes seemed to always enhance a passage beautifully. He would also play double-stops to complement the chord progressions when backing a vocalist. Many bassists, including Stanley Clarke, Jack Bruce, Anthony Jackson, Chris Squire, Jaco Pastorius, James Jamerson, and Ray Brown influence what bass-players are playing today. They each have a style that was different enough to make people listen and respect what they had to say, and their playing, together with that of many others, will ensure that the electric bass guitar will continue to develop as an essential part of many modern ensembles.

The bass and accessory equipment

At the time of writing this chapter there exist more than 200 different models of bass guitar on the market. There are short-scale and long-scale basses which may be either fretted or fretless. In fact, there are almost as many versions of electric bass guitars as there are of automobiles. This vast array of instruments varies from the very traditional-looking Fender Precision Bass, to the more futuristic approach of the Steinberger Bass.

There are two basic types of bass guitar, one which has frets along the finger-board and the other which has none. The fretless bass has a very smooth, legato sound, of the same character as its older brother, the bass viol. This type of bass guitar enables the player to play glissandi and quarter-tones with ease. By contrast, the fretted instrument has a very percussive attack to its sound. It has each fret marked out by a strip of metal and is the most commonly used of the two. Since the fretless bass has no markings, it is suggested that the beginner start on a fretted bass and become familiar with the neck positions and intonation before attempting to play the fretless bass.

The Fender bass guitar has a very western look. The long horn extending from the top of the body is there to give a balance to the instrument when the player is wearing a strap. The horn brings the strap button down to a favourable point so that the neck rests at about a forty-five-degree angle in its normal resting position—this will support the instrument when playing in a standing position. There are some instruments that are unbalanced owing to poor design by the manufacturer and trying to play these instruments will usually result in the uncomfortable task of simultaneously trying to play with, and also support, the neck of the instrument with the left hand.

The Steinberger, on the other hand, has no head-stock and the tuning keys are a group of round knobs located at the bottom of the instrument. In addition, the body is made of a reinforced graphite and fibreglass, which makes the instrument much lighter in weight than its wooden predecessor. This is of a great consideration to any bassist who has developed spinal or back problems due to supporting the weight of a heavy wooden instrument over the years. This instrument is supported by an attachment at the waist and a strap for balance. At present the Steinberger costs about £1300·00 and the Fender Precision (copy) costs about £300·00. I would advise the beginner to start on an inexpensive bass and work up to the more sophisticated model as their playing requirements demand.

The most common types of string in use today are the round wound, flat wound, and half round (sometimes called half wound) strings (see Fig. 11.1). These strings all have a core of hi-carbon steel wire that may be either round or hexagonal in shape. Wrapped at an angle around that core is a smaller thread of nickel or stainless steel material. The amount of winding over the core determines the sound of the string, the E string for example has as many as three outer windings. The alteration of this outer casing and the thickness of the inner core gives each string its sound. The round wound string has a very round outer casing with very deep grooves in between each winding. The flat wound string has an outer casing that is similar to that found on the round wound string, except that the windings are far lighter and closer together. The half round strings are actually round wound strings that have had the outer casing ground down. Most bassists use the round wound strings for live performances, the half round for studio recording, and the flat wound strings for playing the fretless bass. The gauge of the string to be used should be determined by the degree of comfort required by the player. Obviously heavy gauge strings will offer more resistance than lighter gauge strings and the lighter gauge strings will not have as big a tone as the heavier ones. I might suggest that the beginner try different gauges and experiment to see which strings are the most comfortable—maybe start out on the lighter gauge and then after a month or so, move up to a heavier

Fig. **11.1**

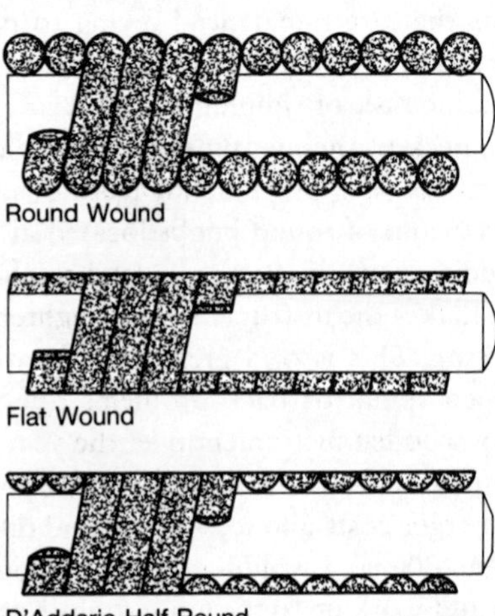

gauged set. It is recommended that a beginner use a round wound set of strings; for example, D'Addario XL220-Super Soft for a fretted bass and D'Addario S-HR70 Super Soft for a fretless bass. A notebook should be kept to hand and notes kept as to when a certain string has been started on and which strings have been used. It should also be noted when it was necessary to change the strings and the reasons for such a change. Strings made by different manufacturers may then be tried until one is found which is liked. After years of trying different strings, I am sure that every bassist will have their own personal reasons for why they use the equipment that they do.

The setting up of an electric bass guitar is not that difficult although it is something that most seem to prefer to leave to an experienced repair shop. After purchasing a brand new bass it is far more exciting to begin playing rather than properly setting it up. It is, however, worth considering what is involved because a minimum amount of time will give a maximum amount of quality playing time. Firstly, it will be necessary to put on a new set of strings. For this, a few tools will be needed; a small Phillips screwdriver, a set of Allen keys, an ordinary screwdriver, a wire cutter, a small bottle of lemon oil, and a tuning scope (electronic tuner).

The instrument should be placed on a flat surface with the top of the neck (just under the nut) supported by something which will elevate the neck enough to give access to the tuning pegs. Usually, a hand towel rolled and placed under the neck with the head-stock hanging over the edge of a table will be sufficient as long as great care is taken not to put any extreme pressure on any one part of the instrument. It should be kept in mind that the bass strings are very thick and create a lot of tension on the neck. I recommend loosening the middle two strings (A and D) before loosening and removing the outer strings (G and E). This procedure will prevent tension from warping the neck by uneven stress whenever changing the strings.

After removing all of the strings, a good clean cloth should be used to remove any dirt or residue from the finger-board, back of the neck, and body. Usually, a little lemon oil applied to the cloth and then rubbed over the finger-board will help preserve the wood over the years as the sweat and dirt from playing will eventually destroy the plastic film coating. It should be made sure that the bridge and pick-ups have been wiped clean and any burrs (rough edges in the saddle of the bridge that may cause a string to break) have been smoothed. The new set of strings should be threaded through the opening at the base of the bridge (depending on the type of bridge and its design). The string should be pulled through carefully until the ball at the end of the string has made contact. Great care should be taken not to pull the strings aggressively through the bridge opening. This caution is necessary to avoid scraping the edges of the strings and having the metal shavings fall into the pick-ups. The strings will then need to be threaded through their openings in the tuning pegs. Enough slack should be left in each string for it to be wrapped round the post several times, the first wrap going round the post and then over the top of the string that is sticking through the open part of the post. Each string should then be tightened so that the slack is taken up and there is enough tension to produce a note. It will then be necessary to adjust the bridge.

The bridge should have vertical and horizontal adjustment screws. The string action, or distance between the string and the finger-board, is determined by the vertical adjustment and should be set first. Playing at random across the neck and up and down the finger-board will help the player to determine which height will be comfortable. Sufficient height will be needed to prevent the string from buzzing, yet care must be taken not to make the string so high that it is difficult to press down comfortably. It will then be necessary to adjust the intonation by making the distance from the twelfth fret to the middle of the bridge the same as the distance from the nut to the twelfth fret. This equal distance will allow us to establish the octaves. After each string has been adjusted, the bass can be plugged into a tuning scope. Starting with the D string, the octave of the string should be tuned by playing the note at the twelfth fret and adjusting the horizontal screw on the bridge until the note is in tune with the tuning scope (or tuning fork, piano, etc.). If the string is touched lightly at the twelfth fret and played, a harmonic note is produced. The vertical screw should then be adjusted until this harmonic note is in tune.

The procedure of tuning the octave and the harmonic notes should be repeated until both are as closely tuned as is possible. There are, however, no two sets of strings that are exactly alike and it may not be possible to achieve a perfect tuning. Further adjustment should therefore be made by playing and listening to the different octaves along the finger-board, as well as scales and double stops.

The following comments should serve as a short reference section for the beginner. When choosing an instrument for the first time, the beginner should try to take along another musician who has some experience with bass guitars, perhaps a teacher. Some general comments on choosing a guitar are to be found in Appendix IV of this book, but more specifically, it should be made sure that the bass has an adjustable bridge (with vertical and horizontal screws) and a neck with an adjustable truss rod, and it is recommended that the beginner choose a bass with one pick-up, which will help to keep the cost of the instrument down. The choice of amplifier is not as difficult as it may seem. It is important to decide whether the amplifier is to be used solely for practice or if it is to be used for some live performances as well. The former will, of course, require less power although it should be borne in mind that it takes more power to reproduce bass accurately than may be thought (I am sure that many will have turned up the radio in the car only to hear the sound become more distorted). What usually happens is that the power amplifier does not have enough wattage to reproduce the lower frequencies of the sound accurately. If the amplifier is to be used for live performance work it should be remembered that the amplifier will need to be carried around. Thus, weight and size are also important factors. Usually, the bass amplifier will come as one unit with a speaker cabinet and a power/pre-amplifier unit (a box that contains both the power and the tone controls) which normally sits on top of the speaker cabinet. Some companies make units that have everything in one enclosure. This type of system is a good unit for the beginner to consider although it will restrict the player as far as being able to add different components later on. All of this will depend on budget, the size and weight required, as well as other personal needs. As with the guitars, as many different amplifiers should be tried as is possible and it should, of course, be made sure that the sound is pleasing to the ear. Make sure, for example, that the amplifier will reproduce a good definition of the low notes (as well as the highs), and it should not sound distorted unless there is a special effect built into the amplifier for that purpose. It is a good idea to turn the amplifier all the way up to make it distort, and then to turn it down to see where the maximum volume level will be without distortion. This is important for establishing how much can be expected from the amplifier during performance. Finally, the price of amplifiers will vary with their features and so the beginner should try to establish ahead of time exactly what it is that the amplifier is to do.

Sound and technique

It seems that every other year or so, there comes along a bassist who has developed a style that is considered unique. Most of the time, it is their particular way of playing something that has already been done before that distinguishes them. It is, therefore, this ability to adapt technique that will usually set one bassist apart from another. Let us take a look at some aspects of bass guitar playing that will be of value to the beginner as well as to the professional bassist for developing some techniques that will enable them to establish their own unique styles.

There are a few items that deserve attention when setting up the equipment to play. First, it should be made sure that the playing environment is supportive of creating music. Far too often we find ourselves unable to practise because of peoples' complaints or just not enough inspiration. Pick a place, such as a garage or a bedroom, where there is little disturbance from traffic or other noise and set up the amplifier in a position so that the sound is not blocked by any object in front of the speaker cabinet. I would also advise that the student get in the habit of playing in a standing position as well as in a sitting one. In preparing to play, it is a good idea to decide beforehand just what is to be accomplished. Practice time should be used wisely and this can be assisted by the setting out of a schedule, perhaps as follows:

Warm-up and scales (standing)	8.00–8.15 a.m.
Improvisation	8.15–8.30 a.m.
Reading and studies	8.30–9.30 a.m.
Rest period	9.30–9.45 a.m.
Practice technique	9.45–10.30 a.m.
Research and technical studies	10.30–11.45 a.m.
Warm-down and scales (sitting)	11.45–12.00 noon

Of course, many people will not be able to set aside this amount of time; others will have to split their time into a morning and afternoon/evening session. It is, therefore, up to individuals to determine their own needs based upon their daily life-styles. Clearly, there are always going to be sacrifices that have to be made and it will be important for a beginner to keep in mind that once a system has been developed, the rate of progress will be improved over a period of time.

In addition to the features of setting up the instrument given earlier, the bass should be adjusted so that the volume control is turned all the way up on the bass; the volume and all tone controls on the amplifier should be given a mid-way setting, usually at 5. What we are trying to achieve is a 'flat' setting on the amplifier which can later be fine-tuned to the settings which suit a player's personal needs.

As we discussed earlier, developing a sound requires the application of various techniques, and the sound is affected by how the bass is played. If, for example, we have a right-hand instrument but are left-handed, and simply turn the instrument around, we shall soon find out that we sound different from other bass-players. This approach is used by many great players and is not considered incorrect. As far as the right hand is concerned, there is a choice of using a pick (plectrum) or the fingers. A pick will give the player a very clean sound with a bright attack; the fingers will give a closer feeling with the strings and many different responses.

Usually the bass (for right-handed players) is held with the left hand wrapped around the neck, cupped between the thumb and the index finger. The left hand should be kept as loose as possible in order to obtain the maximum amount of speed and dexterity. The thumb should be in the middle of the neck, pointing towards the tuning pegs and the nut. Try to keep an arch to the hand as if you were holding a ball in the palm on your hand. Naturally left-handed players should apply the same approach, but using the right hand to hold the neck. As I stated before, there is nothing wrong with trying different approaches, so please experiment to find what suits your needs the best.

The right hand should be placed over the strings with the fleshy part of the palm (just under the thumb) resting over the E string. If a pick is to be used, then this technique should be practised, in the beginning, sitting down. The student should try to keep the wrist as flat as possible, holding the pick firmly and using an up-and-down motion with the wrist. The forearm and elbow should hug the upper part of the body and this same position should be maintained when slapping or using the finger-picking technique. When playing with the middle and index fingers, the player should try to keep the right hand arched, with the thumb damping the lower strings so that they do not vibrate. 'Slapping and popping' the strings with the right hand is another technique that a player can use. For this, a string is slapped with the thumb and then popped with the middle and/or index finger. One such example is to slap the E string with the fleshy part of the thumb near the middle joint. While holding down a note with the left hand, the G string may then be pulled up with the tip of the middle finger and then released. This technique is usually used very rhythmically and creates the effect of a drummer and a bassist playing at the same time. One of the first bassists to really develop this style of playing was Larry Graham who can be heard on recordings by the group, Sly and the Family Stone (available on CBS records). Alternate plucking of the strings with the middle and index fingers is yet another technique used to develop the bass sound. Many bass-players use this approach because it puts them in direct contact with the strings and how they respond to one another. Of course, one could play a string with both fingers simultaneously, but I feel that this does not really give a player any distinct advantage. It takes more energy and concentration to move two fingers when one finger can do the job. Below, I have given some examples of the many different styles of bass playing today.

Pop Music

This term refers to a style that has a light feeling with easy going bass patterns. It can also be played in a shuffle rhythm or just a straight $\frac{1}{8}$th note (quaver) rhythm (see Ex. 11.1).

Ex. 11.1

Rhythm 'n' Blues

This style of music has probably had the biggest influence on current popular music over the last twenty years. The electric bass had a very important part in establishing the feeling in this style of music which is also sometimes referred to as soul music and has a very rhythmic approach (see Ex. 11.2).

Ex. 11.2

Reggae

The bass is a very important part of this very spiritual music. Reggae music comes from Jamaica, and it has a very heavy feeling in the bass. The rests are just as important as the notes in this style of music and the bass guitar usually has a big, low sound and is very rhythmic and heavy in its approach (see Ex. 11.3).

Ex. 11.3

Soft Rock

This style is more rock sounding than pop music, but it still has a good swing feeling and a light approach. Many groups from California made this style popular (see Ex. 11.4).

Ex. 11.4

Jazz grew out of a 2-beat dixieland and ragtime style to go towards a 4-beat swing feeling. This style was very popular during the big band era in the 1940s and is still played by those musicians who are musically capable. The bassist must be adept at interpreting chord structures and playing sometimes at very fast tempos (see Ex. 11.5).

Ex. 11.5

Montuno

The montuno style comes from the latin community and has a very rhythmic approach. The bassist is expected to play off the beat (on the 'and' of the second beat) and still keep good time with the drummer. It is a very difficult style to play, but also very challenging (see Ex. 11.6).

Ex. 11.6

Rock 'n' Roll

This style came out of the music of the fifties and the bass parts usually have a very straight quaver feel, with many rhythmic variations. The shuffle-feel is also used a lot. There are many different types of rock 'n' roll playing (psychedelic, acid, heavy metal, etc.) (see Ex. 11.7).

Ex. 11.7

Gospel

This musical style originated from the male vocal parts sung during the slave trading era. The male with the lowest voice would sing the moving harmony parts. These parts were adapted into music being written for the church and later adapted for musical instruments. The bass parts are played with a lot of spirit (see Ex. 11.8).

Ex. 11.8

Usually, different styles of music call for a different type of technique to be applied, but there is no reason why any of these techniques cannot be used for any style of music. As long as the player learns to play with control, imagination, and a feeling for dynamics, any music can be enhanced by using different styles. It is always important to keep an open mind when music is involved. Because it is a language that communicates ideas from one person to another, it is important to be open to new and different ideas no matter how strange they may seem at first. It is this author's wish to have each player examine his or her playing and try to find new ways of discovering things about music that may have gone unnoticed before. Being a musician takes a lot of practice, patience, and good luck. There is also a lot to be said about the person who has accepted the responsibility that goes along with that profession. The bassist with the successful career is the one who knows how to be on time, who can contribute useful ideas, and maintain, as far as possible, a positive attitude and outlook. The ideas discussed in these pages are only a small (yet very important) part of what it takes to be a good musician and it is this author's wish that these ideas will inspire its readers to want to be creative in every step of their lives.

Below is a list of books and videos that I recommend as an approach to playing the bass. These books and cassettes will give the beginner, as well as the professional player, many years of satisfactory music. For the benefit of the UK reader, I have provided the address (in parentheses) of the most recent publisher.

Further Reading

Blazehvich, V. (1957). *Studies in Clefs for Trombone*, International Music Company, 511 Fifth Avenue, New York, NY.

Hindemith, P. (1949). *Elementary Training for Musicians*, Schott.

Kaye, C. (1969). *How to Play the Electric Bass*, Gwyn Publishing Company (PO Box 2030, North Hollywood, Calif. 91602).

Nanny, E. *Enseignment complet de la contrebasse* (1925). Henri Eklan, 1316 Walnut Street, Philadelphia, Pa 19107.

Shear, C. *The Improviser's Bass Method* (1979) Sher Music Company, (PO Box 15–489, San Francisco, Calif. 94115).

Simandl, F. *New Method for the Double Bass* (1964). Carl Fischer Inc. (62 Cooper Square, New York, NY).

Videos

Al Jarreau Live in London (with Nathan East) (Warner Brothers).

Joni Mitchell Live (with Jaco Pastorius) (Electra Records).

Star Licks Master Series with Louis Johnson (video, cassette and instruction booklet (Star Licks Videos).

12 Folk Guitar

Bert Jansch and Michael Stimpson

In some respects, folk music and the involvement of the guitar is one of the most difficult areas of music to define. It is a term that is somewhat ambiguous and varies in its meaning and relevance from country to country. In some, as in the United Kingdom, folk music implies both a traditional form of music that has been passed directly from one generation to another, and a more commercial style that is often performed by a singer/guitarist. It is distinguished from other styles of music by, for example, the nature of the ensemble, the form of the music, and even its social setting. In other countries, many of those in Africa for example, the term embraces almost all of the music that has been produced and hence has less significance as a distinguishing term. In 1955 the International Folk Music Council formulated the following definition and although this most certainly contains the essence of what folk music is, it now conflicts in part with a present-day understanding of western folk music.

> Folk music is a product of a musical tradition that has been evolved through the process of oral transmission. The factors that shape the tradition are: (i) continuity that links the present with the past; (ii) variation which springs from the creative inpulse of the individual or the group; and (iii) selection by the community which determines the form or forms in which the music survives.
>
> The term can be applied to music that has been evolved from rudimentary beginnings by a community uninfluenced by popular and art music; and it can likewise be applied to music which has originated with an individual composer and has subsequently been absorbed into the unwritten, living tradition of the community.
>
> The term does not cover composed popular music that has been taken over ready-made by a community and remains unchanged, for it is the re-fashioning and re-creation of the music by the community that gives it its folk character.[1]

Because this book is predominantly concerned with the representation of the guitar in schools and colleges of the United Kingdom, it is necessary here to take a somewhat looser, westernized, 1980s viewpoint of folk music. This should therefore reflect both the breadth and development that the style has undergone, particularly since World War II. The point has been made elsewhere in this book that the guitar is all-too often seen only as a simple means of accompanying a folk song; it is equally possible for the folk guitarist to argue that this area receives transient attention.

British folk songs, melodies, and dance-steps have been well documented, the process getting seriously under way towards the end of the nineteenth century and the beginning of the twentieth. Among the most famous collectors were Ralph Vaughan Williams and Cecil Sharp, and much of their work applied to folk song that had not only been orally transmitted but could not be traced to any specific composer. As the twentieth century progressed, popular songs in a folk idiom that were written by named songwriters became increasingly established. The advent and refinement of the gramophone and tape recorder, and in particular, amplification, played a vitally important role in hastening this process. These and other factors instigated a folk revival in the 1950s and 1960s, in America at the hands of Woody Guthrie, Pete Seeger, and Bob Dylan. There are many parallels that can be drawn between the stimulus for their work and that of the earlier blues-players (for example, Huddy Leadbetter (Leadbelly) and Elizabeth Cotton), and all brought about a far more diverse folk music, of the 'now' rather than of the 'then'. These changes, together with a sometimes close association with the world of pop music also gave rise to a highly productive period in Britain. The work of Martin Carthy, Dick Gaughan, Davy Graham, Bert Jansch, John Martyn, John Renbourn, and Martin Simpson amongst many others, has all been highly innovative. In addition, some folk groups, such as Pentangle and Fairport Convention, received considerable recognition. Meanwhile, more traditional folk musicians have found a vast array of venues and the concept of the folk club has become firmly established as a vital part of this musical style.

The guitar and accessory equipment

When choosing a guitar it will be necessary for the student to be absolutely clear in his or her mind on which style of music is to be pursued. If it is likely that at some time the potential player may wish to explore music other than folk, then it is advised that a classical guitar be purchased, i.e. with nylon strings. Even if interest lies solely with folk music, it may still be appropriate to use this type of guitar, either because of a preference for the sound or because the nylon strings are a little less painful for young fingers. In this section, however, it is the steel-string guitar that is to be considered.

As with some other types of guitar, a range of sizes of folk guitars is available. Half and three-quarter size guitars are made for children, but the need for the smaller size should of course be assessed carefully. The body shape tends to be based on, for example, a jumbo Gibson, Martin Dreadnought, or Martin 000, that is, a waisted, acoustic body with a central sound-hole. The different woods used are similar to those of other guitars, i.e. a body of rosewood, mahogany, or maple, with a spruce or cedar top, and a neck of mahogany and ebony. Less expensive woods are used (for example, the table may be made of plywood), although the sound is obviously affected and will not mature in the same way. The neck of the guitar will be narrower than the classical variety, both in width and depth. In addition, the length will be different, the folk guitar usually possessing fourteen frets to the point at which the neck meets the body of the guitar. A finger-plate is usually provided to protect the table of the guitar.

Some folk guitarists will wish to amplify their guitar, there being three methods of doing this. The first is to purchase a guitar with the pick-up built into the bridge, such as the Thinline model made by Barcus Berry. This pick-up, and the cheaper detachable 'bugs', are transducers, i.e. they pick up the vibrations of the wood and convert this into an electronic signal. Amplification may also be achieved by using either a magnetic pick-up (which responds to the steel strings) or the C-ducer, a small microphone that is built into a tape that may be fixed just below the bridge. (It is worth noting that a magnetic pick-up is less effective with bronze strings, as opposed to nickel. Bronze strings, however, produce a brighter acoustic sound.) All must be connected to an amplifier and sometimes a pre-amp.

Two other types of guitar deserve attention, the National and the Dobro. Both guitars, which are steel strung, have a resonator—a metal disc that is normally set at the position of the sound-hole. The two guitars differ by the shape of the resonator (concave or convex) and the body construction; the National is all-metal, the Dobro is made of wood. These features give a very bright, loud, almost banjo-like sound to the National guitar, whereas the Dobro gives a more mellow tone. Thus the former has often been used for blues-playing (that straight southern character), the latter is associated with the country and bluegrass field. The Dobro was designed to be played on the lap (lap-steel), having a very high action and requiring a solid, bullet-steel slide. The reader is referred to the playing of Josh Graves and Mike Aldrich; for National guitar-playing, Sammy Mitchell.

Steel strings are available in two forms, wound and unwound. It is usual to have a wound sixth, fifth, fourth, and third string and an unwound second and first. For the player who wishes to bend notes on the third string, as in the blues, an unwound third string is preferable. These strings, like those for an electric guitar, have different gauges (thicknesses) and are generally classified as medium gauge, light, or extra light. Within each classification the gauge varies for each string, examples of which are as follows:

String		*Gauge (thou)*	
	Medium	Light	Extra Light
first	13	12	10
second	17	16	13
third	26	24	20
fourth	36	32	26
fifth	46	42	36
sixth	56	52	46

When fixing to the guitar, the ball-end of the string should be placed at the bridge-end and secured with bridge pins. The strings should be wiped after playing to remove any perspiration and help preserve the quality. In addition, the upper strings may be cleaned with white spirit and the lower, wound strings may be snapped against the finger-board to dislodge any dirt that may have collected. As with any other type of guitar string, their life is finite and spare strings should always be available.

There are many general points that could be made about the purchasing of a folk guitar and for these the reader is referred to Appendix IV. Prices of folk guitars obviously vary considerably, but as a guide it is recommended that at least £100·00 be spent if possible. This would provide a basic model such as those made by Yamaha, Takamine, Washburn, or Sigma. There are many specialist makers such as Robert Armstrong, David Bourne, Andrew and Hugh Manson, Tom Mates, and Fylde. The price of guitars from these and other makers is upwards of £375·00.

A capo is a device that fits on the neck of the guitar across the finger-board and alters the pitch of the strings according to the position at which it is placed. The two main functions are to alter the pitch of the strings to that suitable for higher-pitched voices and/or allow a player to use 'basic' chord shapes in higher positions, thus avoiding the need for a barré. An example of this is as follows: the E major chord indicated in first position gives a chord of G major when played above a capo placed at the third fret, and a chord of A major when placed above a capo at the fifth fret (see Fig. 12.1).

Fig. 12.1

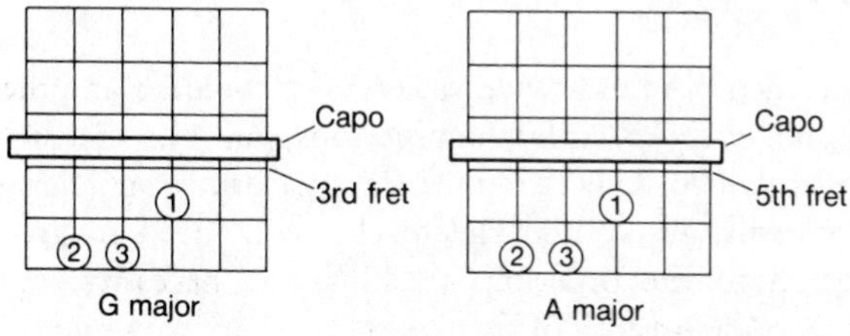

Capos can be made of quite different materials that range from chrome-plated brass to just elastic. The resulting variations in their weight and size are an important consideration for the player, and in addition it should be checked that there are no parts of the capo that will scratch and damage the neck when it is fitted or adjusted. It should also be noted that the fitting of a capo does affect the tuning and some adjustment will be necessary each time it is used or removed. Prices vary from approximately £2·00 (for example, the capos made by Dunlop or Gibson) to £12·00 (Shubb).

Slide-guitar (Bottleneck) is that characteristic sound reminiscent of a Hawaiian guitar. It is achieved by slipping a finger through a tube of glass or metal and sliding this along the strings as they are sounded. This way of playing was seen by sailors visiting Hawaii and brought back to the United States where slaves adopted the crying-like qualities of the effect. It was literally the broken top of a bottle that was used (after drinking the contents!), although a knife or even a cigarette lighter can be used when the guitar is rested horizontally on the lap as the instrument is in Hawaii. A heavy-gauge string is used to give greater sustain and a high action is necessary to avoid the bottleneck rubbing against the frets. The exact height of the strings above the finger-board is more important when some individual fingering is to be done; if the guitar is to be used solely for sliding, the action is less important. This applies to the Hawaiian guitar which has no frets and the strings may be an inch above the finger-board. It is most usual for slide-guitar players to use an open tuning, a subject that will be dealt with in more detail at the end of this chapter. A manufactured bottleneck of glass or metal costs in order of £3·00. Glass is generally more suitable for the acoustic sound; metal bottlenecks do vary in thickness and weight, the heavier tube (for example, brass) giving more sustain.

Technique

Folk guitar incorporates a wide variety of techniques and the playing of strums, finger-styles, scales, hammer-ons, pull-offs, etc. are all skills that a player will be likely to require. Many features are relevant to the learning of folk guitar and the teacher will need to give careful consideration to the ordering of skills, the necessity, or not, of exercises, and the breadth of the repertoire. The strumming of chords does, however, deserve special mention because for many folk guitarists and/or singers, it will form a major part of right-hand technique. Essentially there is a choice of sounding the strings with the thumb, finger or fingers, or a pick. Relevant to this choice is the nature of the accompaniment (whether the chord is broken or not), the volume required, and whether the beat necessitates an up or down stroke. Some work on either open strings or a single chord will be appropriate, as will the gradual development of more complex rhythms. For the playing of single strings folk guitarists use either thumb, fingers, or pick(s), or any combination. Finger-nails may be as important to the folk player as, for example, to the classical guitarist (particularly if nylon strings are used), and, as with this style, different guitarists use different parts of the nail and/or finger-tip to achieve the tone that they wish. The quality of note that is almost solely confined to folk style is the snapping sound that is produced by lifting the string a little as the finger passes across it.

There are many parallels to be drawn between the right-hand fingering of folk and classical guitar, and the general rule of the thumb looking after the bass notes and the fingers the upper strings, still applies. It is not uncommon for a player to use a thumb-pick, that is, the type of pick, usually made of plastic, which fits over the thumb. This not only counteracts the problem of a broken nail, but also enables the player to achieve slightly heavier bass notes easily. This contrasts with the lighter style of, for example, Ralph McTell, and also facilitates the flatter wrist of folk guitarists. This position brings the heel of the thumb closer to the strings and thus provides an effective means of damping the sound and tightening a chordal accompaniment. As will be seen later in this chapter, a common form of accompaniment is to pick out notes of a chord with the thumb or insert fragments of a melody in the bass. The thumb pick therefore serves to pronounce this a little more. Picks that fit over the fingers are used by the country 'n' western players, blues players, and other folk guitarists. They are generally made of metal and give a clearer, louder sound than that produced by the finger-nail or finger-tip. A pick that is held rather than fitted over the fingers or thumb varies in both shape and hardness. It is usually held between the index finger and thumb and thus leaves the remaining fingers free (except the little finger which is not normally used) to play the upper strings, if necessary. Occasionally the pick is 'stored' between the middle and ring fingers of this hand, thus leaving the thumb and index finger free. Clearly, however, with flat-pick players it is the pick that predominates, and a mixture of up and down strokes are used for single notes, chords, and cross-picking (the playing of notes on non-adjacent strings). The reader is referred to the flat-pick playing of, for example, Doc Watson, Jimmy McGregor, Mark O'Connor, Dan Crary, Tony Rice, and Norman Blake for expert illustration of the art.

For slide-guitar playing with a hollow slide, the little finger of the left hand is commonly used, i.e. the slide is fitted on the little finger. This tends to allow for more varied fingerings with the remaining fingers, although some players do use the middle or ring fingers to fix the slide. When playing a Dobro, lap-style with a solid 'bullet', the index finger must be straight enough to fix it underneath, the middle finger being used to help balance it. The slide should be placed over the fret to avoid a departure from the true pitch (the sharpening or flattening of the sound is however sometimes deliberately used by blues players). For vibrato in this style (slide), it is important to give the note a moment at its pitch before moving the left-hand finger. As with other styles of folk guitar, a flat pick (with or without the fingers) may be used to sound the strings, or finger-picks. The latter will give a stronger sound, particularly when a bass syncopation is required.

Repertoire

Folk guitar accompaniments are often very repetitive due to the repeated use of a melody and the verse form of most songs. For the accompaniments it is common for the student to turn initially to the chord shapes found in first position. Aspects of this subject have been discussed in other chapters and the reader is referred to Chapters 3 and 6. A series of chord diagrams is to be found in Appendix III. It should, however, be noted that in school, in-service course, and college of education, the term 'classroom song' is often synonymous with 'folk song'. The following discussion will often therefore encounter the difficulty of definition referred to in the introduction, and for practical reasons may lie closer to the former term. References are given in parentheses, primarily to provide a source for the words and chords. However, many of the songs will be found in other publications.

For the beginner, it is appropriate to choose from the small selection of songs which only require an accompaniment of one chord, strummed in an even rhythm. The Canadian folk song *Land of the Silver Birch* (*Flying Around*, A. and C. Black) is one example, a D minor chord or E minor chord being a suitable harmony for the whole piece, strummed for the moment with down-strokes only. (Note, for a full D minor chord the sixth string may be tuned to D.) *Frère Jacques* (*Seventy Songs with Ostinati*, Albert Chatterley, Novello), is one example of a song which requires just one major chord for the accompaniment. Although not strictly a folk-guitar publication this source gives useful ostinati, the rhythms of which may be used for the chord accompaniment. Other one-chord songs include *Freedom Train*, *Mr Rabbit*, *Shalom*, and *Old Abram Brown* (the latter by Benjamin Britten), all of which may be found in *Flying Around* (A. and C. Black).

There are a considerable number of songs for which two chords will be sufficient, still for the moment played with a single downward strum. *Hush Little Baby* (*124 Folk Songs*, ed. Moses Asch, EMI) is one example, shown below (Ex. 12.1) in the key of E major.*

Further songs that can be played with the same accompaniment (but not necessarily the same two chords) are *Tom Dooley, Pick a Bale of Cotton, Gypsy Davy* (*124 Folk Songs*, ed. Moses Asch, EMI) and *Mango Walk* (*Ta-ra-ra Boom-de-ay*, A. and C. Black). Also suitable for young children are the songs *What shall we do with the Drunken Sailor?* and *Zum Gali Gali* (*Flying Around*, A. and C. Black) and *Going to the Zoo* (*Ramblin' Boy and other songs*, Tom Paxton, Oak Publications).

*The publications are intended as a source only. The chordal accompaniments are the authors own suggestion (Ed.).

Ex. 12.1

Going to the Zoo is the first example in this section of a song that requires three chords for its accompaniment (for example E major, A major, and B7, or D major, G major, and A7). Also by Tom Paxton is *The Last Thing on my Mind*: other songs at this level of difficulty (three chords) are *Blowing in the Wind, Michael Row the Boat Ashore, This Land is Your Land*, and *Colours* (*The Complete Guitar Player Songbook*, Russ Shipton, Wise Publications), and *This Train* (*124 Folk Songs*, ed. Moses Asch, EMI).

Up to this point some distinction has been made between the relative difficulty of chords in first position, and assuming that the pitch of the singer(s) allows, chords such as F major have been avoided. However, the building up of a repertoire of songs with the easier changes will eventually allow the player to take on more difficult sequences. One suggested here is A major, E major, D major, and F major which will be suitable for *Bottle of Wine* (*Ramblin' Boy and other songs*, Tom Paxton, Oak Publications). Other sequences of four chords will permit the accompaniment of *Mr Tambourine Man* (*Bob Dylan's Greatest Hits*, Warner Brothers). A longer sequence will be appropriate for another Dylan song from the same publication, *The Times They Are A-Changing* and one by Pete Seeger, *Where Have All the Flowers Gone?* (Harmony Music).

The songs have, up to now, been presented as playable with simply a downward strum of either the thumb, index finger, more than one finger in a light brush stroke, or with a pick. The different tones that these give invite some combination of action, thus enabling the player to vary the emphasis of the strum. It would, of course, be well before the above repertoire had been completely considered that the player would wish to introduce a faster accompaniment. The first to be suggested here is a combination of the thumb and fingers and the incorporation of an upstroke in the strum as shown in Ex. 12.2. This

Ex. 12.2

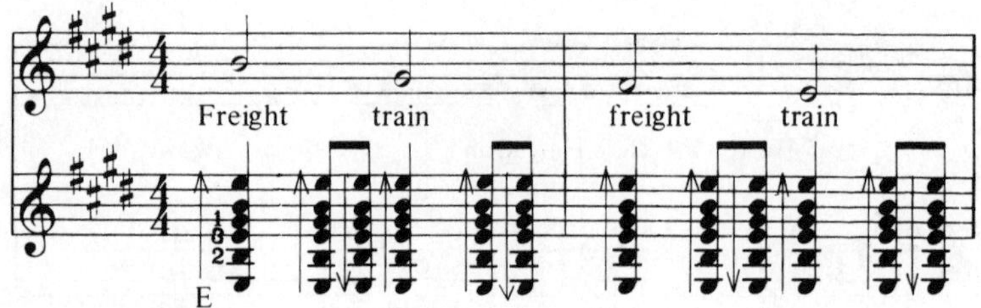

would be suitable for a song such as *O Sinner Man* (*Flying Around*, A. and C. Black) and *Freight Train* (*The Complete Guitar Player Songbook*, Russ Shipton, Wise Publications). Alteration to a dotted rhythm provides an accompaniment that would be suitable for a song such as *I'd Like to Teach the World to Sing* (*Apusskidu*, A. and C. Black).

Tambour, a technique which involves the striking of the strings and the bridge (see Chapter 9) may also be used to give a softer, more percussive accompaniment. This type of accompaniment would be appropriate for *Kum-Ba-Ya* (arr. Frank Walsh, F. & R. Walsh). A chordal accompaniment will soon, of course, require further variation, and one of the most straightforward is to sound the root of the chord with the thumb on the first and third beats of a bar, in common time. One or more of the right-hand fingers may then be used to play the remaining notes of the chord as indicated in Ex. 12.3.

Ex. 12.3

The strum in this accompaniment can easily be doubled via an upstroke with one of the fingers; this and other variations are shown in Ex. 12.4, including accompaniments in triple time, the use of bass notes other than the root, and the linking of two chords by a short, bass run.

Ex. 12.4

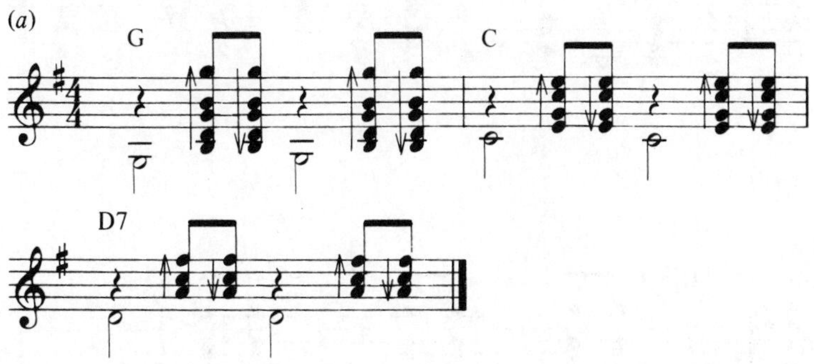

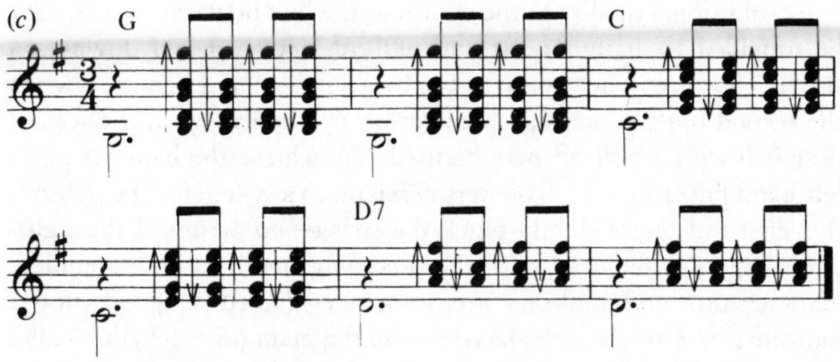

An additional quality to the chord, or the link between chords, may be provided by hammer-ons and pull-offs (upward and downward slurs). They are indicated on music by a small curved line (◡); when the second note is higher, a hammer-on will apply; when the second note is lower, a pull-off may be used. To achieve the hammer-on, a left-hand finger literally hammers down on to a string; for the pull-off, the left-hand finger should pluck the string—no action of the right-hand fingers is required once the preceding note has been sounded. Hammer-ons and pull-offs are sometimes linked to grace notes, indicated by a small note placed before the main note. Rhythmically, they may be very short (indicated ♪◡♩) or take half the value of the note that is 'graced' (indicated ♪◡♩) (see Ex. 12.5).

Ex. 12.5

(*a*)

G

C

D7

(*b*)

The emphasis of the discussion so far has been placed on the strummed chord but in many cases it will be more musically appropriate to pluck the notes of a chord with the fingers. This not only provides a different texture to the accompaniment but, in some respects, allows for easier use of the thumb because the position of the hand is not displaced by the strum. This more mobile accompaniment is given in Ex. 12.6, although songs such as *Little Boxes* (Tro Essex Music) and *Morning has Broken* (*Cat Stevens Easy Guitar*, Freshwater Music) will be acceptable with a more static waltz accompaniment. For this, the thumb plays the root of the chord on the main beat of each bar and the remaining harmony notes are plucked with the fingers. (Ex. 12.6a)

Another option that is open to the singer/accompanist is the finger-style or pick; that is, the breaking up of the chord shapes into single notes. For this, a right-hand movement that involves the thumb and some of the fingers, is used. The exact combination will depend on the time-signature of the song, the texture and tempo of the piece, and the extent to which the melody is to be reflected in the accompaniment. An evenly played pick for the thumb, index, middle, and ring fingers is a suitable starting-point. When applied to the chords of A major, D major, G major, E minor, and F♯ minor, this pick gives an appropriate accompaniment to a song such as *Scarborough Fair* (*Simon and Garfunkel's Greatest Hits*, Music Sales) (see Ex. 12.7). The dotting of

Ex. 12.7

the rhythm of this movement gives the well-known backing to the song, *The House of the Rising Sun* (*The Complete Guitar Player Songbook*, Russ Shipton, Wise Publications). Example 12.8 shows the

Ex. 12.8

pick with different bass harmony notes, giving an accompaniment that may be used for Ralph McTell's song, *The Streets of London* (Essex Music) and *Bright Eyes* (Mike Batt, April Music). There are many other variations. For a slightly heavier bass the thumb can be used to sound more than one string at a time. The combination of the fingers, for example the middle and ring, gives a clearer top (Ex. 12.9): this can be used for the aforementioned *Mango Walk* and *The Wreck of the John B* (*The Jolly Herring*, A. and C. Black), and *Yellow Bird* (Marilyn Keith, Alan Bergman, Norman Luboff, Chappell).

For the incorporation of melody into an accompaniment, some mention of clawhammer technique is warranted. For this, the thumb is used to play on each of the main beats of the bar, alternating between the root and fifth of a chord or perhaps the root and third. The melody or remainder of the harmony is played by the fingers. The technique can be used in most keys in first position with relative ease, and when linked with the hammer-ons and pull-offs referred to earlier it provides

Ex. 12.9

a considerable number of combinations. A short example is provided in Ex. 12.10 and this type of accompaniment will be suitable for songs such as *Homeward Bound* (*Simon and Garfunkel's Greatest Hits*, Music Sales), and *Moonshadow* (*Cat Stevens Easy Guitar*, Freshwater Music).

Ex. 12.10

For some relatively easy examples of blues, and a clear and informative discussion, the reader is referred to *Masters of Instrumental Blues Guitar* (Donald Garwood, Oak Publications). Subjects covered include melodic structure, blues progressions, rhythmic units, and instrumental breaks. The same publisher may be considered for *The Country Blues Guitar* and *Delta Blues Guitar* (by Stefan Grossman), and *Robert Johnson* (by Samuel Charters). *Beginning Blues Piano* (Eric Kriss, Acorn Music, Music Sales) contains plenty of relatively easy pieces and because each one contains chord diagrams this may also be considered by anyone looking for basic instrumental ensemble.

Among the most popular pieces of solo folk guitar has been *Anji* (Davy Graham, Young Music). Two well-set-out publications, *The Irish Collection, Volumes 1 and 2* (John Loesberg, Ossian) may also be considered, as should *Guitar Pieces* (John Renbourn, Oak Publications) and *The Songs and Guitar Solos of Bert Jansch* (New Punchbowl Music/Cramer Music).

Tunings

It is relatively common when playing folk guitar to use tunings that vary from the normal E, A, D, G, B, E. These adjustments range from the straightforward to the obscure; in the former category lies the adjustment of the fifth and fourth strings so that the open strings form an E minor chord (Ex. 12.11*a*). This will, for example, allow a melody to be played on the upper string(s) while using the remaining strings as a drone. The further adjustment of the third string can alter this tuning to an E major chord (Ex. 12.11*b*). This was favoured by delta-blues players (for example, Elmore James) although many singers prefer to lower this tuning by a tone to form a chord of D major (Ex. 12.11*c*). The basic Hawaiian tuning widely used by slide-guitarists forms an A major chord (Ex. 12.11*d*). As with the E tuning, some players prefer to lower each string by a tone to form a G major chord (Ex. 12.11*e*) because this gives a deeper tone than the more ringing A tuning. In addition, with the A tuning, if a heavy gauge string is used, the third string is more liable to break. Thus, many blues players use the G tuning and any performer will prefer to use more than one guitar to reduce the difficulties of re-tuning accurately. The extra tension that the Dobro guitar can withstand allows the tuning shown in Ex. 12.11*f*. A somewhat less usual tuning is also shown below (Ex. 12.11g) with an accompaniment (Ex. 12.11*h*). For a more complete account of the subject and pieces which use different tunings, the reader is referred to *The Book of Guitar Tunings* (Stefan Grossman, Amsco). Finally, it should be stressed that care should be taken with re-tuning because some instruments do not cope well with raising the pitch and strings may break.

Outside the category of repertoire but worthy of reference because of its considerable information, is *The Folk Directory* that is published by The English Folk Dance and Song Society. This book, published

Ex. 12.11

(*a*)

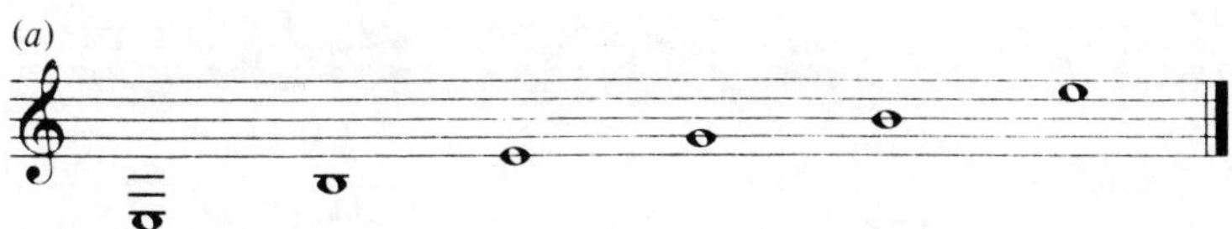

(*b*)

(*c*)

(*d*)

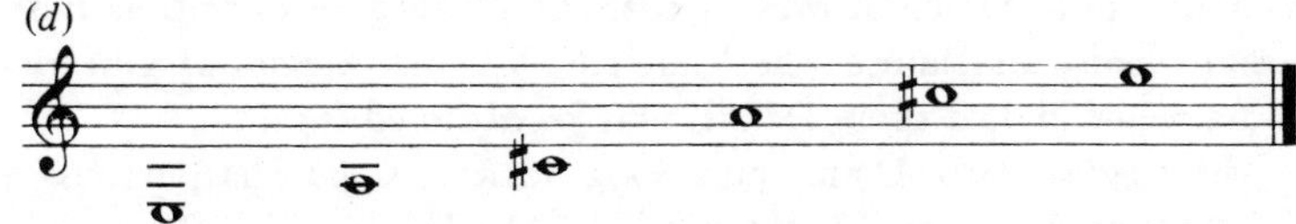

(*e*)

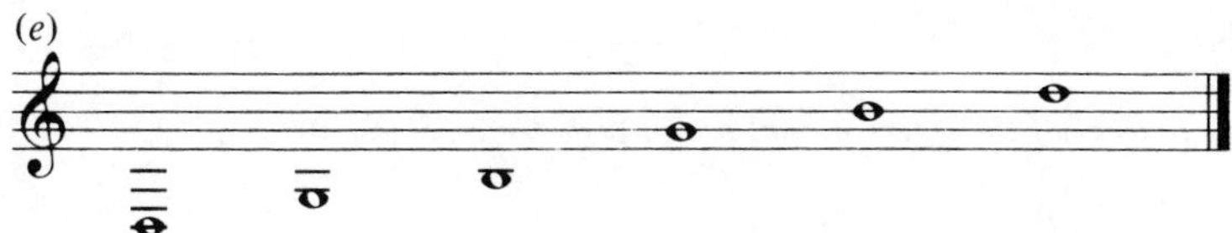

(*f*)

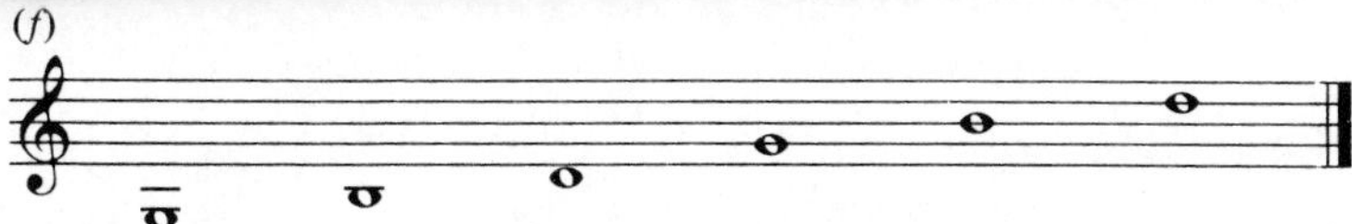

(*g*)

each year, contains details of, for example, archives, libraries, museums, clubs, bands, conferences, and agents. The society itself, membership of which at present costs £13·25, organizes tuition and social events, and houses the Vaughan Williams Memorial Library and a well-supplied shop. Details may be obtained from:

The English Folk Dance and Song Society, Cecil Sharp House, 2 Regents Park Road, London NW1 7AY; Tel. 01-485 2206.

Note

1. *Journal of the International Folk Music Council*, vii (1955), p. 23.

13 Flamenco Guitar

Paco Peña

BY virtue of its strong dynamic character, flamenco has long been a popular form of singing, dancing, and guitar-playing, which like bullfighting, has become a symbol of Spanish culture. Yet its origins lie completely in just one region of Spain—Andalucía—in the south.

Some of the fascination for the guitar in flamenco over the past few decades undoubtedly stems from the popularity of the classical guitar, which has attracted the attention of many music-lovers to all forms of guitar-playing. In flamenco, they find a unique musical experience in which the 'western' characteristics of the guitar provide an accompaniment to the stranger, exotic sounds that exist in the music, particularly in the flamenco song. Such a combination of 'east' and 'west' is hardly surprising given Andalucia's heritage as a melting-pot of many different cultures from Europe and the Mediterranean. The result, musically, has now crystallized in what we know as present-day flamenco.

The guitar is the only instrument used in flamenco, and rightly so since it is able to combine percussive, rhythmic elements with a softer, lyrical line essential to the performance of this music. Thus, the appeal of the flamenco guitar is widespread, and there are a great many *aficionados* from every nationality keenly involved in the art of playing flamenco. Because flamenco guitar is part of the musical heritage of a specific geographical region of Spain and its people, it is very important that anyone wanting to know and master the art of flamenco guitar becomes familiar with its history and development. Nevertheless, a degree of caution must be exercised in trying to describe flamenco guitar, because otherwise one can end up giving a distorted picture.

Flamenco is a culture with its own philosophy and life-style. Music is the main mode of expression of that culture and the guitar plays a very important part in the production of that music. Yet this music emerges in history, not as a form of guitar-playing, but as a particular form of singing—*Cante Flamenco*. Although the guitar played a major part in the music's development, it was the singers throughout flamenco's history that were considered the main exponents of the art. Indeed, it was by their innovative contributions that the development of flamenco was measured. In fact, when describing the music, the word flamenco used on its own actually represents nothing other than the singing. Therefore, the singing can be described as *Flamenco, Cante Flamenco*, or even just *Cante*. The Spanish word for singing is *canto* or *canción*; *cante* specifically refers to flamenco singing. Despite the overriding importance of the *cante*, flamenco would be inconceivable without the guitar in accompaniment. In effect, the guitar does not merely accompany the singer, but forms an integral part of the song; singer and guitarist are one in creating the *cante*. No other instrument has the inherent capacity to parallel the harsh, Oriental-like cadences of the flamenco singer while simultaneously providing a strong staccato drive to the rhythm. Fernando Quiñones, an authority on the subject, sees the guitar as 'the canvas on which the *cantaor* gradually sketches out the lines and colours of his *cante*'.

On the other hand, flamenco's recent history has seen a new dimension come into being with solo guitar-playing. This is, in many respects, a departure from the old tradition of accompanying the singer, and it has brought significant changes in terms of technical facility on the guitar for both solo and accompaniment playing. Furthermore, being a largely novel art form, it has reached a new section of the public, making flamenco more popular than at any time in the past.

History

Flamenco guitar's history differs from that of the classical guitar in that the latter's past is well documented in a multitude of writings that go back many centuries. Musicians wrote down their ideas and even treatises on how to play. In contrast, flamenco is an oral art handed down from one generation to the next; no written records exist to enlighten us as to its origins. This is, of course, true of folk and rock or electric guitar as well. However, with electric guitar we have a very clear idea of its history because it has all happened in our own time and in the time of recorded sounds. Nor is flamenco the folk music of Andalucía in a general sense. It is a musical phenomenon that results from the mixture of many different elements and circumstances against a background of very particular social conditions.

Flamenco, as a distinct type of music, emerged in the eighteenth century. Nevertheless, Andalucía has had a strong musical tradition from ancient times and it would be naïve to dissociate flamenco from that heritage. Ricardo Molina, a well-respected writer on the subject, asserts that 'the substratum of the *cante* is so profound that it intermingles with the native Andalucían disposition for singing and dancing', and reminds us that Andalucía has been called 'the eternal singing land'. Indeed, Molina captures the notion of flamenco's ancient links, despite its relatively recent history, by comparing it to 'certain desert plants that produce an intense flower just above the soil, but whose roots penetrate mysterious geological depths'.

During the time of the Roman Empire, the people of Betica (Andalucía) became renowned for their songs and dances which they came to perform in the capital city of Rome itself. One thousand years later, during the Western Caliphate, when Córdoba was the flourishing centre of Islamic art and where poetry, architecture, philosophy, and music reached an apogee of achievement in the Islamic mode, it would seem from the evidence that the indigenous music of Andalucía held its own. None the less, the music heard by either the Roman or the Arab conquerors was by no means flamenco as we know it. Throughout the centuries, Andalucía has come to absorb peoples of very different cultures and backgrounds, and has integrated elements of their music into the indigenous prevailing music.

The culmination of that influx, and a vital ingredient for the creation of flamenco, was the arrival of tribes of nomadic gypsies who, after wandering for several centuries, came to Spain and Andalucía during the fifteenth century. In Andalucía, it seems that the gypsies found something in the music that they did not find elsewhere in their migration throughout North Africa, Spain, and the rest of Europe, and which undoubtedly stirred the very fibres of their own Oriental ancestry. It is often stated that flamenco is gypsy music. However, flamenco is not ethnic music but a phenomenon of geography and culture. As far as I know, there is no such thing as a separate gypsy music culture anywhere else in the world that remotely resembles flamenco. When the gypsies arrived in Spain, the country was in great turmoil. The last Moorish stronghold, Granada, fell to the Christian forces of Isabel and Fernando in 1492. Soon afterwards there followed the expulsion from Spain of both Arabs and Jews. Undoubtedly, many Jews and Moors stayed behind (hardly surprising as they were Andalucíans for many generations past), fleeing into the hills with other rebellious Andalucíans who were dispossessed of their land by the conquering northerners. All minorities, not least the gypsies, suffered discrimination.

The gypsies found the land saturated with seeds from Oriental cultures. They, in turn, contributed not with a culture of their own, but 'an ability to interpret, the gift of innate musicianship, an inclination to dramatize art and a vital life style that echoes the traditional Andalucían way of life'. So the gypsies became the vehicle through which all the cultural elements dispersed in the countryside were crystallized into a new form of expression. This emerged in the gypsy home and against a background of social misery—akin in many respects to the later origins of the blues in the deep south of the United States.

Today, the guitar is such an integral component of flamenco that it is hard to imagine the *cante* without it. Yet, flamenco historians have not found any evidence to date that the guitar was used initially to accompany flamenco singing. Even now, some of the most dramatic forms of *cante* (for example, *Carceleras* and *Martinetes*) are invariably performed *a palo seco*—totally unaccompanied. But by the late nineteenth century, guitar accompaniment for flamenco was an established fact. And it is hardly surprising that the guitar should, more than any other instrument, take on that role, as it was widely played in Andalucía throughout all that early period in the history of flamenco, and certainly was being used as accompaniment for the traditional songs and dances of southern Spain. This is well exemplified in paintings of such artists as the eighteeenth-century French painter, Watteau. When it became the close partner of the flamenco singer, the guitar helped the primitive flamenco song take a more organized form. The embryonic melodies of the lone singer were pointed in the right direction by the harmony of the guitar, and the instrument's rhythmic possibilities helped to decide the rhythmical structure of the songs and dances—the *compás*.

Around 1860, flamenco came out of its original secluded environment and started to be performed in public. Special places opened up called *Cafés Cantantes*, dedicated exclusively to the performance of flamenco. Initially, the guitar was used to do little more than to accompany the song and dance rhythmically, but soon, public exposure and the spectacle on the raised stage of such places, led to guitarists striving to achieve a wealth of expression and technical facility. This culminated in today's virtuosi.

The guitar

The flamenco guitar is basically the same instrument as the Spanish classical guitar. However, they belong to different traditions (at least in the last few centuries) and play very different kinds of music, each with its characteristic range of sounds. A somewhat different approach is therefore followed in their construction. With the classical instrument, the general aim is to achieve a rich, full-bodied tone, a wide variety of musical colours, and long sustained sound. The flamenco guitar is made to produce a sharp, percussive sound suitable for the original role of the instrument, i.e. providing a strong rhythmic accompaniment to the dance, and echoing the peculiar textures of the flamenco voice. Its sound, unlike that of the classical guitar, must die fairly quickly as there are often many notes played simultaneously (*rasgueados* etc.) and the sustaining of all those notes at once would not be desirable in the character of flamenco music.

The front or top of the guitar (the most important part as it is that which vibrates in sympathy with the strings) is traditionally made of pine or cedar in both flamenco and classical instruments. However, the back and sides are different. In a flamenco guitar, cypress (a light wood in colour and weight) is used for those parts of the guitar, producing a bright, sunny kind of sound. Classical instruments use a hard wood (almost invariably rosewood).

That two different types of Spanish guitar should exist is a curious phenomenon, for there is no evidence to suggest that anything other than one type was used in the past for all forms of guitar music. The guitar has an exceedingly long history in Spain, having probably been brought there by the Romans who themselves derived that kind of instrument from the Greeks. Throughout the Middle Ages, and even after 800 years of Moorish domination (and lute music), the guitar remained the instrument of choice (in both cultured and popular circles). Thus, Spanish composers such as Milan and Mudarra wrote for the vihuela de mano, the progenitor of the modern guitar. Meanwhile, the same instrument was being used at the more popular level, Spaniards generally finding it best suited for the accompaniment of their traditional songs and dances. Given this history, it would appear then that the sound of the flamenco guitar is probably closer to the sound of the guitar a century or so back. However, since then, greater demands have been placed upon classical guitarists who have to perform in large halls and are expected to produce considerable volume despite small movements of the fingers. Moreover, they must assert the distinct character of the music they are playing. Consequently, guitar-makers have striven to make an ever more sonorous instrument that can preserve the beauty of sound and intimate nature of guitar music. In the meantime, flamenco guitars, by not requiring such a sonorous quality, have basically retained the original character of the sound and remain in essence unchanged. José Romanillos, the renowned guitar-maker, has carried out much research on the subject and helped me to arrive at the above conclusions. According to him, in the past, guitars were all the same in construction and in the types of wood used. He argues that cypress is a local tree in Andalucía whereas rosewood would have to be imported from either the Far East or South America. It would then seem natural that the readily available materials should be used in making such a popular instrument rather than imported ones.

Apart from the woods used, some constructional features distinguish flamenco guitars from classical; the flamenco guitar is, for example, usually a little shallower in depth of body. The action is lower, i.e. the strings are closer to the frets. Thus, apart from producing a different sound to the classical guitar, this facilitates the playing of *ligados*, *rasgueados*, and other aspects of technique that are distinctly flamenco. Flamenco rhythms very often require sharp accentuations of given beats; this is achieved by tapping the front of the guitar near the bridge, below the first string, with one, two, or three fingers. In order to protect the wood from being damaged, a plastic tapping plate (*golpeador*) is glued on the appropriate place of all flamenco guitars. The strings used in either classical or flamenco are the same; plain nylon for the first three strings and metal-wound nylon for the three basses. Mechanical tuning pegs are used in classical guitars. In flamenco guitars, the traditional wooden pegs continue to be used by some makers.

Technique

The technique for flamenco and classical guitar is very similar. Indeed, today there is considerable interchange of technique and many classical compositions utilize some of the characteristics of flamenco guitar; it is also common for flamenco guitarists to take classical studies in order to improve their technique. However, flamenco music is learned orally, with the result that particular aspects of technique follow a natural selection process dictated by the requirements of the music. Thus, while many classical guitarists (sadly, not all) have put their ideas down, making them available to all, flamenco is a more closed circle and guitarists have worked in isolation.

One important difference between the two is shown by the playing position. No footstool is used by the flamenco guitarists, and the lower bout of the guitar is rested on the top of the right thigh. The position (angle) at which the guitar is held is less rigid than for a classical guitarist, and this undoubtedly reflects the history and character of the music. The exact position depends on the size of the player, and in any case it is not fixed during the performance of a piece. This position must be flexible enough to allow for the freedom of movement of both hands, and this can be somewhat awkward for a beginner. Support of the guitar is mainly from the upper part of the right arm, although by virtue of the fact that notes are always being fingered by the left hand, the pressure of the thumb and the fingers does play a role in holding the guitar. There is far more space between the guitar and the body of the player (the upper bout of the guitar is not held against the chest), and this, too, adds to the flexibility and freedom of position.

The technical demands on, and the requirements of, a flamenco guitarist's left hand are the same as that for a classical guitarist (and others). The right hand is also basically the same, but with subtle differences. Right-hand fingers play at right angles to the strings and move from the knuckle; they draw an arc during their movement and find the string 'on the way'. Some flexibility does exist in the joint nearest the tip of the finger, although the control is not completely released and all the pressure is not abandoned. This type of action is used for all plucking techniques—arpeggios, tremolo, and plucked chords, etc. Runs (scales) too, except that the arc mentioned earlier is stopped when the finger hits the string, as the string is always played using rest stroke.

Runs are commonly played strongly, with a pronounced attack. They should be regarded as musical ideas, as important to the melodic line as any other single-note line. But when played in the flamenco way, runs often burst out aggressively, like an explosive force in which the player almost seems to fight the guitar.

Tremolo is yet another technique that arises in both flamenco and classical guitar, and the reader is referred to discussion of this and other techniques in Chapter 9 of this book. However, the tremolo used in flamenco music contains an extra note, played by the index finger (see Ex. 13.1).

Ex. 13.1

One important function of the fingers in flamenco is to play outwards. For this, the finger sounds the string during a movement away from the hand; this action is, however, only used during *rasgueados* and is not used for sounding single notes. *Rasgueados* are a form of strumming which provide flamenco with much of its characteristic sound. The simplest form of *rasgueado* uses all the fingers, striking the strings with each finger in turn, beginning with the little finger (marked x). Before the little finger has completed its action, the ring finger (a) commences the same movement, followed by the middle finger (m) and finally the index finger (i). The action is not a sudden shooting-out of each finger separately, but a continuous sliding of the fingers (using the outside of the nails) across the broad area of the strings. The basic hand position should be maintained, i.e. the hand itself should not move unduly. The thumb is rested lightly on an unused bass string, thus providing an anchor and preventing the accidental sounding of unwanted notes. All these features should provide a percussive, rhythmical sound (see Ex. 13.2). Observe that all the notes fit into the time of one beat and form one basic *rasgueado*.

Ex. 13.2

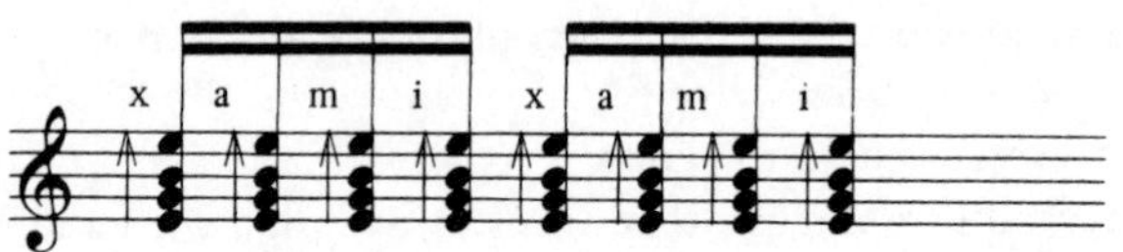

In order to finish a continuous sequence of *rasgueados* of this kind on a beat, it is necessary to adjust the speed of the *rasgueados* slightly so that the final stroke (with i) falls on the beat (see Ex. 13.3). There are a number of ways in which *rasgueados* may be adapted to achieve specific rhythmic effects. For example, a more rhythmic variation of the basic *rasgueado* involves the incorporation of a backstroke played with the index finger, as shown in Ex. 13.4. Note that all five notes fit into the time of one beat or one basic *rasgueado*.

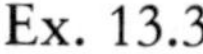
Ex. 13.3

Ex. 13.4

Another alternative is to add an extra forward stroke (played with i) at the very beginning, thus creating a group of six notes (see Ex. 13.5). This variation is used to make the beginning of the *rasgueado* more forceful. *Rasgueados* may also be used for the embellishment of a chord as in Ex. 13.6. In these the *rasgueado* is played very rapidly, with the last stroke falling on the beat. Another type of *rasgueado* requires a different approach. Here, the hand abandons the basic position and moves (rotates) from the wrist. Only the thumb, index, and little fingers are used (see Ex. 13.7).

Ex. 13.5

Ex. 13.6

Ex. 13.7

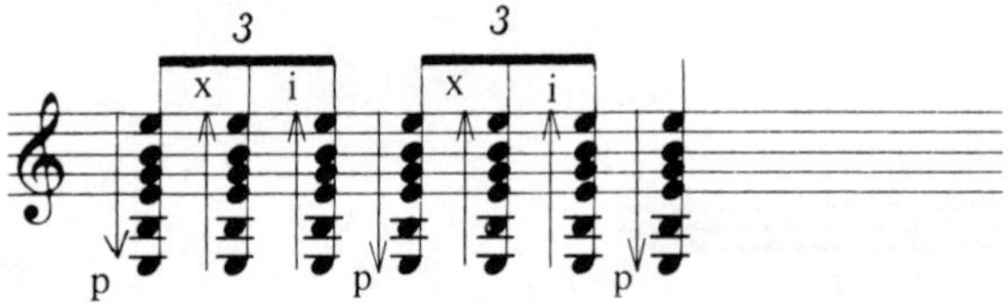

Golpe refers to the tapping of the guitar with one or more of the right-hand fingers. This is usually carried out just below the first string near the bridge—on the tapping plate. It is used to stress or emphasize certain beats of a *compás*, and is always a unified sound. Usually, it is the ring finger that is used, although on occasion the ring and middle fingers, the ring and little fingers, or even all three are used. The sound of the tap generally coincides with the sounding of the strings, this being done by either the index finger or the thumb (which play outward across the strings). It should be noted that *golpe* may be used with either chords or single notes, and that it is indicated on music by the symbol X, written above the chord, note, or rest which it accompanies (see Ex. 13.8).

Ex. 13.8

Two other technical devices, *ligados* (slurs) and the use of open strings, warrant attention because they too contribute to the character of the music. *Ligados* are important because they provide the means for more personal expression in one's playing. Where they are placed says a great deal about how the phrase is to be played, varieties of accent, flow, and syncopation being possible. Similarly with the use of open strings; rather than being avoided, the fingering is often adjusted to bring out the sound of the open strings.

The use of the right-hand thumb is another very important aspect of flamenco technique. The sound of notes played with this digit in the flamenco fashion has a particular texture which any serious student should endeavour to discern clearly, to feel, and to imitate. As with the playing of runs, the thumb uses rest strokes, producing a sound with a quality that is hard to describe—a mixture of mellowness and firmness, of sharpness and roundness, but unique to flamenco.

The role of the thumb is not limited to playing the bass strings. It very often crosses over into the range of the upper strings in order to bring out the sound required by particular *falsetas*. At times, this digit is used as a plectrum or pick (*alzapúa*), having an up-stroke that is used for strumming any number of strings. This is a rapid movement (working from the wrist) that gives a unified sound rather than allowing the individual notes to be heard.

To complete this section on technique, it is appropriate to refer to the subject of sound quality, and the relationship between technique and the music itself. A proper knowledge of accompaniment with all the implicit understanding of song, dance, and the meaning of it all, is what makes a flamenco guitarist, rather than the ability to 'throw' a solo piece. However, in playing solo, one has to try and find new, interesting sounds. For this, the player must draw from his or her own cultural roots, as well as from other things. This makes flamenco a dynamic art form, open to new techniques if necessary. Some guitarists, in developing the music, arrive at a very classical sound or approach. This is not a natural development from the inside but an affectation from contact with the outside. It has a certain value in terms of technical accomplishment but it does not come directly from the roots of the music. Admittedly, one wants to make a good sound—one wants the guitar to sing. But the quality of sound is dictated by the character, and historical and social background of the music. In flamenco, there is a certain roughness which has to do with uncompromisingly expressing strong human emotions. It contains tragedy and happiness, both in the extreme. The flamenco singer is unconcerned about the world around; not concerned with looking or even sounding good; neither with triviality. The soul is opened up to communicate feelings to no one and everyone. If the message is tragic, it arrives as a shocking, emotive cry; if it is happy, an explosion of happiness bursts out. The sound quality on the guitar is also related to the emotive content and the fundamental aim of communicating to the listener the universal message of flamenco. That quality has to be preserved, and if studious practising takes one too close to the purity of tone required for classical guitar-playing, there is a danger of becoming *less flamenco* in the process.

Repertoire

Just as technique in flamenco guitar is largely dictated by the sounds one wants to reproduce, and just as guitarists have constantly striven to find technical means to express the emotions in the message of flamenco, the repertoire has been modelled into its present form because of the social conditions that initially gave birth to the music. It is also true that the repertoire of the flamenco guitar has grown out of the possibilities of the instrument; the way the right hand strums or plucks the strings is a very natural, guitaristic way to play without seeking to create gratuitous difficulties. Equally, the left hand uses the most natural keys of the instrument, not only in the open position but with the free use of the *cejilla* (capo) anywhere along the finger-board (when the pitch of the singer's voice so requires). This means that guitarists can use the same chord shapes, and fingering, yet produce completely different pitches without added difficulty. This approach has largely dictated the group of traditional flamenco *toques* that are known (any flamenco forms when sung are called *cantes*, when played on the guitar they are called *toques*). Even though the *toques* are widely played as guitar solos, we must always remember that they were originally the accompaniment to traditional songs and dances (particularly the former). Thus, they cannot be studied in isolation. If we want to find the guitar repertoire, we must trace the development of the *cante*.

First, a proviso: we must not be dogmatic; the history of flamenco is quite elusive and absolute facts are hard to come by. Furthermore, flamenco is essentially a living art form which not only adapts itself to the times but depends on that very quality of adaptability and spontaneity for its survival. There are, however, strict rules—rhythmic and otherwise—which will be considered.

The beginning of the music is unaccompanied *cante*, and the first name of which we have any written memory is a man called Tio Luis el de la Juliana, who, it is generally believed, was born in Jerez around 1750 and who was an excellent singer of *Tonás*. So, there we have the name of the first group of *cantes* or definite flamenco forms, viz, *Tonás*. The word *toná* comes from the way any Andalucían person would pronounce the Spanish word *tonada*, which was the name given to any popular or traditional song during the seventeenth, eighteenth, and nineteenth centuries. According to the writer Angel Alvarez Caballero, the primitive *Tonás* consisted of all the unaccompanied *cantes* with the exception of *Saetas*—the songs of Easter—which came from a different source. Therefore, included in the group that we call *Tonás* are: the *Martinetes* (supposedly the songs of blacksmiths in their forges); the *Carceleras* (songs of people in prison); and the *Debla* (a distinct type of *Martinete*). In all probability the *Seguirilla* (*Siguiriya*) in its primitive form was also part of that group, having previously been called *Playera*, from the word *plañidera* which means 'hired mourner' for funerals (indeed, at times the guitar accompaniment evokes the sound of bells tolling). From the earliest days of flamenco, the main interpreters of *Tonás* have been gypsies. In fact, a traditional name for such cantes is *Tonás Gitanas*. As Caballero points out, the main theme of the songs concerns the obscure, tormented world of the gypsies, who found themselves persecuted and humiliated in a hostile environment. Very few *Tonás* have been handed down to the present-day, the exceptions being *la Grande*, *la Chica*, and *la toná del Cristo*, which, thanks to the efforts of venerable singers such as Juan Talega in the 1950s and, more recently, of Antonio Mairena, have been preserved.

But if *Tonás* was unaccompanied, at least until it developed into *Seguirillas*, there were other occasions, particularly festive ones involving dancing and light-hearted singing, in which the guitar was a vital ingredient. From that lineage, flamenco developed a distinct set of forms based on a much more rhythmic structure than was inherent in the free style singing of *Tonás*. The complex rhythms of today, underscored by guitar accompaniment, have thus derived from simpler music as used in the dance. Some of the most important flamenco forms probably stem from a drum-like, somewhat rudimentary measure of early flamenco rhythms, i.e. the simple three-beat structure with an accent on the third, such as *Alboreá*. From this the music moved in two closely related directions, *Bulerías* (with fast, festive rhythm, full of syncopations and very well suited for dancing), and *Soleares* (a majestic song that can also be danced to, full of drama and emotive content). Both *Soleares* and *Bulerías* have a definite *compás* (a rhythmic structure) of twelve beats with accents on beats three, six, eight, ten, and twelve, although, of course, adjusted at different speeds:

```
    >     >   >   >     >
1 2 3 4 5 6 7 8 9 10 11 12
```

This pattern applies, obviously, only to the rhythm; however, when using it in combination with different keys, it produces a whole family of flamenco forms varying in mood, harmony, emotive content, speed, and range of possibilities on the guitar (to be listed later).

Before discussing any flamenco *toques*, I must state that none are traditionally taught with the help of written notation, and so there is not a conventional, definitive way to write down what goes on in the *compás* of whichever form. Notation may be used to aid the memory and to try and convey what is generally played and learned by ear. But difficulties arise, and I would like to clarify some points. The meaning of the word *compás* has different, subtle connotations. First, as I said earlier, the *compás* in an abstract sense is the rhythmic structure that rules the piece and which in the case of *Bulerías* and *Soleares* consists of twelve beats with the accents described. Second, to play the *compás* means strumming chords in certain combinations, strictly adhering to the given rhythmic structure and following a conventional harmonic pattern that represents the basic or traditional character of the form being played. And so, one of these rhythmic strumming sequences constitutes one *compás*. When playing such sequences, one is usually said to be playing *compás*, as opposed to melodic interludes (or indeed preludes) which are called *falsetas* and which traditionally fill in the spaces between the verses of the singer (*falsetas* must, of course, also fit the rhythmic structure perfectly).

The keys that are used in flamenco have clearly evolved from the most natural sounds that the guitar produces. Only a handful are widely used. The main ones are those based on E and A, which incidentally, are not called by their letter names but are known simply as *por arriba* (E) or 'up', and *por medio* (A) or 'around the middle'. These terms simply allude to the physical position of the hand on the finger-board. So, when in E, the hand reaches 'up' to the low sounding strings and exploits the inherent musical possibilities of E and the related chords. Similarly, 'around the middle' refers to approximately the middle register, i.e. from the fifth to the second strings.

It should be noted that when talking of keys we must bear in mind that we are really talking of chord shapes which can be played anywhere up the finger-board with the help of the *cejilla*. Some of the most common keys used in flamenco (not in any order of importance) are as follows: E major (which has four ♯s); E minor (one ♯); A major (three ♯s); A minor (no accidentals); C major (no accidentals); D major (two ♯s); D minor (one ♭). The most characteristically flamenco keys are those which are based on the Phrygian mode, or what is generally known in flamenco as the 'natural' scale. The chords and harmonic cadences derived from this mode are rather different from the tonic, subdominant, dominant possibilities associated with the keys listed above.

The tonic is a major chord; nevertheless, the whole character of the harmony is mournful and 'minor sounding'. The fundamental cadence is not from dominant to tonic but a falling resolution to the tonic from the major chord one semitone above it. So, in the key of E natural, which is very common, this resolution would be F major to E major. Usually, this chord above the tonic is embellished by some dissonance or dischord of various qualities. This will depend on which key is being played, as all keys, or separate chord shapes, offer different possibilities of sound.

Apart from the chords involved in that fundamental cadence, there are others related to them when playing in these 'natural' keys. They correspond with the minor chord on the fourth note of the scale (or the relative major) and the major chord on the third note of the scale. That would be A minor in the case of the E natural, the relative major of A minor being C major, and the major chord on the third note of the scale, which would be G major in this case. So, in the key of E natural, the complete cadence is A minor (or C major), G major, F major, which finally resolves to E major.

The second most used key in this 'natural' mode is A, and the equivalent chords under the above structure are B♭ to A major for the fundamental resolution. The other chords are D minor (or F major), and C major. Other common keys are: B 'natural', which in written notation would have one ♯; the resolution would be from C major to B major, the extra chords being E minor (or G major) and D major. Finally, there is the key of F♯ natural, which in written notation would have two ♯s. The resolution would be G major to F ♯ major and the extra chords B minor (or D major) and A major. Apart from all the keys listed above, other possibilities exist and indeed, guitarists must always explore new ones in their search for new musical excitement. However, these are the most important.

Over the years, flamenco singing has been classified in many different ways. The lack of documented history has meant that authors categorize the various *cantes* according to their views on importance, transcendental quality, and/or emotional or artistic demand on the performer. Needless to say, these criteria are not universally agreed upon.

And so we find, for example, that some *aficianados* group a particular list of songs which display the greatest strength of feeling, the deepest expression, into *Cante Grande*, or *Cante Jondo* (Deep Song). At the other end of the spectrum, *Cante Chico* lists the lighter forms. We find further divisions into *Cante Festero* (happy, for the festival), *Cante Corto* (short tercios), *Cante Largo* (long *tercios*), *Cante Gitano* (gypsy), *Cante Campero* (of the Andalucían countryside), *Cante de Fragua* (of the forges), *Cante Liviano* (light-hearted), *Cante Alante* (to be sung in front of the stage, i.e. to be listened to as opposed to accompanying the dance), *Cante Atrás* (for the dance), *Cante de Faena* (while working), *Cante de las Minas* (of the mines), *Cante de Levante* (the eastern provinces of Andalucía), *Cante de los Puertos* (the sea port region around Cádiz) and so on. Clearly, space does not permit discussion of such divisions and so for the guitarist the flamenco *toques* will be divided into two main groups; those which have a well-defined rhythmic structure, *toques a compás*, and those in which the rhythm is very loose and plays only a secondary role on account of the free nature of the songs they accompany—*toques libres*. In both groups, variations are expected from the guitarist.

The four most important rhythmic forms within *toques a compás* are: (i) *Soleares*; (ii) *Bulerías*; (iii) *Seguirillas*; (iv) *Tientos*. Apart from these basic forms, there are others that are associated with them, sometimes just because they use the same rhythm, and other times in a much closer relationship in terms of the emotive character.

(i) *Soleares* heads the list of all flamenco forms. It has the most perfect balance of majesty, drama, self-assuredness, and variety of expression—it is the quintessence of flamenco. The rhythm, as mentioned earlier, is a clear *compás* of twelve beats (analogous to one bar) (see Ex. 13.9).

A number of flamenco forms have been based on this rhythm, such as *Cañas* and *Polos*. *Cañas* uses exactly the same guitar accompani-

Ex. 13.9

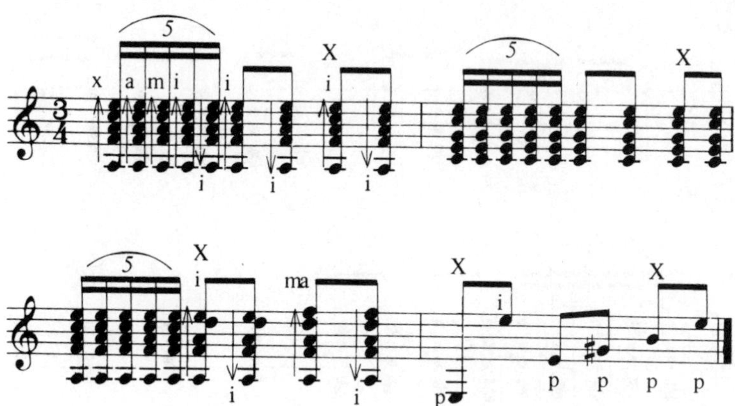

ment as *Soleares* although the song itself is different. It has been widely suggested, and accepted, that *Cañas* is an older form than *Soleares*, being placed at the beginning of flamenco. It is a melancholic song with a clear melodic line and is distinguished from *Soleares* by the latter having a vast number of variations that lend themselves to change with the different interpretation of singers. This fact made the *Soleares* leap forward to become a world of music within flamenco. The *Cañas* has largely been forgotten and it remains sung only as a kind of museum piece.

The *Polos* has a similar history to the *Cañas* and has suffered a similar fate. It is accompanied exactly the same as *Soleares* and *Cañas*, the only difference being its own particular melodic line.

Next in this family come the group of *Cantiñas* and *Alegrías* which use the same rhythmic structure but with a totally different approach and nuance. They are much more lively and are played in the straight major key. *Cantiñas* originate as little folk songs from the region of Cádiz, which became impregnated with the flamenco character. *Caracoles*, *Mirabrás*, and *Romeras* also fall within this category (see Ex. 13.10a and b).

Finally, there is the *Alegrías* which is a very important group of *cantes*. Originally, they were to accompany the dance, but later, due to the special interpretation of some singers, they have become very important *cantes* to listen to as well. The *Alegrías* originated in the region of Cádiz and it seems that their origin is in the *Jotas*. These were traditional folk dances from Aragón which were brought to

Ex. 13.10

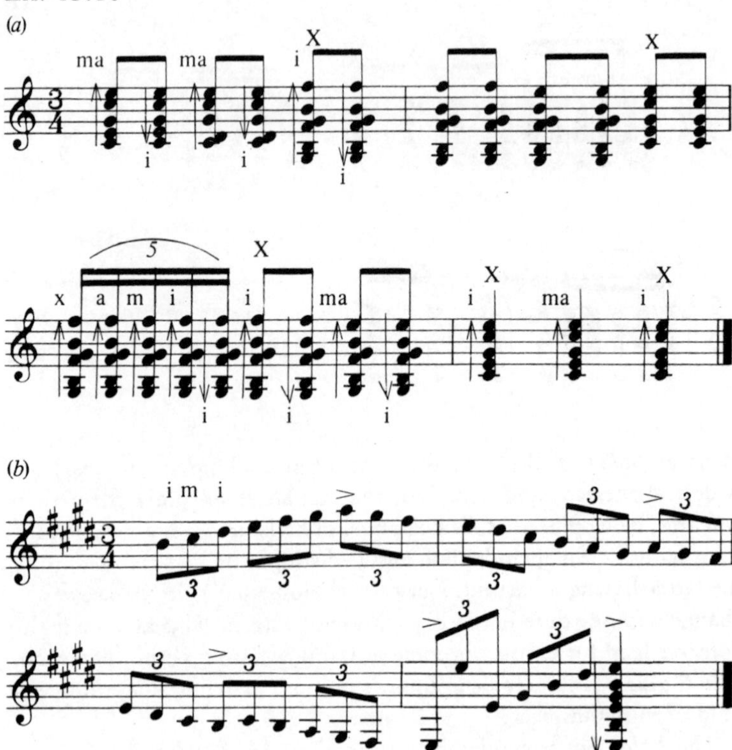

Cádiz by soldiers during the War of Independence in the early nineteenth century (see Ex. 13.11). All the *Alegrías* and different types of *Cantiñas* are always played in the normal major keys but sometimes they also modulate to the minor or to the Phrygian mode.

(ii) The *Bulerías* is probably the most exciting flamenco form on account of its fast, syncopated rhythm and continuous variations that occur within that rhythm. It can be played in any key or mode but the most common one is A natural. Like *Soleares*, *Bulerías* has a twelve-beat structure with the same accentuation. In general it is the syncopation produced by the displacement of the accents in the second half of the unit that provides the source of the excitement. However, this is just a beginning; the rhythm offers such possibilities that guitarists constantly add new variations, thus keeping the performance alive and full of tension. The improvisations can be melodic (*falsetas*) or just variations of the *compás* itself. Ex. 13.12

Ex. 13.11

Ex. 13.12

1 2 3 4 5 6 7 8 9 10 11 12

a.

b.

c.

d.

e.

f.

g.

h.

shows some of the latter. The natural ending of the *compás* is on beat ten; beats eleven and twelve come as a kind of tail after the resolution. They are usually called beats one and two, not eleven and twelve, and with practice they actually become the beginning of the next *compás*:

    >   >   >   >   >   >
1 2 3 4 5 6 7 8 9 10 1 2 1 2 3 4 5 etc.

(iii) *Seguirillas* is a most dramatic form of singing with beautiful, solemn guitar accompaniment. The rhythm is a combination of 3/4 and 6/8, and the *compás* may be thought of as a repeating unit of five beats of which two are slow and three are faster.

* * * * * * * * * * * *	Even beats
1 2 3 4 5	Beats of *Seguirillas*

The *compás* may appear as in Ex. 13.13.

Ex. 13.13

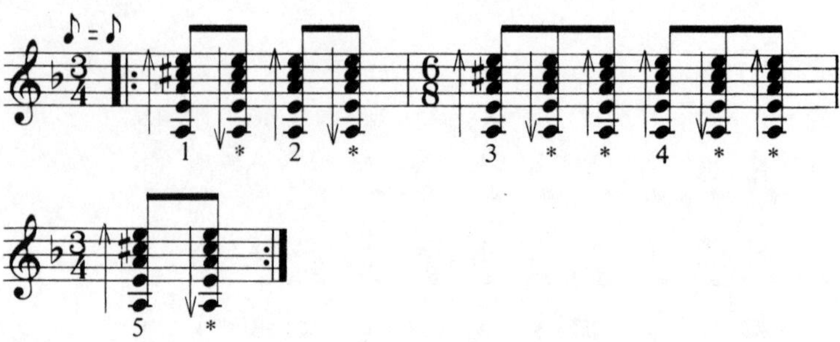

Example 13.14 shows ways in which *falsetas* may be fitted into the above rhythmic structure. *Seguirillas* is commonly played in A natural Phrygian mode.

Also in this group is the *Serranas*, which uses the same rhythm and is played in the key of E natural. It is a very beautiful song that also makes an interesting guitar solo (see Ex. 13.15). The *Peteneras* also follows the same rhythmic pattern but with a slightly different approach to the harmony, although still played in the natural keys (see Ex. 13.16).

(iv) *Tientos* has its origin in the lighter, more popular flamenco form called *Tangos*. The rhythm is 4/4 with subtle accentuation and anticipation of different beats. *Tientos* usually ends with a faster section in the rhythm of the closely related *Tangos*. In general,

Ex. 13.14

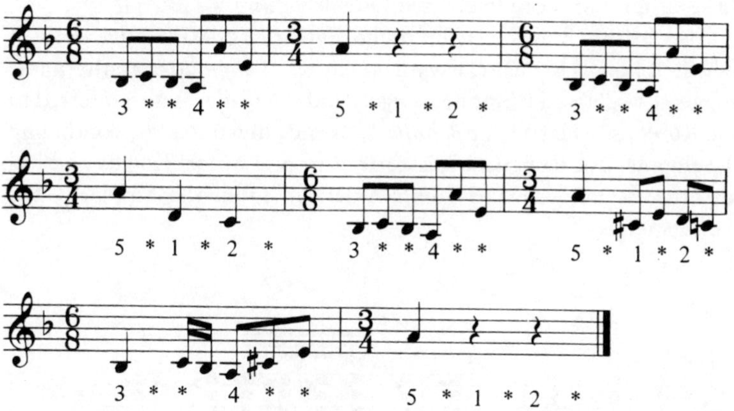
3 * * 4 * * 5 * 1 * 2 * 3 * * 4 * *
5 * 1 * 2 * 3 * * 4 * * 5 * 1 * 2 *
3 * * 4 * * 5 * 1 * 2 *

Ex. 13.15

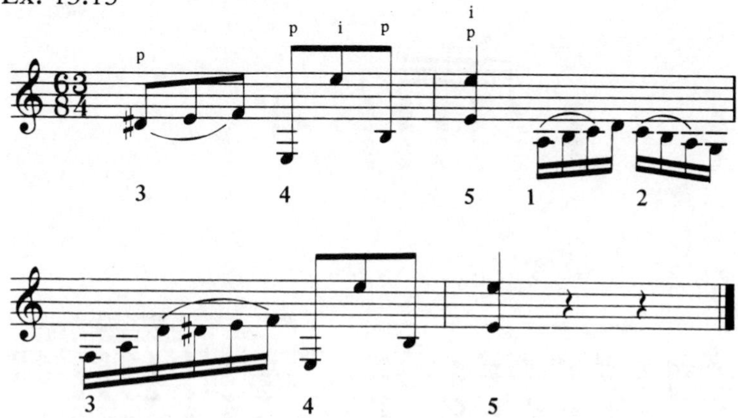
p
p i p
i
p
3 4 5 1 2
3 4 5

Ex. 13.16

♪= 126
ma ma ma ma
p
r r
r r

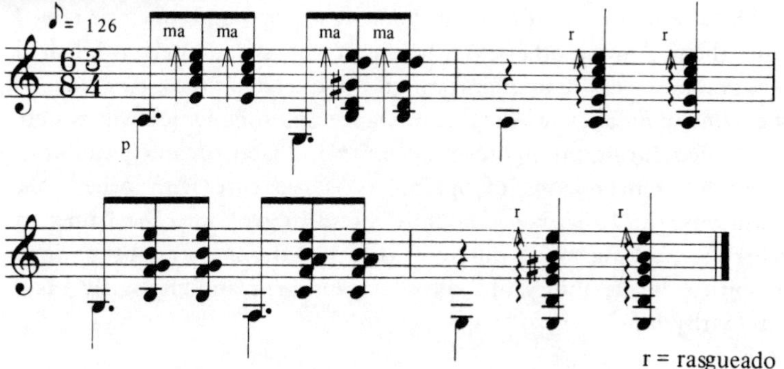

r = rasgueado

Tangos have a more straightforward rhythm than *Tientos*, being a little faster and more lively (see Ex. 13.17a and b).

Also in this family can be found *Farruca* and *Garrotin*, both of which follow a straightforward 4/4 time. *Tanguillos*, as the name suggests, is derived from the *Tangos*, and the reader is also referred to the *Rumbas*. The style of *Rumba Flamenca* illustrates the continuing development of flamenco; it is derived from *Tientos/Tangos* and has absorbed a modern and South American influence. Similarly, the *Colombianas*.

Ex. 13.17

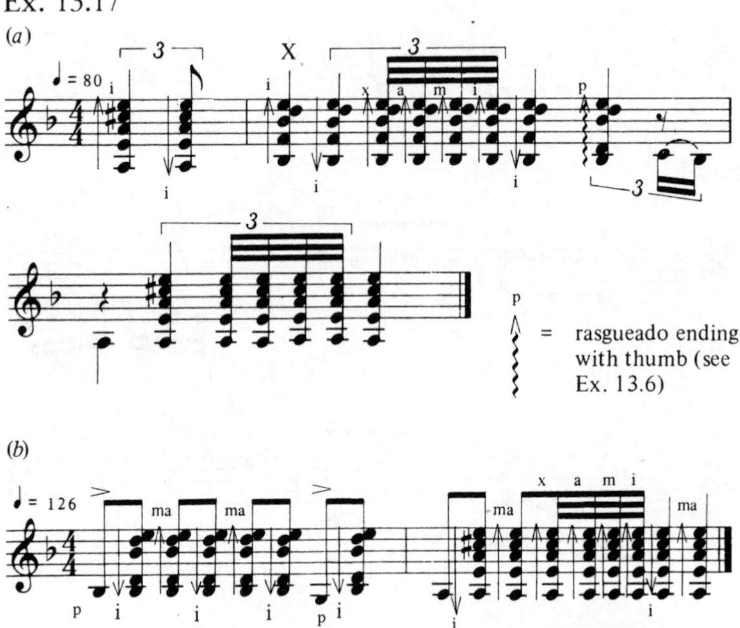

The above are the four main flamenco forms and groups derived from them. Among others that belong to the living repertoire, I shall mention one remaining important group, the *Fandangos*. *Fandango* is the name of an ancient Andalucían dance and song which was widely performed during the eighteenth century and later became popular in many different regions of Spain. As is the case with other folk traditions, the *Fandango* gradually found its way into the flamenco repertoire, taking many different local variations or manifestations owing to the flexibility of expression within it and the fairly easy, catchy rhythms.

Of the various types of flamenco *Fandangos*, I would like to make one fundamental division, that is, *Fandangos a compás*, with a set metric rhythm (predominantly triple time) and *Fandangos* with a very free form which only tend towards triple time—our first example of *toques libres*. In both varieties, the form of the music evolves around the *Copla*, i.e. the song itself which consists of four verses of which two are repeated, or sometimes five verses of which one is repeated, making a total of six musical lines called *tercios*. In both free and rhythmic forms, the Fandango starts with the guitar playing a prelude consisting of a number of measures, or *compás*, which may be more rigid or loose depending on which kind of *Fandango* it is. They are always in a natural key.

The basic *compás* of the main rhythmic *Fandangos*, i.e. *Fandangos de Huelva*, and the free *Fandangos* which are otherwise known as *Fandangos Naturales* or *Fandango Grande*, consists of four triple-time bars divided into two units of two bars (in the key of E natural) (see Ex. 13.18).

Ex. 13.18

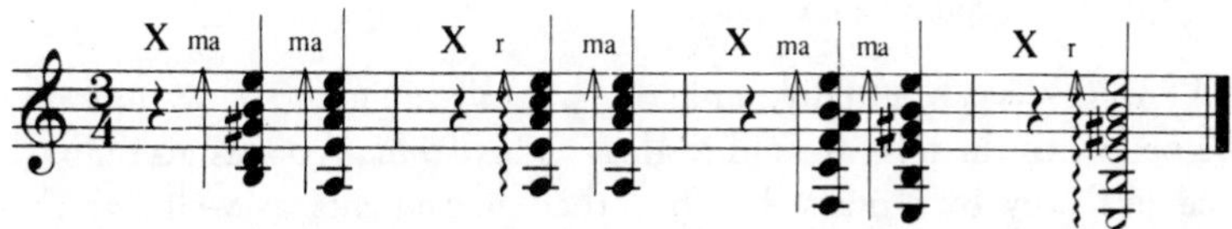

Falsetas may be played during this prelude, i.e. before the singer starts (and of course during the intervals and between songs or *coplas*). The *falsetas* usually start on beat number eleven or number one, but all possibilities are open to the performer. That leads to the *Fandango* itself, the song, which has a particular chordal structure. In the key of E natural, the structure would be as shown in Ex. 13.19.

Of the rhythmic variety (*a compás*) there is a vast repertoire of *Fandangos* according to the region or locality, and where they have developed a particular cadence or turn in the song—or even according to personal styles of individual singers who have changed the melody line significantly. However, from the guitarist's point of view, there is very little difference between most of these songs. I shall list only two fundamental types of these *Fandangos*: (i) The *Verdiales*—a *Fandango* of Málaga going into the province of Córdoba (Lucena) and including also the *Fandango* of Almería; (ii) The *Fandango de Huelva* which has many sub-divisions.

Ex. 13.19

	E major ________________________ C major*
1st verse	1 2 3 · 4 5 6 · 7 8 9 · 10 11 12 (tonic to major chord on the 6th note of the mode)
	C major ________________________ F major
2nd verse	1 2 3 · 4 5 6 · 7 8 9 · 10 11 12 (to major chord on the 2nd note of mode)
	F major ________________________ C major
3rd verse	1 2 3 · 4 5 6 · 7 8 9 · 10 11 12 (back to 6th note of mode)
	C major ________________ G major (or G 7)
4th verse	1 2 3 · 4 5 6 · 7 8 9 · 10 11 12 (to major or 7th chord on 3rd note of mode)
	G major (or 7th) ________________ C major
5th verse	1 2 3 · 4 5 6 · 7 8 9 · 10 11 12 (back to 6th note of mode)
	C major F major ________________ E major
6th verse	1 2 3 · 4 5 6 · 7 8 9 · 10 11 12 (to 2nd note–to tonic)†

Verdiales was originally, and still is, a folk song and dance among the people of the hills around Málaga. This *Fandango* was accompanied not only by guitars, but by other instruments as well (which might even include violin, tambourine, drum, and other percussive instruments). In becoming flamenco, these aspects of the music were left out and it became a flamenco song accompanied only by the guitar. Ex. 13.20 is the rhythm of *Verdiales* which applies also to the *Fandango de Lucena* and *Almería.*

Coming to the rich group of the *Fandangos de Huelva*, the rhythm is different from that above. From that simple structure, a wealth of

* Note 1: In practice and after a lot of accompaniment playing, one begins to 'hear' passing chords between E and C (G 7), between C and F (C 7), between F and C (G 7) and C and G (D 7). These should not be played by system but only when one actually discovers that they are needed.

† Note 2: Singer and guitarist follow this set structure when accompanying the dance. However, as a song it is much more relaxed and likely to change, even in the rhythmic form. In the case of the free *fandango* form the chordal pattern remains but with no concern for rhythm. The singer is completely free to lengthen or shorten his *tercios,* while the guitarist will simply stand by ready to follow and echo and heighten the singer's nuance at the end of each verse.

Ex. 13.20

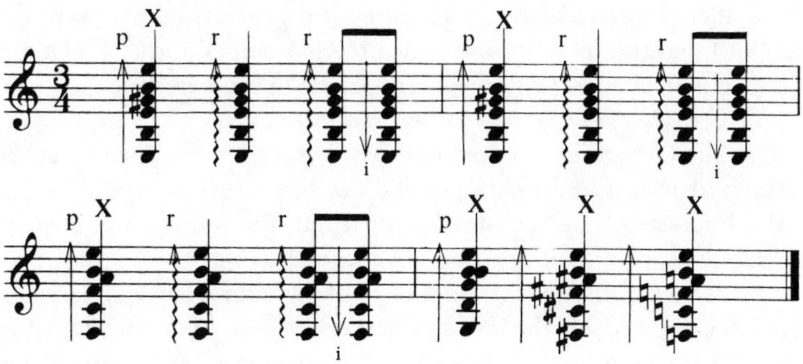

variations spring (see Ex. 13.21). As mentioned earlier, the *falsetas* usually start on beat number eleven or number one, and the natural ending of both the rhythm and *falsetas* is on beat number nine, followed by a chordal reiteration of the resolution during beats ten and eleven. The last beat is left silent except for the continuing sound of the chord just played. The *Fandango de Huelva* is a very popular form of the lighter type of flamenco (very similar in rhythm and spirit to the other famous dance, the *Sevillanas*) on account of their infectious gaiety and the feeling that they convey of the joy of being alive and in appreciation of nature, the country, and the sea. Indeed, there is a well-known division of these songs which depends on whether their source of inspiration is the sea, the *sierra*, the mines, or the marshes around Huelva.

Ex. 13.21

Turning back to the free *Fandangos*, we can group them as follows. First, there is the *Fandango* itself, already described and played in the key of E natural or A natural. Then there are three forms which are very similar in construction but are played in different keys:

(i) The *Malagueñas*, played in E natural.

(ii) The *Granadinas*, played in the key of B natural which is rather calm and lyrical and offers possibilities for a very beautiful guitar solo. Interestingly, when playing B natural, the top open E is often sounded in unison with a D♯ on the second string.

(iii) The *Tarantas*, played in the key of F♯ natural and again strings are left open, notably the B which clashes with the A♯ of the F♯ major chord, as well as the top open E. This relaxing of the chord of F♯ major gives *Tarantas* a dark, mysterious character which is perhaps in keeping with the background of this particular kind of *Fandango*, the mines in the eastern part of Andalucía.

Flamenco, then, is an art form that has a rich and varied repertoire, although one that is continually changing. The conditions that gave birth to the music have altered, the suffering has reduced, and thus the motivating forces will not be the same. Different stimuli are therefore present for today's flamenco guitarists, and flamenco will continue to reflect the influence of modern, popular (or otherwise) styles that have evolved in the twentieth century. But it is an influence that is always kept in check by flamenco's true identity as a unique type of music, forever linked to the roots of its cultural heritage.

The forms that this process of self-discovery will take, will obviously be varied. This is not, however, to say that every great player invents a new vocabulary—this leads to the solipsisms of the avant-garde. The musician, like everyone else, aims (consciously or subconsciously) to balance his or her own aspirations with society (i.e. other people with whom relationships will be formed). To move too far one side or the other produces either the musical equivalent of a psychopath or, at the other extreme, a timid sheep. In this consideration of the collective and the individual, I think we can find common ground to enable the teacher truly to help a pupil to discover, in jazz-playing, a way towards real enjoyment and to participate in fruitful relationships with other players. This process obviously involves facility and an understanding of the accepted tools of musical language—scales, arpeggios, and chords etc. It is, however, very important that these do not become an obstacle. At all stages of discovery, the student must be playing and improvising. Jazz is not something that is played after certain precepts have been mastered, but it is a way of operating. The jazz player must be capable of ad hoc reaction; aware and sensitive, not merely armed with carefully rehearsed licks and phrases. Thus it is as much a reactive, responsive process—an art for the Einsteinian age that is ever changing, expanding, contracting, leading, and following. The model student should therefore have a thorough understanding of the language—diatonic and chromatic harmony, rhythmic flexibility, technical facility, a confidence to follow a line of thought, and an ability to reflect and flow with the requirements and influence of the moment. If the playing of composed music is akin to delivering a speech, jazz is a conversation—one which preferably involves the audience as well as the participants. This definition, of course, hints at the failure of much modern jazz playing in the last thirty years. If the musicians are conversing in a language which only they understand, then the audience cannot participate. This is the 'taught' language which the listener cannot appreciate. What can be appreciated, and what is characteristically jazz, is the individual character of the playing and the electricity that is generated by a live, spontaneous relationship between the players. This is really what differentiates jazz from most other branches of popular music. In rock music, for example, the accent is on the premeditatively effective, the dramatic, the emotionally manipulative. Rock is about power, jazz is about flow.

The reason for this lengthy introduction is as much to provide a warning to teachers as anything else. Jazz is not an activity amenable to the usual music school disciplines. Although much of this chapter will be devoted to a discussion of those areas which can be covered by normal teaching methods, i.e. what has been done in the past by jazz guitarists with the material that was available to them, a large part of teaching time must be spent on uncovering the proclivities of the individual. Someone may wish to play, for example, with the thumb, a pick, or on any type of guitar. The common criterion will, however, be musicality in an improvisatory context.

History

The following brief account of the most important aspects of the guitar in the history of jazz is intended to bring to the attention of class music teachers and guitarists of other styles, the main features and characteristics of the players that have shaped the instrument's development. It is undoubtedly true that in what has been commonly described as the major trends in jazz, the guitar has not been the pioneer instrument (as it has in blues and rock). The major instruments of jazz have been the trumpet and the saxophone, and the guitar in this context has shown itself to be an adaptable follow-up in many instances.

The first important guitarist that I am aware of was Lonnie Johnson, who recorded with Louis Armstrong in the middle 1920s. He recorded a number of duets with Eddie Lang, and in these he takes most of the single string work, his use of pull-offs and hammer-ons sounding quite modern. In contrast, Lang's playing sounds at times a little contrived, and all his work gives the impression of being less spontaneous. It is, however, the more fluent Johnson who has been confined to the no-man's land that lies between blues and jazz, and it is Lang that has been given the accolade of 'founding father'. The reasons for this are understandable. Although to the unhistorical ear, Lang's playing may sound a little stilted, it contains in fact the seeds of what came after. Johnson played with the fingers, at this time at least, and Lang used a pick. He played an arch-top guitar of the type which is still considered to be the standard (either electric or acoustic) jazz instrument. He was, in a European sense, also much more harmonically sophisticated. He played a number of chord-melody solo arrangements which established a tradition that led through George Van Eps to Ted Greene. He was a fine accompanist, playing picked chords with variable bass notes, using passing notes to move between chords. This strongly influenced Django Reinhardt's rhythm guitar work. Lang's single-string work, in as much as it consists mainly of arpeggio notes with some chromatic passing notes, is in some ways the equivalent of the Louis Armstrong trumpet style. The notes are given a full attack, but his style is more European in the sense that the phrasing stays very close to the beat. This is the same foundation that Reinhardt built on.

The chord style became dominant in America in the 1930s. The arch-top acoustic guitar could provide a good rhythmic propulsion and was loud enough to play unaccompanied introductions. Soloing against the ensemble really required high chord-playing in order to overcome volume limitations, and so, many of the good players of the period (for example, Dick McDonough, Carl Cress, and George Van Eps) became masters of a style which involved playing rapidly changing chords on the top four strings with some melodic embellishment.

In 1934 the first recordings of the Hot Club Quintet of France were published. In this, Django Reinhardt was the first guitarist to play mainstream jazz without the limitations of the instrument being apparent. He has been the greatest improvising guitarist in history and was the first to have the technical facility to make instant connections from the brain to the fingers. His extemporizations were truly spontaneous, yet clearly articulated and perfectly organized. This was supreme jazz playing of the conventional kind, that is, the instant creation of coherent variation through a given harmonic framework. His harmonic thought, with strong use of diminished and augmented chords, was very advanced for the time and much of it predates the be-bop innovations of the 1940s, although his expression was characteristically different.

Django Reinhardt used a much louder guitar (Maccaferri/Selmer) than that used by the Americans, and this, together with his enormous physical strength, enabled him to produce enough volume to project a single line. However, without the invention of amplification, it is doubtful whether the guitar would ever have truly moved up to the front line. Reinhardt was really a unique phenomenon and his group was set up to project him, whereas American players were still struggling to compete with the trumpet, saxophone, piano, and drums.

The liberation began for the guitar in the late 1930s, when the adoption of the electric guitar immediately changed the technique and approach of guitarists. Although not by any means the first to use amplified guitar for jazz, it is usually considered that Charlie Christian was the first master of electric jazz guitar. With Christian, we first hear a guitarist playing long, quaver lines. A typical solo would have a riff-phrase in the first sixteen bars with long even lines over the middle-eight bars. Thus, tension is provided by the riff and released through the long line. The predominance of line sometimes becomes excessive with more modern guitar players: with Christian the contrast is quite distinct. As soon as the guitar was amplified, the player quite naturally imitated the great stylists of the day, saxophone players. Charlie Christian is, to some extent, Lester Young on the guitar. In this way, whole areas of the instrument's potential were neglected. Chord-playing was jettisoned to be revived in the late 1950s by Barney Kessel, and as be-bop took a hold of the jazz world, guitarists became more and more involved in acquiring the single-string technique that was required to cope.

Barney Kessel, together with Tal Farlow, were the two major guitarists of the 1950s. During the course of the decade, Kessel developed one of the most effective trio styles by mixing a Christian-inspired single-note style with chord style, reminiscent of the 1930s. Farlow usually played with piano accompaniment and, together with Jimmy Raney, was the first guitarist to develop the technical facility to sound really confident at the faster, bop tempos. This line of development culminated with the early recordings of Joe Pass, the most accomplished single-string bop player in the instrument's history. These players had by now departed some way from the basic chord sounds, using chord alterations and substitutions to embellish the fundamental harmony.

Wes Montgomery appeared at the end of the decade and became the most popular guitarist in jazz history, alongside Django Reinhardt. He played with the thumb, managing to employ both up and down strokes, probably in a 75/25 per cent ratio of down and up. Playing up strokes with the thumb is awkward but, using the thumb gives a connected feeling which helps the phrasing considerably, and also gives a much warmer tone than a pick. Wes Montgomery's solos usually follow the formula of single line, followed by passages in octaves, winding up with block chords. Thus the sound density is constantly increased and tension is maintained throughout.

The mainstream tradition, that is, playing extemporized solos over the chords of standard tunes, reached its acme in the early 1960s with the recordings of, for example, the Bill Evans Trio and the Miles Davis Quintet. Once again, the guitar seems to have been noticeably absent from the front line, and the guitarist who has had the sensitivity to play in this ultra-loose, rhythmically emancipated environment, is Jim Hall. It was in the mid-1970s that a new generation of improvising guitarists, Metheney, Scofield, and Abercrombie, developed a more subtle phrasing. Wes Montgomery died in 1968, the year when rock-playing heavily began to influence and shape jazz. Players such as Larry Coryell and John MacLaughlin became established, and from them the fusion players of the 1970s. The aim was to marry the rock sound and attack with more sophisticated harmonic thought. This brings us to the present-day when the most forward-looking players combine a feeling for jazz tradition, a thorough knowledge of scales, chord substitutions, and an interest in the discoveries of rock players that are largely to do with tone production and treatment of individual notes—string bending, echo effects, and amplification overdrive etc.

It is important to sum this up succinctly so as to place the succeeding teaching material in a historical context. By staying close to the arpeggio notes of the chords, an early jazz feeling will be evoked (including, of course, the syncopation). By emphasizing non-chord notes (i.e. other notes in the scale of a chord aside from the arpeggio) and some chromatic notes with less syncopation, a more mainstream-modern sound will be achieved. If the emphasis is heavily on chromatic altered notes against the basic chord sounds, a modern sound is created that is, however, recognizably connected to an improvising tradition (for example, the playing of John Scofield). A scalic, linear approach, with accent on all the scale notes and little reference to the arpeggios, gives rise to jazz–rock–fusion sounds.

The guitar

The guitar used by Charlie Christian was an arch-top guitar, with a mounted pick-up. These guitars were commonly used until the mid 1960s, but they do impose certain limitations. The guitar does not respond well to being strummed, nor is it sensitive to an increase in right-hand attack. Thus, many of the possibilities of the acoustic guitar are lost without a commensurate gain. The amplified arch-top guitar seems to fall between two stools. Nevertheless, it does have certain unique tonal qualities that have become associated with a particular style of music for which it seems to be best suited. This type of guitar—the f-hole arch-top—gives probably the most centred note. For a long line of quavers or semiquavers, it produces the clearest, most articulate tones. Because the note decays quickly, it is the most clean for rapid chord changes. The acoustic sound, although not loud, is very distinct and projects much further than a round-hole jumbo. The Maccaferri/Selmer guitar, used by Django Reinhardt, is an attempt to combine the sonority of the round-hole with the clarity and projection of the arch-top instrument. When amplified with a magnetic pick-up, the guitar produced a lot of overtones, so that the less resonant f-hole instrument seemed to be more suitable because of its flatter response. The development of transducer pick-ups in the last fifteen years or so, has allowed a fairly consistent reproduction of the round-hole guitar. Many jazz players now use this particular type of instrument, for example the Ovation.

It has always been possible to produce reasonable conventional jazz tones from solid guitars, particularly those made by Fender. Joe Pass, for example, recorded *Sounds of Synanon* on a Fender Jazzmaster and Ed Bickert uses a Telecaster. If the strings are heavy enough, the essential quality, namely a round, centred note which rapidly decays, will be obtained. However, a jazz guitar tone produced on a solid guitar usually lacks something in the bass, and can sound too bland because of the extremely even response of the strings. The vibrating top of the conventional jazz guitar gives the tone an increased vitality. The reader is referred to the playing of Jim Hall. This is a true amplified acoustic tone—the natural sound of the instrument exists alongside the electric sound—both are audible. This gives a very intimate atmosphere; a quiet, personal quality. All the major guitarists from Charlie Christian to Joe Pass use this type of instrument—Barney Kessel, Jimmy Raney, Tal Farlow, Sal Salvador, Wes Montgomery, Jim Hall, Kenny Burrell, George Benson, and Herb Ellis.

The following comments are intended for the relatively inexperienced student. A solid-bodied or semi-acoustic guitar is acceptable, such as those made by Ibanez, Yamaha, or Fender. A heavy-gauge string is suggested for a conventional jazz tone. Also, the amplifier should have a closed-back speaker cabinet. This will enable a clean, sharp note to be obtained. A transistorized amplifier, in contrast to a valve amplifier, gives a flat response that is most appropriate for this conventional jazz tone. For clean jazz-playing, no trace of distortion is required and a minimum of 50 watts is therefore recommended. On many amplifiers the tone settings are relatively 'active', which means that quality will be lost as the setting is reduced. Relatively high settings are therefore advised for the amplifier with some reduction made on the guitar. The sound is, however, dependent on a variety of factors, notably the requirements of the player. Some may, for example, prefer a trace of distortion which with many modern amplifiers can be blended successfully. Nowadays, some players use two amplifiers and a delay mechanism, digital or analogue, to produce a bigger, stereophonic sound. A chorus pedal is also used in this context. The size, shape, and material for the pick will vary, but generally the heavier the pick, the better the tone that can be produced. A heavy pick is, however, less manageable and some compromise will therefore be necessary—about 1 mm. thick should suffice.

Technique

Conventionally, jazz guitar has been played using a pick. Each great player developed their own refinements to right-hand positioning and attack, but the student should note the two major distinctions, that of either resting the fingers on the pick-guard or leaving the right arm loose and free. A guitarist such as Django Reinhardt used the latter approach, but the modern electric guitars that require less attack favour the former. Here, movement is reduced and mostly confined to the thumb and first two fingers (which hold the pick), thus facilitating more refined articulation. Of prime concern is the matching of the up-and-down strokes of the pick because the quality is unbalanced and dependent on the angle of attack on the strings. The down stroke of the pick corresponds approximately to the classical rest stroke; the up stroke to free stroke. Historically, all guitarists up to Joe Pass used a predominance of down strokes because of the superior note quality. With modern guitars, particularly solid-bodied ones, an even tone can be produced with regular up-and-down picking. This allows more rapid playing.

There are, however, a number of chord voicings that are unobtainable with a pick. Further difficulty with this technique is found when playing a walking bass line against chords. As a result, more and more players use a classical-style right hand which allows the notes of a chord to be played either as an arpeggio or simultaneously. Thus, modern players have been evolving many different techniques to expand the range of the instrument, although there is a sense in which a jazz player's technique is as personal as the manner of phrasing. For example, Wes Montgomery used the right-hand thumb to sound the strings, Lenny Breau used thumb-pick and fingers, whereas Stanley Jordan plays by tapping the finger-board with both hands. A wide latitude must therefore be allowed to the student in his or her technical approach to the right hand.

Left-hand technique is equally individual and once again, all the great masters have had their own fingerings. Many players now are less dependent on picking every note and rely on the left-hand fingers to hammer on the notes during fast scale passages. Both approaches are applicable.

Teaching: scales and chords

In a sense, it is necessary for a student to have reached a certain level of sophistication before he or she can enjoy the process of improvisation. For a beginner, imitation will be one of the most rewarding activities, so perhaps at a basic level the most useful skill which can be acquired, and later be put to use in improvisation, is the development of the ear. For a player beginning the instrument, the teacher may therefore wish to teach without reference to notation (for example, short well-known tunes). This emphasizes the relationship between sound and the finger-board. Like every other musical faculty, the ear will develop with practice and exposure. In jazz it is one of the most important aspects and the development of good relative pitch is essential. Later on, aural transcription should be attempted of solos by great players; this has been the most important way that jazz has been passed on and absorbed. The following comments are applicable for the student who has been playing for a few years, but feels impeded from further progress in the area of improvisation. A student who is historically minded may discover that once he or she has understood basic harmonic theory, development can be microcosmically analogous to the evolution of jazz guitar-playing. However, following the opening comments of this chapter, it is the extemporization and manipulation of given melodies that is of fundamental importance.

Jazz has seen an unfolding into complete chromaticism, but to appreciate this the student must first have a thorough understanding of diatonic scales and harmonies. The western major scales may be taken as the basic tool. From the C major scale, for example, there emerges the triad; C major from the first degree of the scale, D minor from the second, etc. If a four-note chord is made on each degree of the scale, the following chords are obtained: C major 7, D minor 7, E minor 7, F major 7, G 7, A minor 7, B minor 7–5. In diatonic playing, i.e. playing music with an obvious key centre, these chords are often designated by Roman numerals. Thus C major is I, D minor is II etc. This has the advantage of always demonstrating the relationship between the given chord and the tonic. A large percentage of popular songs, old and new, are based on these chords, the I, VI, II, V progression being especially common. Many songs have variations on the diatonic chords for sixteen bars, then a bridge eight bar section in another key, before returning to the original key for the last eight bars. The evolution of harmonic thought in jazz has seen the embellishment of these chords with more and more chromatic additions, and the development of this discussion is with just this in mind.

If the student is asked to improvise on the given chords of a standard jazz tune, the recognition of the relationship of the harmonies to the tonic is essential. For example, a tune such as Jerome Kern's *All the Things You Are*, seems at first sight quite complicated: | F minor 7 | B♭ minor 7 | E♭ 7 | A♭ major 7 | D♭ major 7 | G7 | C major 7 | C major 7 | C minor 7 | F minor 7 | B♭ 7 | E♭ major 7 | A ♭ major 7 | D7 | G major 7 | G major 7 |—to quote the first sixteen bars. This sequence can, however, be played by using four major scales only: A♭, C, E♭, and G. F minor 7, B♭ minor 7, E♭ 7, A♭ major 7, and D♭ major 7 are all diatonic chords in the key of A♭. Similarly, C minor 7, F minor 7, B♭ 7, E♭ major 7, and A♭ major 7 are in the key of E♭. Thus, the first weapon a student needs is a thorough knowledge of major scales and arpeggios. (It should be noted that technical facility is not the main issue here but the recognition of their relationships.) These should be absorbed by the process of discovery, by improvising over simple diatonic chord patterns in different keys, and finding which notes of the parent scale fit particular diatonic chords (see Ex. 14.1). A convenient way to learn these scales all over the finger-board is to employ the four basic chord shapes (plus one intermediate which is more useful as a scale position) (see Ex. 14.2). By moving these shapes up the finger-board (with the addition of a first finger barré), and adding or subtracting various notes, all the

Ex. 14.1

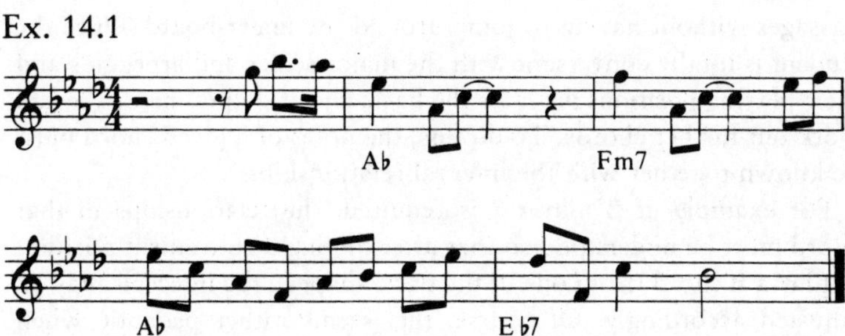

Ex. 14.2

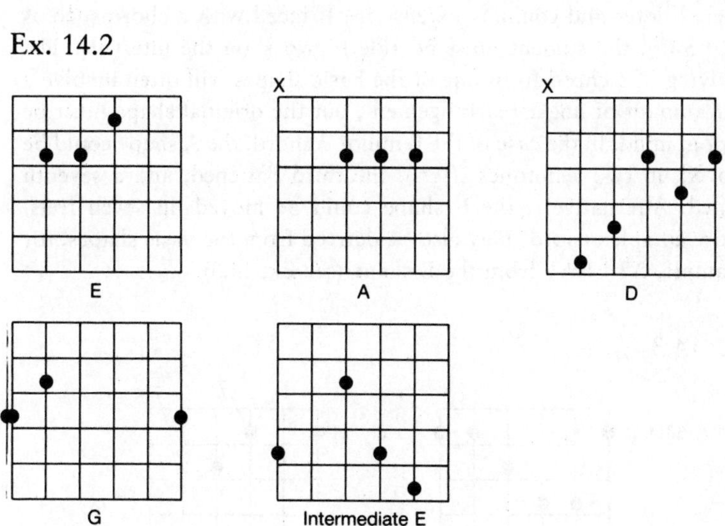

common chords can be found. (Most importantly, there is also a complementary scale in each position.) It follows, therefore, that there are five positions for playing every major chord and its associated arpeggios and scale, and a student should be able to play (in one position at a time) an improvisation over a simple diatonic chord pattern. Furthermore, when a student wishes to employ extensions and upper intervals as well as the basic arpeggios, they can all be extrapolated from the basic positions.

A student should also be able to play a chord in all the positions and then be able to play different chords in as close to the same position as possible. The same should apply with the associated scales and arpeggios and a player will then be able to flow smoothly between passages without having to jump around the finger-board. Once the student is totally conversant with the major scales and arpeggios and their playing positions *vis-à-vis* the basic chord shapes, he or she can work out further chords. To do this, the notes of a given chord must be known together with the interval relationships.

For example, if B minor 7 is required, the relationships in that chord must be understood so that after finding a convenient position to play a B chord (from one of the basic shapes), the intervals may be adjusted accordingly. Of course, this seems rather pedantic when dealing with simple chords, but it is absolutely vital when using altered notes and complex extensions. If faced with a chord such as A7+5+9, the student must be able to work on the intervals. The deriving of a chord from one of the basic shapes will often involve a fair amount of finger rearrangement, but the original shape must be kept in mind. In the case of the B minor 7 chord, the A shape could be moved up two semitones (frets), the third flattened, and a seventh added. Alternatively, the E shape could be moved up seven frets. More complex chords may also be derived from the basic shapes, for example, A7+5+9 from the E shape (see Ex. 14.3).

Ex. 14.3

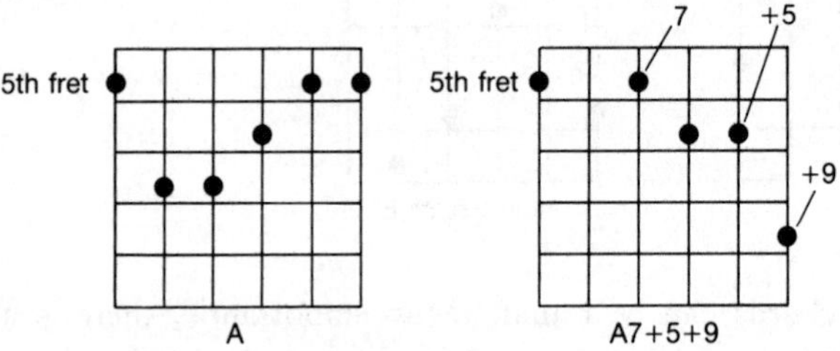

Clearly, the student will not immediately be able to derive chords such as this, but it is very important that this approach should be developed rather than rely on a so-called 'chord encyclopedia'. The same applies with scales and arpeggios. Once the major scale and arpeggios relating to a chord shape in a given position have been understood, other scales can be derived (for example, the minor scales). The process for finding a scale may be begun with a chord shape, the B minor 7 chord previously mentioned being suitable. The arpeggio, i.e. the constituent notes of the chord, provides four of the notes (B, D, F♯, A) and now the student must decide which other notes are required to complete the scale. The relationship of the chord to key is important. The B minor 7 chord is found as II in the key of A, III in G, and VI in D. Considering the first example (A) as our tonic, the appropriate scale will be B, C♯, D, E, F♯, G♯, A (A scale). In G it would be B, C, D, E, F♯, G, A, B (G scale).

This was implied when it was stated that the major scale would fit over any of the related chords in the diatonic chord family relative to that scale. The diatonic chord sequence given earlier may now be reconsidered—F minor 7, B♭ minor 7, E♭ 7, etc. It is already known that two scales, A♭ major and C major fit the first eight bars of the passage. However, this gives a diffuse relationship to the actual chords involved for each has its essential arpeggio notes. So it is preferable to treat each chord individually. In the first bar, F minor 7 has an arpeggio and related scale of A♭. By approaching it as an F sound by using the arpeggio, there is more feeling of movement when the B♭ minor 7 is arrived at. This gives the improvised line (or chord line) a more vertical structural feeling (see Ex. 14.4).

Ex. 14.4

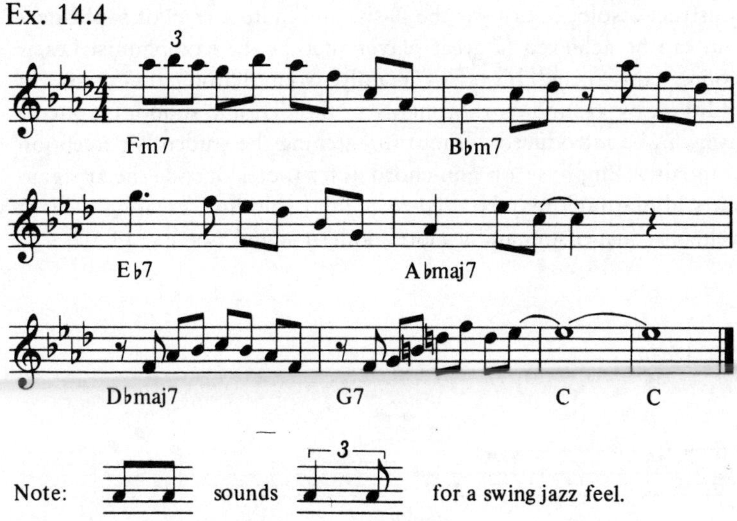

Similar principles are involved if chord voicings are to be played over the basic sequence. For chords played on the top four strings (30s style), each chord may be taken and notes from the scale added. For example, for F minor 7, the chords of F minor 6, 9, and 11 may be found; for E♭ 7–E♭ 9, 11, and 13. (It should be noted that only diatonic notes are being used.) Similarly, a chord with a walking bass line can be produced by always working from these primary chord shapes. For F minor 7, the scale notes should be added on the bass strings as shown in Ex. 14.5. This may be repeated for the remainder of the sequence.

Ex. 14.5

No jazz performer would use only this wholly diatonic method to construct a solo, but this is the basis, and quite a level of sophistication can be achieved (a great player such as the saxophonist Lester Young constructed his solos mainly from diatonic material). In addition, by grounding thoroughly in the diatonic sound, chromaticism can be introduced without threatening the student's perception of tonality. Emphasis on non-chord notes (notes outside the arpeggio but still diatonic) may be used to build a solo line, creating a slight feeling of suspension and a more modern sound (see Ex. 14.6).

Ex. 14.6

This is, of course, most effective when the basic chord is provided in the accompaniment. There are also ways of playing both the melody note and the chord with spacing so that both are clear. Ex.

14.7 shows a wide interval between melody note and chord so that it almost sounds like two instruments. This would have to be played with either the right-hand fingers or pick and fingers (it should be remembered that the fundamental chord shape should be borne in mind).

Ex. 14.7

The next stage harmonically is to introduce passing notes. This means that for the first time, notes outside the parent scale may be employed to provide extra emphasis to the chord structure (see Ex. 14.8). Passing notes always work well from a semitone below chord notes, and often from a semitone or a scale tone above.

Ex. 14.8

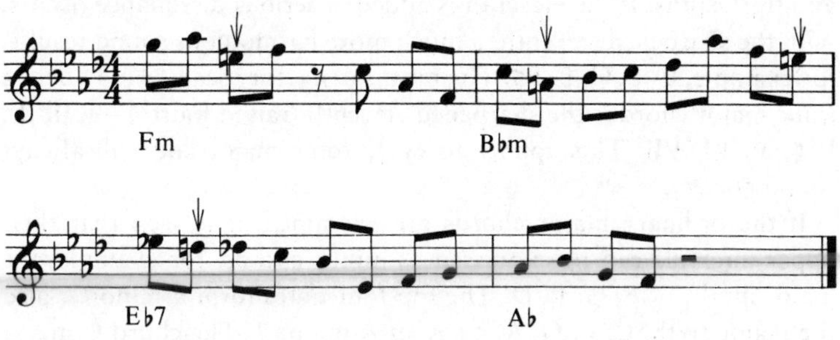

Harmonization of passing notes brings us to the area of chord alterations (diatonic chords with chromatic upper intervals) and chord substitutions (the use of different chords altogether). As a first step, it is usually true that a chord can be passed into from the same chord shape a semitone above or below, just as with the single line. After this stage, chromatic notes can be given more weight so that finally, in the most 'advanced' playing, the diatonic framework is more or less abandoned, i.e. each chromatic note is capable of equal stress to the diatonic notes. The following section is applicable to the student whose ear is sufficiently developed to be able to accommodate dissonances. However, the diatonic material should be well assimilated first.

Before giving some examples of the common guidelines for chord alterations and substitution, it should be noted that in diatonically-based harmony as it applies to jazz, there are really only two types of chord—the resolved chord (true tonic) and the resolving chord (dominant). The minor sevenths, minor seventh flat-fives, dominant sevenths, altered dominant sevenths, diminished, and augmented chords are all unstable, resolving chords, i.e. they want to move to a stable chord, a tonic. The tonic chords are the major type—major sevenths, major ninths, or minor type—minor/major sevenths, minor/major sixths etc. Historically, jazz has been played using the harmonies of the standard tunes of the time, which have shown a distinct preference for the V–I progression. The IV–I progression is fairly common, but is much more characteristic of rock and blues. If this is understood, the following material will be easier to assimilate.

Alterations and substitutions on the tonic chord are less frequent than with the dominant. The former, being the 'home chord', stands on its own. A major seventh chord can be extended to include ninths and thirteenths. If the eleventh is added, a serious dissonance occurs; with the sharpened eleventh, a much more harmonious sound results, for example, C, E, G, B, F♯. The most satisfactory scale to play over a tonic major chord is the sharpened eleventh (raised fourth)—I, II, III, IV♯, V, VI, VII. This applies to every tonic major and will always sound correct.

If the ordinary major chords are examined, it is seen that their upper intervals can be expressed as minor chords, for example, the major ninth, C, E, G, B, D. The top four notes form E minor 7; also the major sixth, C, E, G, A, gives an A minor 7. The chord C major 7 + 11 (C, E, G, B, D, F♯) contains B minor. Although these chords on their own do not suggest a tonic, when played against C in the bass, they give the sound of an enhanced major chord. It follows, therefore, that a sequence such as: | C major | D minor 7 G 7 | C major | D minor 7 G 7 | may be expanded to form: | C major A minor 7 | D minor 7 G 7 | E minor 7 A minor 7 | D minor 7 G 7 |. These tonic substitutes work best where the tonic chord is about to be abandoned. The only extension really satisfactory at a final tonic chord is the sharpened eleventh. In fact, where the tonic is weak, further substitutions are often possible. The A minor 7 and E minor 7 substitutes can themselves be treated as resolving chords, thereby supplying the V–I relationship that jazz prefers: | C major 7 A 7 | D minor 7 G 7 | E 7 A 7 | D minor 7 G 7 | C major 7+11 |

In the same way with dominants. The top part of a G 11 chord (G, B, D, F, A, C) produces a D minor 7 chord. G 13 produces the chord of D minor 9. Because resolving (dominant) chords are inherently unstable, they are more prone to allow scale notes to be altered. Hence, when the range of altered sound (G 7+5−5+9−9) is combined with the G 7 scale, it produces a chromatic scale without the F♯. Some landmarks around a potential chromatic quagmire are therefore required. It is to be noted that G 7−5 has the same notes as D♭ 7−5; many altered seventh chords can be substituted in this way—G7+5−9 for D♭ 9 with a root of G. If D minor 7 substitutes for G 7 chords, then A♭ minor 7 can be stretched to substitute for D♭ chords. So, over a given resolving chord, there are four possible substitutes. These must, of course, be used with discretion and whether they sound good or not will depend to a large extent on making the upper melody line coherent. So the progression quoted above could become something like this: | C major 7 F major 7 E minor 7 A 7 | D minor 7 E♭ 9−5 A♭ 13 G 7 | E 7+9 B♭ 13 E minor 7 A 7 | D minor 7 G 7 A♭ minor 9 D♭ 9 | C major 7+11 |.

Another useful way of organizing chromaticism on dominant chords employs diminished chords. For example, the top four notes of a G 7−9 chord (B, D, F, A♭) produce a diminished chord. B diminished, D diminished, F diminished, and G♯ diminished are all the same chord, so it follows that over a dominant seventh G, those four chords can be substituted. A synthetic diminished scale is formed by connecting the chord notes from a semitone below, for example, G♯ diminished scale is G♯, A♯, B, C♯, D, E, F, G, G♯. This is one of the most useful scales for improvising over a dominant chord because it is easy to work out a pattern which can then be transposed up and down in minor thirds. The diminished scale starting one semitone up from the root will exactly fit the dominant seventh, 13, and 11−9 chords (see Ex. 14.9).

A second scale which fits the +5−5 alterations can be derived. This is a scale built on the most removed of our initial dominant substitutes, for example, A minor can be substituted for G 7. If A♭

Ex. 14.9

melodic minor scale is played starting on G, it will be, G, A♭ (−9), B♭ (+9), B, D♭ (−5), E♭ (+5), F, G. This takes us even further away from our original sound of G 7, but works well if the connections are understood. The implications and possibilities of substitutions are endless. For example, if a phrase or chord is moved up a semitone, a I–V motion (IIb substitutes for V) is essentially made. A shift down of a semitone creates a I–IV motion (see Ex. 14.10).

Ex. 14.10

Transposition is one of the advantages that the guitar enjoys, so it should be taken full account of. Another fruitful avenue is to unlock the triads contained in the diminished scale. For example, the G♯ diminished scale contains E, G, B♭, and D♭ triads. So, if judiciously used, those triads can be played against a G dominant sound. This brings us to the area of polytonality. Often the older system of chord symbols is abandoned and a symbol more indicative of polytonality is used, for example, A 13−9 could be written as $\frac{F\sharp}{A7}$ or A 7−5−9 becomes $\frac{E\flat}{A}$. There still remains the problem of working out the appropriate scales. In both examples the diminished scale outlined above will fit.

The introduction of this type of material must obviously be a slow and gradual process especially as harmony can be among the least interesting areas for a young player. If the student is approaching from the classical perspective, i.e. there is an emphasis on learning 'set' pieces, the working out of arrangements of standard tunes using the principles of alterations and substitutions would be an appropriate task. The student who approaches from the rock area who may wish to expand his or her single-string improvising, will probably be more amenable to blues examples. These use the same premisses for their construction. Blues is a useful vehicle because it is generally easier for a player to retain the basic chord pattern in the mind while appreciating the shifts and alterations that create the feel of a jazz performance.

It is, however, vital that a student learns to apply this material creatively, in a variety of contexts and not just in 'standard' jazz but also latin, funk-fusion etc. It should be clear, however, that the above material is quite difficult to absorb. Many students will not be particularly interested in players such as Wes Montgomery and Joe Pass; they may, however, be responsive to players such as Pat Metheny, Larry Carlton, and Lee Ritenouer who work in a much more accessible environment but who have absorbed the same knowledge. All students are most likely to appreciate harmonic sophistication when applied to a melody they know and like. It is therefore important that the teacher selects material carefully (for example, many of Stevie Wonder's tunes can support altered chords).

In conclusion then, the emphasizing of the idea of relating to the basic chord forms, is important. Everything that has been discussed—scales, chords, altered chords etc., should be extrapolated from this. The altered notes should be sounded against the diatonic chords. Scales should always be practised against a chord sound. If there is nobody available to play the chords, they may be recorded on tape and the single line extensions played against them. Finally, the ear should be gradually taken away from the basic chord sound so that the dissonant tones can be heard and their relationship to the basic chord understood. All of this, combined with aural transcriptions of recorded solos, will help develop the ear, which is of course the most essential requirement for the jazz player.

Appendix I
General Information

Open Strings

The following open strings are those of a six string guitar such as a classical guitar, lead guitar (electric), or flamenco guitar.

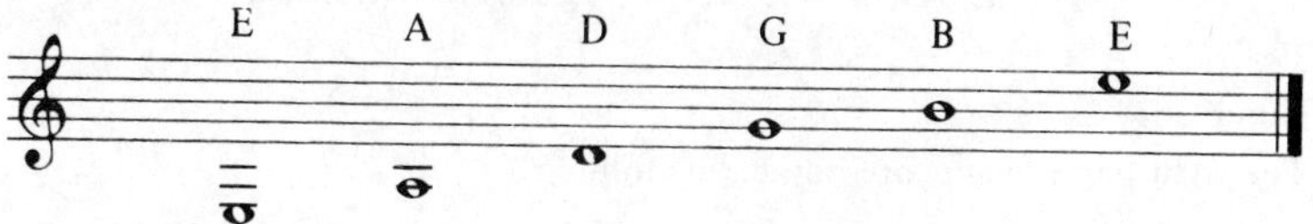

The following open strings are those of a bass guitar.

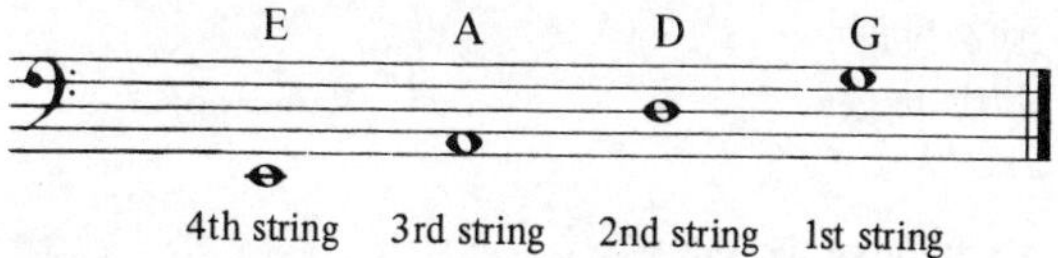

String numbers

A number set in a circle indicates the string

(1) = first string

(6) = sixth string

Tablature

This is sometimes found in place of the more usual form of music notation. The six horizontal lines represent the six strings of the guitar.

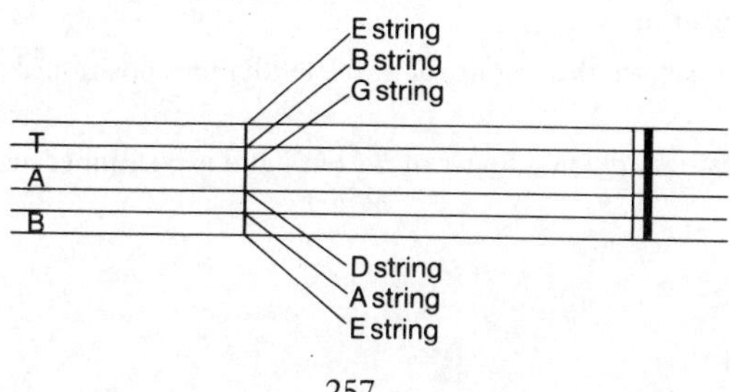

A number indicates which fret should be pressed. The line on which the number is placed shows the string that is to be played. The rhythm may also be given.

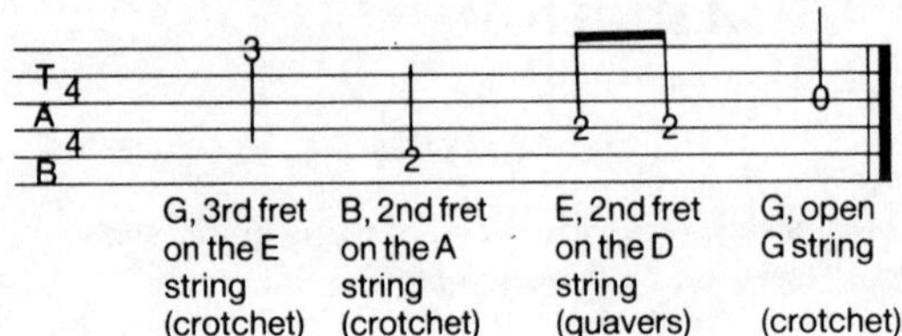

Fingering

The right-hand fingers are notated as follows.

thumb	p	
index finger	i	
middle finger	m	
ring finger	a	
little finger	x	(flamenco)

The left-hand fingers are notated as follows.

index finger	1
middle finger	2
ring finger	3
little finger	4

⊓ indicates a down-stroke of a pick.
V indicates an up-stroke of a pick.

Position numbers

A Roman numeral indicates a given position of the left-hand fingers. The number shows the fret that is to be pressed by the first finger and assumes that the second, third, and fourth fingers will 'look after' their respective frets above the position.

II Second position, the first finger of the left hand is positioned at the second fret.

V Fifth position, the first finger of the left hand is positioned at the fifth fret.

Appendix II
Note Positions

Note positions for frets 1–4

Note positions for frets 5–8

	5th fret	6th fret	7th fret	8th fret
1st string	A	A sharp B flat	B	C
2nd string	E	F	F sharp G flat	G
3rd string	C	C sharp D flat	D	D sharp E flat
4th string	G	G sharp A flat	A	A sharp B flat
5th string	D	D sharp E flat	E	F
6th string	A	A sharp B flat	B	C

Note positions for frets 9–12

	9th fret	10th fret	11th fret	12th fret
1st string	C sharp D flat	D	D sharp E flat	E
2nd string	G sharp A flat	A	A sharp B flat	B
3rd string	E	F	F sharp G flat	G
4th string	B	C	C sharp D flat	D
5th string	F sharp G flat	G	G sharp A flat	A
6th string	C sharp D flat	D	D sharp E flat	E

Note positions for frets 1–4 of a bass guitar

	open string	1st fret	2nd fret	3rd fret	4th fret
1st string	G	G sharp A flat	A	A sharp B flat	B
2nd string	D	D sharp E flat	E	F	F sharp G flat
3rd string	A	A sharp B flat	B	C	C sharp D flat
4th string	E	F	F sharp G flat	G	G sharp A flat

Note positions for frets 5–8

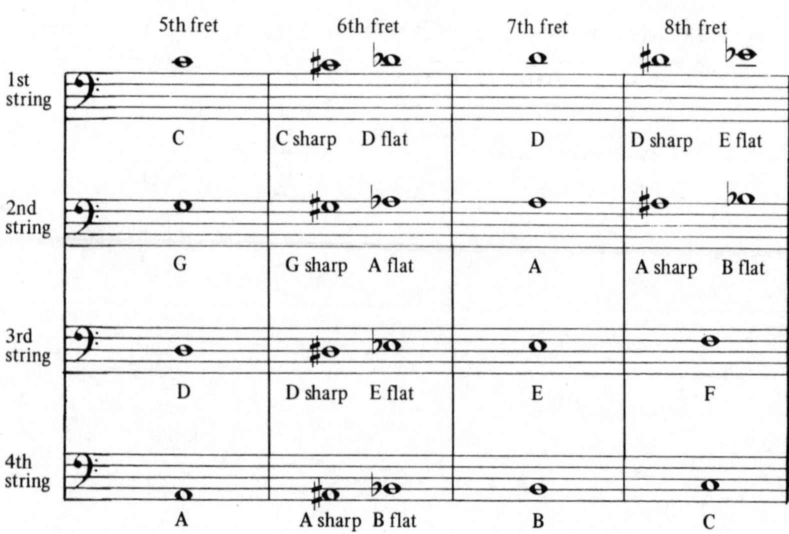

Note positions for frets 9–12

	9th fret		10th fret	11th fret		12th fret
1st string	E		F	F sharp	G flat	G
2nd string	B		C	C sharp	D flat	D
3rd string	F sharp	G flat	G	G sharp	A flat	A
4th string	C sharp	D flat	D	D sharp	E flat	E

Appendix III
Chord Diagrams

Chords are often presented 'visually', without the use of music notation.

(i) The vertical lines represent the strings.
(ii) The horizontal lines represent the frets.
(iii) X indicates a string that is *not* to be played.
(iv) ○ indicates that a string is open.
(v) A circle with a number inside shows where a finger should be pressed and which finger is to be used.

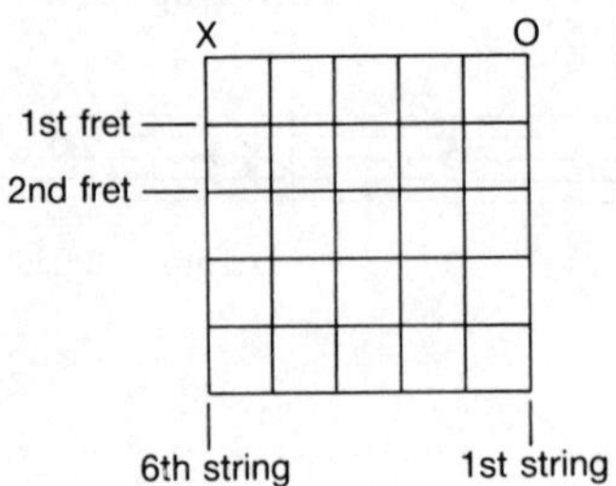

Chord shapes in first position

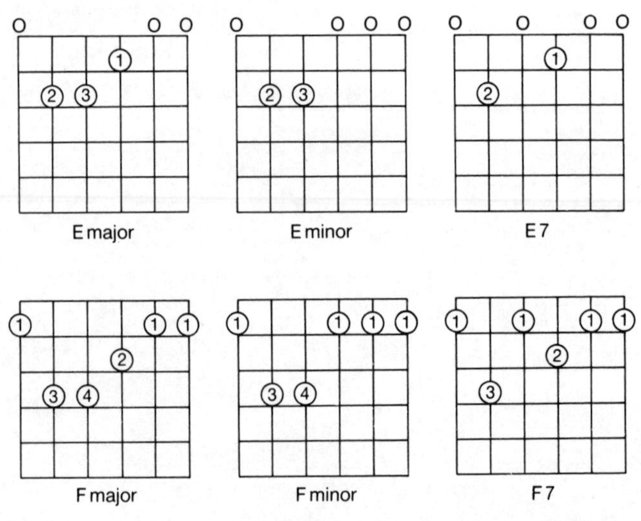

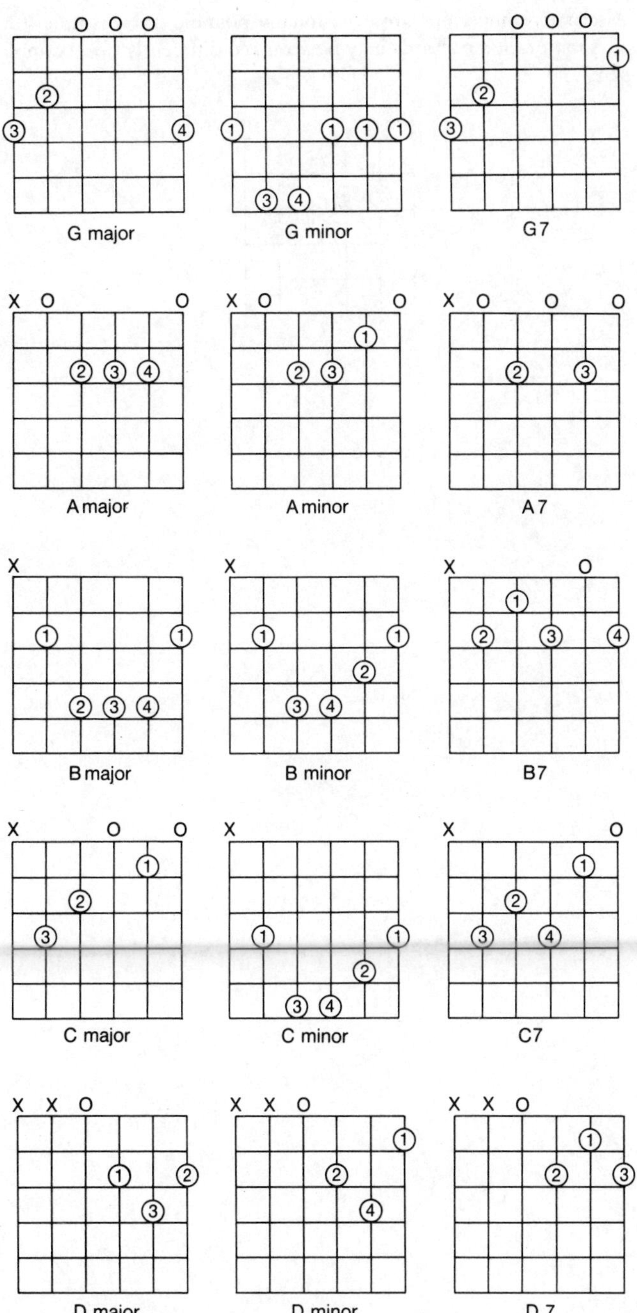

G major G minor G7

A major A minor A7

B major B minor B7

C major C minor C7

D major D minor D 7

Note. Alternative fingerings are occasionally possible, for example, for the chord of A major. Some chords may be arranged differently, for example the chord of E7.

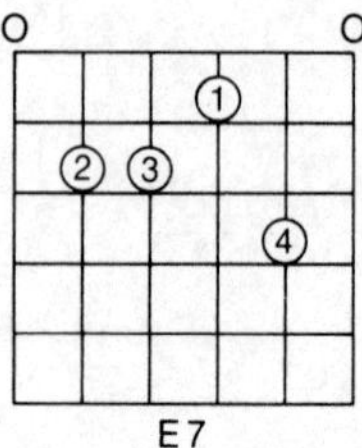

Appendix IV
Buying a Guitar

Although each type of guitar has its own specialized features, there is a small number of points that even the inexperienced player may look for.

(i) The construction of the guitar should be sound, particularly at the points where the neck of the guitar joins the body and where the bridge is fixed to the table (front). No cracks in the wood should be evident, nor should any scratches or other marks of damage.

(ii) The tuning of the instrument should be accurate. As well as listening to the open string tuning the purchaser should check the tuning of chords, preferably at different positions on the finger-board. In addition, each open string should be compared with the note found at the twelfth fret – a true octave should be heard. If possible, the harmonic should also be played at this fret (twelfth) and compared with the pitch of the stopped note at the same fret.

(iii) If the strings are too high off the finger-board, they will be difficult to press down. If the strings are set too low, stopped notes will 'buzz' when sounded. To check the latter, the strings should be played strongly.

(iv) A degree of balance should exist in the overall sound. The bass strings should not, for example, sound far louder than the treble strings, or one treble string sound louder than the others.

(v) The tone should, of course, be pleasing, and as consistent as possible.

(vi) The neck should not be warped. This may be checked by looking along the neck from the head-end.

(vii) The tuning mechanisms should work truly and there should not be points where the tuning pegs are turned and nothing happens to the pitch of the strings.

Appendix V

Some Makes of Strings

Classical: D'Addario Pro Arte, Aranjuez, Augustine.
Electric: Rotosound, G.H.S., Ernie Ball.
Bass: Rotosound, Guild, Frontline.
Folk: Martin, D'Addario, Ernie Ball (Earthwood).
Flamenco: Juan Martin, Flamenco D'Addario, La Bella Flamenco. (Many flamenco guitarists, however, prefer to use classical guitar strings.)
Jazz: D'Addario Chrome, D'Addario Half Round, D'Angelko Smooth Round.

Appendix VI
Music Publishers

Ariel Music, Sibford Ferris, Banbury, Oxon OX15 5RG.

Ashley Mark Publishing Company, Saltmeadows Road, Gateshead NE8 3AJ.

Associated Board of the Royal Schools of Music, 14 Bedford Square, London WC1B 3JG.

Belwin Mills Music Limited, 250 Purley Way, Croydon CR9 4QD.

Boosey and Hawkes Music Publishers Limited, 295 Regent Street, London W1R 8JH.

Broekmans and van Poppel. Sole United Kingdom Agent is Universal Edition.

Cambridge University Press, The Edinburgh Building, Shaftesbury Road, Cambridge CB2 2RU.

Chappell Music Limited, 129 Park Street, London W1Y 3FA.

Chester Music J. & W./Edition Wilhelm Hansen London, 7–9 Eagle Court, London EC1M 5QD.

Cramer Music, 99 St Martin's Lane, London WC2N 4AZ.

EMI Music Publishing Limited, 138–140 Charing Cross Road, London WC2H 0LD.

Eschig. Sole United Kingdom Agent is Schott & Co. Limited.

Faber Music Limited, 3 Queen Square, London WC1N 3AU.

Fentone Music Limited, Fleming Road, Earlstrees, Corby, Northants NN17 2SN.

Hampton Music Publishers, Northampton Guitar Studios, 46 Brookland Road, Northampton NN1 4SL.

International Music Publications, Woodford Trading Estate, Southend Road, Woodford Green, Essex 1G8 8HN.

Island Music Limited, 22 St Peter's Square, London W6 9NW.

Kalmus (Alfred A.) Limited, 38 Eldon Way, Paddock Wood, Tonbridge, Kent TN12 6BE.

Music Sales Limited, 78 Newman Street, London W1P 3LA.

Musical New Services Limited, Guitar House, Bimport, Shaftesbury, Dorset.

Novello & Co. Limited, Fairfield Road, Borough Green, Sevenoaks, Kent TN15 8DT.

Oxford University Press, Walton Street, Oxford OX2 6DP.

Peters Edition Limited, 10–12 Baches Street, London N1 6DN

Ricordi (G.) and Co. (London) Limited, The Bury, Church Street, Chesham, Bucks HP5 1JG.

Schirmer (G.) Limited, Stockley Close, Stockley Road, West Drayton, Middx. UB7 9BE.

Schott & Co. Limited, 48 Great Marlborough Street, London W1V 2BN.

Southern Music Publishing Co. Limited, 8 Denmark Street, London WC2H 8LT.

Tecla Editions, Preachers' Court, Charterhouse, London EC1M 6AS.

Thames Publishing, 14 Barlby Road, London W10 6AR.

Universal Edition (London) Limited, 2–3 Fareham Street, Dean Street, London W1V 4DU.

Wise Publications, 78 Newman Street, London W1P 3LA.

Appendix VII

Further Reading

Achard, Ken, *The Fender Guitar*, Musical New Services.

Achard, Ken, *The History and Development of the American Guitar*, Musical New Services.

Bishop, Ian C., *The Gibson Guitar from 1950* Vols. I and II, Musical New Services.

Bone, Philip J., *The Guitar and Mandolin*, Schott.

Brosnac, Donald, *The Electric Guitar: its history and construction*, Omnibus Press.

Clinton, George, *Andrés Segovia*, Musical New Services.

Delaunay, Charles, *Django Reinhardt*, Ashley Mark.

Denyer, Ralph, *The Guitar Handbook*, Dorling Kindersley.

Duarte, John W., *Melody and Harmony for Guitarists*, Universal Edition.

Duncan, Charles, *The Art of Classical Guitar Playing*, Sunny-Birchard Music.

Evans, Tom and Mary Anne, *Guitars, From the Renaissance to Rock*. OUP.

Hiscock, Melvyn, *Make Your Own Electric Guitar*, Blandford.

Mongan, Norman, *The History of the Guitar in Jazz*, Oak Publications.

O'Brien, W. E. (trans.), *Segovia, an Autobiography of the Years 1893–1920*, Marion Boyars.

Otero, Corazón, *Manuel M. Ponce and The Guitar*, Musical New Services.

Siminoff, Roger H., *Constructing a Solid-Body Guitar*, Hal Leonard.

Sloane, Irving, *Guitar Repair*, Omnibus Press.

Summerfield, Maurice J., *The Classical Guitar*, its *Evolution and its Players since 1800*, Ashley Mark.

Summerfield, Maurice J., *The Jazz Guitar*, Ashley Mark.

Taylor, John, *Tone Production on the Classical Guitar*, Musical New Services.

Turnbull, Harvey, *The Guitar from the Renaissance to the Present Day*, Batsford.

Tyler, James, *The Early Guitar*. OUP.

Wheeler, Tom, *The Guitar Book*, Macdonald Futura.

Index